The
Bozeman Trail
Volume I

RED CLOUD, THE GREAT OGALLALA SIOUX WAR CHIEF
Photo taken at Washington, D. C., 1875. An exceptional
picture, showing the noted Sioux leader at the age of 53.

The Bozeman Trail

Historical Accounts of the Blazing of the Overland Routes into the Northwest and the Fights with Red Cloud's Warriors

VOLUME I

by
Grace Raymond Hebard and
E. A. Brininstool

with Introduction by
General Charles King, u.s.v

Introduction to the Bison Book Edition
by John D. McDermott

University of Nebraska Press
Lincoln and London

First Bison Book printing: 1990
Most recent printing indicated by the last digit below:
10 9 8 7 6 5 4 3 2 1

Library of Congress Cataloging-in-Publication Data
Hebard, Grace Raymond, 1861–1936.
The Bozeman trail: historical accounts of the blazing
of the overland routes into the Northwest,
and the fights with Red Cloud's warriors /
by Grace Raymond Hebard and E. A. Brininstool:
with introduction by Charles King.
p. cm.
"Introduction to the Bison book
edition by John D. McDermott." Reprint.
Originally published: Cleveland: A. H. Clark, 1961.
ISBN 0-8032-7249-9 (v. 1).—ISBN 0-8032-7250-2 (v. 2)
1. West (U.S.)—History.
2. Bozeman Trail. 3. Indians of North
America—West (U.S.)—Wars. 4. Overland journeys
to the Pacific. 5. Red Cloud, 1822–1909.
I. Brininstool, E. A. (Earl Alonzo), 1870–1957.
II. Title.
F591.H4 1990 978'.02—dc20
90-12364 CIP

Reprinted by arrangement with the Arthur H. Clark Company
The original index, which appeared at the end of Volume II, has been
divided, in the Bison Book, into separate indexes for the two volumes.

TO THE MEN WHO BLAZED THE TRAIL

The Scouts, Frontiersmen, and Soldiers of the
United States Army of the Plains, who led the
Van in the March of Civilization, that
the Prairies, Mountains and Valleys
of the Great West might be redeemed, this volume is most
gratefully dedicated

Contents of Volume I

Illustrations, Volume I

MAPS

Introduction to the Bison Book Edition
By John D. McDermott

They seem a rather odd couple in retrospect, Grace Raymond Hebard and Earl Alonzo Brininstool. The first was a highly trained academician and early feminist who championed woman suffrage before the Wyoming State Constitutional Convention in 1889. The second was a California newspaperman and outdoorsman, a writer of poetry and self-confessed romantic who, like Miniver Cheevy, cursed his fate that he had been born too late.

Grace Raymond Hebard in her era was one of the best educated women living in the American West.[1] Born July 2, 1861, in Clinton, Iowa, she attended the University of Iowa, earning her B.A. and M.A. degrees. In 1891 she joined the faculty of the University of Wyoming, where she remained for the rest of her academic career. In 1893 Illinois Wesleyan University granted her a Ph.D., and five years later she earned admission to the Wyoming bar. In 1908 she became a full professor and head of the University of Wyoming's Department of Political Economy, serving in that capacity until her retirement in 1931.

Her early interest in Wyoming history resulted in the publication in 1904 of a primer for students, entitled *The History and Government of Wyoming*, which went through eleven editions. A regional text, *The Pathbreakers from River to Ocean*, followed in 1911. In 1922 Hebard wrote *Teaching Wyoming History by Counties*, followed by *Civics for Use in Public Schools* in 1926.

Her interest in Wyoming history extended to the places where significant events occurred, and she became a pioneer in identifying and marking historic sites and early trails. As State Regent of the Daughters of the American Revolution, she was a successful lobbyist for funding from the Wyoming legislature to purchase stone markers and monuments to commemorate the state's frontier heritage. As secretary of the Wyoming Oregon Trail Commission, she arranged for and presided over many dedicatory ceremonies, including several for Bozeman Trail sites.[2] Her later work centered on the Shoshoni experience, including *Washakie* (1930), a biography of the tribe's remarkable warrior chief, and *Sacajawea* (1932), a study of the Indian woman who proved a valuable guide and interpreter to Lewis and Clark.

Hebard's accomplishments brought her many admirers, but her affirmative style offended some with whom she came in contact. Walter M. Camp, who is remembered for the numerous accounts that he collected of participants in the Indian Wars, said of her in a moment of exasperation: "She is an intelligent woman . . . but is so full of conceit and extravagant self-esteem that she can not disguise it."[3] But upon her death in Laramie, Wyoming, on October 11, 1936, the entire city seemed to mourn, and the many tributes in eulogy testify to her ability to inspire students and to the respect held by her peers.

Born in Warsaw, New York, on October 11, 1870, Earl Alonzo Brininstool attended public schools and business college before moving west in 1895 to become a newspaper reporter for the *Los Angeles Times*.[4] From 1904 to 1915 he wrote a column for the *Los Angeles Express* in which he published five thousand poems on western themes. A selection of these appeared in *Trail*

Dust of a Maverick: Verses of Cowboy Life, the Cattle Range and Desert (1914). After 1915 he made his living as a freelance writer.

Long interested in the U.S. military–Indian conflict on the Northern Plains, Brininstool initially visited scenes of the 1866–68 Sioux war in 1913. At Fort Phil Kearny, he was able procure a three-foot section of the old stockade, which he eventually offered to share with James Carrington, the surviving son of the military post's first commander.[5] Twenty-three years later, he wrote Grace Hebard that he still had the relic and that nothing had a more prominent place in his den.

Brininstool's interest in the Old West led to the publication of many articles and books on cowboy and Indian history, first in such periodicals as *Hunter-Trader-Trapper* and *Winners of the West*. By the time of his death on July 28, 1957, he had produced a significant body of work. His major studies include *The True Story of the Killing of "Billy the Kid"* (1923), *A Trooper with Custer* (1925), *Fighting Red Cloud's Warriors* (1926), *Chief Crazy Horse: His Career and Death* (1929), *Dull Knife, A Cheyenne Napoleon* (1935), *Crazy Horse, The Invincible Ogalalla Chief* (1949), *Troopers with Custer* (1952), and *Fighting Indian Warriors* (1953).

Brininstool readily admitted that he was a romantic, longing for bygone days. In 1917 he wrote Grace Hebard, "I certainly am sick and tired of 'civilization,' and nothing would suit me better than to spend the rest of my life in a log cabin way back in the hills somewhere away from all this ceaseless rush and worry. I hate it. My mother always was remarking that I am 'the only Indian she ever saw born of white parents.' And if there is anything that I constantly regret it is that I did not live in the buffalo days and the days when the plains were at their height."[6]

It is not clear when Hebard and Brininstool decided to collaborate on a history of the Bozeman Trail, but we do know that the work had been in process for a number of years prior to 1919. Originally conceived as a modest monograph on the Wagon Box Fight, the study grew into a lengthy manuscript, sometimes referred to as "The Powder River" or "Fighting Red Cloud's Warriors in Wyoming."[7] The origin of the book as a pamphlet helps to explain in part its rather disjointed form, being a series of essays on various aspects of Bozeman Trail history with little or no transition between chapters. After Scribners rejected the manuscript, the authors contracted with the Arthur H. Clark Company, a new firm specializing in western history, and the two-volume set appeared early in 1922.

Charles King (1884–1933) was the third writer involved in the production of *The Bozeman Trail*.[8] King had not been selected by the publisher to do the introduction, but rather solicited by Hebard and Brininstool. Famous for his many novels of the Indian Wars, such as *The Colonel's Daughter* (1883), and accounts of personal experience in frontier service, such as *Campaigning with Crook* (1880), he was without a doubt the country's leading authority on the subject. King rode in the Fifth Cavalry with Wesley Merritt and George Crook before an Apache bullet shattered his arm and led to his retirement in 1879. He had returned to active service as a brigadier general in the Spanish American War and then trained recruits for the army in World War I before retiring a second time. A national figure, he gave the book the stamp of authenticity in introducing it.

The basic assumptions of the authors of *The Bozeman Trail* are quite clear from the beginning. The volume is dedicated "To the Men Who Blazed the Trail: The

Scouts, Frontiersmen, and Soldiers of the United States Army of the Plains, who led the Van in the March of Civilization, that the Prairies, Mountains and Valleys of the Great West might be redeemed." The authors viewed the experience of the Indian Wars as a purely positive one that permitted the spread of white civilization and allowed progress to occur.

The carriers of "civilization," in this case, were the officers and men of the frontier army. In the introduction, Charles King declares: "We were the pioneers of civilization, the defense of the emigrant and the settler, the real agency that made possible the development of a continent." According to the old campaigner, soldiers in the Indian Wars paid a terrible price, suffering much more than in other wars and serving without recognition or reward. In bitter eloquence, King reproached the past:

> In the thankless duty to which so many of my comrades gave their last full measure of devotion, there was neither honor nor glory. It meant death, perhaps by torture, if a battle went against us, and unlimited abuse at the hands of the eastern press and pacifists if the victory were ours. It involved more peril, privation and hardship than did service in the Civil War, and yet, for years, our senators, in Congress assembled, refused to confer brevets bestowed for bravery, on the ground that it was *not* warfare! (p. 23, this volume)

Conversely, little is said of the Indian foe. Although Red Cloud is somewhat sympathetically presented, the text contains such condemnatory phrases as "blood thirsty savages," long since deleted from the historian's lexicon. Especially surprising is the treatment of the Sand Creek incident, summarized by W. C. Coutant:

"The matter, even to this day, remains in dispute as to whether it was honorable warfare, such as the government was urging against the Indians, or a 'horrible massacre'" (p. 129, fn. 37, this volume). It is easy to forget that in 1922 modern scholarship had yet to settle this matter in ringing condemnation of John Chivington and his bloody acts.

Since the publication of *The Bozeman Trail*, a great deal of research has been accomplished, and much new material brought to light that expands and revises the story. Dee Brown in *The Fetterman Massacre* (University of Nebraska Press, 1963) uses a number of contemporary sources to weave a fascinating story of Col. Henry B. Carrington's short-lived command of the Bozeman Trail forts. Robert A. Murray in *Posts on the Powder River Country of Wyoming* (University of Nebraska Press, 1968) uses military records found in the National Archives to discuss problems in administration, policy, strategy, tactics, armament, and supply. And many other studies of the Indian and white groups and participants have enriched and deepened our knowledge of those times.

The readers should be aware of a few minor errors of fact in the text. The discussion concerning Fort Laramie is a bit garbled. There were three posts called Fort Laramie—the log-stockaded Fort William (1834–41), the adobe-walled Fort John (1841–57), and Fort Laramie, the military post (1849–90). Fort John was initially the home of the military, but soon became part of a complex of buildings, numbering over a hundred at various times. Capt. Frederick Brown did not join the command late in 1866, but served as the regimental quartermaster at Fort Phil Kearny from the very beginning. Although Brown's body did show evidence that he may have committed suicide on December 21, that of Capt. William Fetterman did not. According to the post surgeon who inspected the corpse before burial, Fetterman suffered no bullet wounds of any kind but had been clubbed on the head and had his throat cut, which verifies the story of American Horse concerning the ill-fated commander's death.[9] The relief column dispatched from Fort Laramie upon receipt of word of the Fetterman Disaster on December 25 did not leave until January 3, 1867, delayed a week by heavy snow and cruelly cold weather.

Upon the death of Hebard, the publisher Arthur H. Clark wrote that *The Bozeman Trail* was "without exception the most valuable source work on this important highway of westward expansion."[10] And in perspective, its value as a source book containing many eyewitness accounts of the events of the period ensures it a secure place on the list of basic studies of the Bozeman Trail and Sioux War of 1866–68.

NOTES

1. For details of the life and work of Grace Raymond Hebard, see Alfred Larson, "The Writings of Grace Raymond Hebard," *Annals of Wyoming* 10 (October 1938), pp. 151–54; *In Memoriam: Grace Raymond Hebard* (Laramie, Wyo.: The Faculty of the University of Wyoming, June, 1937); and Janell M. Wenzell, "Dr. Grace Raymond Hebard as Western Historian." Master's thesis, University of Wyoming, 1964.

2. *Marking the Oregon Trail, The Bozeman Road, and Historic Places in Wyoming,* 1908–1920 (The Daughters of the American Revolution, a. 1920).

3. Letter to Max Littman, Chicago, February 24, 1920, Littman Papers, Sheridan County Fulmer Public Library, Sheridan, Wyoming.

4. See obituary, *New York Times,* July 31, 1957; *Who Was Who in America,* 1951–1960 (Chicago: The A. N. Marquis Company,

1963), p. 104; Dan L. Thrapp, *Encyclopedia of Frontier Biography,* Vol. 1 (Glendale: Arthur H. Clark Company, 1988), pp. 169–70.

5. Letter to James B. Carrington, Los Angeles, January 3, 1924, Carrington Papers, Sterling Library, Yale University, New Haven, Connecticut.

6. Letter to Hebard, Los Angeles, December 21, 1917, Brininstool File B-B771-ea, American Heritage Center, Laramie, Wyo.

7. Letter from Hebard to King, Laramie, June 3, 1919, Charles King File B-K58-c, American Heritage Center, Laramie, Wyo.

8. The material on King is voluminous. For a sampling, see Hazel Manning Flock, *Frontier Army Life Revealed by Charles King, 1844–1933* (Hays, Kans.: Fort Hays Kansas State College, March, 1965), pp. 1–8; Jack D. Filipiak, "Forgotten Novelists of the Frontier Army," *The 1966 Brand Book,* ed. William D. Powell (Denver, 1966), pp. 31–50; and Oliver Knight, *Life and Manners in the Frontier Army* (Norman: University of Oklahoma Press, 1978), pp. 1–38.

9. Testimony of Assistant Surgeon Samuel M. Horton, Fort Phil Kearny, July 25, 1867, pp. 3–4, Records of the Special Commission to Investigate the Fetterman Massacre and the State of Indian Affairs, 1867," Records of the Bureau of Indian Affairs, Record Group 75, National Archives. For American Horse's story, see *The Bozeman Trail,* Vol. I, fn. 86, p. 312.

10. *In Memoriam: Grace Raymond Hebard,* p. 36.

Preface

The circumstances surrounding the birth of this publication were as unpretentious as were the participants in the battles herein described. A modest pamphlet, to contain only the narrative of the Wagon Box Fight,[1] gradually expanded and developed into a tome of several hundred pages. As eye-witnesses of frontier battles were interrogated; as the Indian fighters of the sixties told their experiences; when original records were investigated; when private letters were read, and when government publications were scrutinized and compared with unpublished manuscripts, the fact was embarrassingly thrust upon the authors that a mere pamphlet would very inadequately delineate the combats between the white man on the one side and the Sioux, Cheyennes, and Arapahoe Indians on the other, in their fierce contests for the possession of cherished lands belonging to neither, but to the peace-loving Crows.

A major portion of this book has never, in any form, been heretofore presented to the reading public; many facts of historical value and significance have gone, in some unexplainable way, unrecorded, until now. The illustrations are, in the main, new to the public, many being productions from original pencil or pen-and-ink drawings made and executed by the artists on the ground, and not from memory or worded descriptions of others, and herewith produced in print for the first time. The map of the Oregon Trail and the

Overland Stage Route has a unique history, as the original draft of the streams and watersheds, the old trails of the Indians and emigrants, and the stations along the road to the West, was made by Jim Bridger in 1863, at the request of Colonel William O. Collins, who, for a number of years, had this greatest of scouts for his special guide while he was fighting to establish the line of the Western frontier. This map was first drafted with a pointed stick, using the ground as a background; afterwards the map was enlarged and made into greater detail by the use of charred embers on the whitened skin of a deer. From these rough outlines, though most accurate and painstaking in their details, Colonel Collins constructed the map on mounted linen paper with pen and ink. This map was given by Colonel Collins to John C. Friend, who, after possessing the drawing for over half a century, donated it to the authors—a cherished possession.

The drawings of Fort Laramie and Fort Halleck, and those of Sweetwater, Horse Shoe, Deer, Platte Bridge, South Pass, St. Mary's and Three Crossings telegraph stations, and Camp Mitchell and Camp Marshall, are all reproductions from original drawings made in 1863 by C. Moellman, a bugler attached to the Eleventh Ohio Cavalry, who was at that time stationed along the Oregon Trail. These drawings, made in colors, are, so far as can be ascertained, the only set of illustrations of the telegraph stations on the Oregon trail. The stations were, in what is now the state of Wyoming, that portion of the country which has at various times been known as Dakota, Idaho, Montana, and Wyoming Territories. The drawings were given by the sister of Lieutenant Caspar Collins to Mr. Friend, who, in turn, donated them to the authors. The picture of Fort Phil Kearney was drawn in 1867 by Antonio Nicoli, a

bugler attached to the Second U.S. Cavalry, and presented to Max Littman, who, that year, sent it to his
parents in Europe, where it remained many years, but
was ultimately returned to the owner, and was recently
graciously loaned to the authors for photographic reproduction.

The map of the Bozeman Trail from the Platte to
Fort C. F. Smith was surveyed by the former student of
one of the authors, Miss Vie Willits, (Mrs. A. L. Garber). To her and Mr. Garber much of the accuracy of
the description of the country around and adjacent to
Fort Phil Kearney, and the location of sites and battlefields, is due, and in this manner acknowledged. Sergt.
Samuel Gibson, who so graphically describes the
Wagon Box Fight, has enabled us to furnish accurate
sketches of the Wagon Box corral, as well as the
ground plan of Fort Phil Kearney. A. B. Ostrander,
F. G. Burnett, Mrs. A. L. Garber and Edward Parmelee
have made possible the reproduction of the plans of
Forts Reno and C. F. Smith. The map of the Hayfield
Fight is from descriptions and information furnished
by F. G. Burnett, who was active in the engagement.[2]

The information furnished by Capt. James H. Cook
regarding Chief Red Cloud places the great Sioux
leader, for the first time, in an entirely new light before
the American people, and shows him to have been a
keen and successful strategist in battle, and a staunch,
unswerving friend in peace.

Many have helped to make this publication a possibility, though those who have particularly rendered
valuable service, aside from those mentioned heretofore, are herewith enumerated, in order that this
form of recognition of their assistance may be publicly
acknowledged:

D. F. Barry, William E. Connelley, James B. Carrington, Frederick Claus, Edward J. Davison, William Devine, F. M. Fessenden, Rev. H. Groetgeers, Michael Henry, John Hunton, Major G. W. Ingalls, U. S. Senator J. B. Kendrick, Captain H. G. Nickerson, E. A. Logan, W. Y. Pemberton, Luke Voorhees, U. S. Senator F. E. Warren, Mrs. G. M. Wells, Agnes R. Wright Spring.

Special words of appreciation are due General Charles King for his instructive introduction.

GRACE RAYMOND HEBARD
E. A. BRININSTOOL

September, 1921

Editor's Notes

1. See Volume II.

2. The sketches of the Wagon Box corral, the reproductions of the plans of Forts Reno and C. F. Smith, and the map of the Hayfield Fight appear in Volume II, as well as the chapter on Chief Red Cloud that is based on Capt. Cook's information.

Introduction by General King

My first look at the Powder River was in the heat and glare of a July morning, in the fateful summer of '76. Custer and nearly half his regiment had been annihilated only a long day's march "as the crow flies" beyond that other fateful field where, ten years earlier, Fetterman and his men had been surrounded and slowly massacred. "Covering the hills like a red cloud" the warriors of Makh-pi-ya-luta had swarmed about the hated soldiery, and there was left no white man to tell the tale.

The folly of going after Indian braves in unknown numbers, with forces both unskilled and inadequate, having been thrice demonstrated, our leaders stopped to think. Within three months, and three days' march, of the scene where Red Cloud had earlier taught us the first lesson, Reynolds, Crook, and Custer had successively met defeat or death. Crook, realizing conditions, fell back upon his entrenched camp in the northeast foothills of the Big Horn and sent for reinforcements. We were the reinforcements.

The Fifth Cavalry had then never encountered Red Cloud. We were on terms of comradeship with his great rival, Spotted Tail, chief of the Brulé band. We came freighted with anything but favorable impressions of the chief who had so defiantly parted from the Great Father's representatives in '66, and had so contemptuously dealt with their successors at Fort Robinson in '75. We knew when we forded the Platte at Fetter-

man that Red Cloud had given fair warning ten years
earlier that he would kill every white man who ventured to invade his hunting grounds beyond Canton-
ment Reno, and we were now beyond. We knew that
he was not present in person the blistering Sunday
morning six weeks earlier, on which Custer had dared
to attack an Indian village six miles in length. Between the outspoken leader of the Ogallalas and the sly,
scheming politician who headed the Uncpapas, and
through them the young men of the six confederated
tribes, there could never be alliance or accord. Red
Cloud, the soldier, Sitting Bull, the schemer, were
chiefs of totally different mould, though we had not
then the appreciation of Red Cloud's virtues that came
with long later years.

We knew him only as the inspiration of the most
brilliant and daring battles the Sioux had fought, and
as the trainer of so many of the young warriors who
had gone to swell the ranks of Sitting Bull. We remembered his warning as we dismounted to bivouac
for the night on the banks of this ash-colored, turbid,
sluggish stream. We were choked with alkali dust
and faint with heat, and we gazed with longing, burning eyes on the snow-clad summits far to the west where
Cloud Peak towered above the fir-crested heights of
the Big Horn. We again recalled it when, three days
later, we drew rein and gazed at the palisaded ruin of
little Fort Phil Kearney, and pictured, silently, the
scene within those wooden walls where the puny garrison and the affrighted, trembling women and children listened, appalled, to the crash of musketry, a mile
away to the west, where, beyond that screening ridge,
the pitiable force sent out to drive away skulking Indians who were annoying their wood choppers, found

themselves presently hemmed in by countless hordes. Oh, well for those poor women that Carrington, post commander, refused to listen to the few hot-heads who urged him to send forth his remaining companies to the support of Fetterman! That would have inevitably led to the massacre of the last man – to the martyrdom of the last woman. We spent ten weeks that summer hunting those red warriors over the prairies of Wyoming, Montana, and the Dakotas, finding them once in such force at Slim Buttes, in September, that we were glad to get away with their pony herd and a handful of prisoners. We "went through the motions," as soldiers say, of deposing Red Cloud from his high estate and designating "Old Spot" to reign in his stead as chieftain of the whole Sioux nation, but it was *"brutum fulmen."* In the hearts of his tribesmen Red Cloud lived and reigned long years thereafter, while Spotted Tail died at the hands of the assassin.

Before ever the ghost dance craze of 1890 brought about the last of the Indian wars, we had begun to realize the truth of the adage that, red or white, you could not keep a good man down. There were fellow men whose character was beyond reproach, whose word was truth itself, and whose experience and knowledge none of our number could question, and of such was Captain "Jim" Cook, the chosen associate, guide and scout of such soldiers as Generals (S. S.) Sumner and Fountain in the trying Geronimo campaigns of the mid eighties. Time was, in the old days of '75 and '76, we left Fort Laramie at daybreak and marched away east by north, over the rolling divide, bound for the Sioux reservation, with a parting glance at Laramie Peak sinking toward the horizon in our wake, and Rawhide Butte at long intervals peeping warily at us from the north of west, and along in the afternoon we would bivouac on the treeless banks of the Niobrara. Something less than a mile away eastward a conical, mound-like butte overlooked the country in every direction, and thither, under careful guard, would go our signal officer and men, while the troop horses and pack mules, shed of their burdens, rolled and kicked on the scanty turf. Look whithersoever you would, in those days, not a sign of foliage was in sight, not even the cottonwood. But, forty-three years thereafter, I rode, one August morning, into a veritable oasis, a bower of beautiful foliage, of shaded vistas and softened lights, where all had been bare and almost barren. Now, soft green turf, vine-clad arbor, rippling streamlets and a modern homestead marked the spot where so often we rolled in our blankets for a night's rest under the summer stars, and not until I had climbed that signal height and gazed over miles and miles of bare ridge and divide, of broad and shrubless valley, could I realize the truth. There were the old landmarks, Laramie Peak dimly visible in the far southwest, Rawhide Butte, storm-scarred and hoary, twenty miles away to the west. Tumbling waves of wind-swept uplands stretched from horizon to horizon, east, west, and north, broken only on the northward skyline by jagged sawteeth – "Inyan Kara" and the kindred cliffs of the Black Hills of Dakota – the Black Hills old Red Cloud would have died to keep, if he could, forever free from the intruding paleface.

And that evening, with all the comforts of home about us, with a fine portrait of old Red Cloud himself, and with many of his prized belongings, in the heart of the family circle, we sat for hours and listened to Captain Cook's story of his years among the Indians, his long intimacy with Red Cloud and his deliberately-formed conception of the old chieftain's actual character. If there were any among us who had come to scoff, they remained to pray.

We heard at last the Red Cloud side of the long controversy. And those of us who had served under, and honored, General Crook—"Wichahnpi Yamoni" as the Sioux called him, not "Gray Fox," as the newspapers had it—wished that he, too, could have known the truth, both as to Red Cloud and to that fierce, untamable but most gallant warrior, Crazy Horse. Crook was the last man to permit injustice to the Indian.

The story of the old Bozeman Road around the Big Horn and through Indian Fairy Land is or was "a tale that is told." The sorrows and sacrifices of the army ordered to hold and defend it, our people have long forgotten, if indeed they ever knew. Solemnly had Red Cloud given his word and warning. It was scoffed at by the powers at Washington, and the army paid with its lifeblood for the blunders of the Interior Department. In the thankless duty to which so many of my comrades gave their last full measure of devotion, there was neither honor nor glory. It meant death, perhaps by torture, if a battle went against us, and unlimited abuse at the hands of the Eastern press and pacifists if the victory were ours. It involved more peril, privation and hardship than did service in the Civil War, and yet, for years, our senators, in Congress assembled, refused to confer brevets bestowed for bravery, on the ground that it was *not* warfare! We were the pioneers of civilization, the defense of the emigrant and settler, the real agency that made possible the development of a continent, yet, east of the Mississippi we had hardly a defender.

In the ten years of profound peace enjoyed by the nation after the final muster-out of the last volunteers of the Civil War, we, the regulars, lost scores of officers and hundreds of men in battle to the death with our red wards. It is comfort to know that there are those in civil life who, even in their sympathy for the cause of the Indian, have learned to estimate at something like its true worth the service rendered to the people of the United States by, and the sacrifices demanded of, their little army of the old frontier, especially along that line of battle and humiliation, the Bozeman Trail by way of Powder River.

CHARLES KING

August, 1921   *Brig.-General*, U. S. V.

The
Bozeman Trail
Volume I

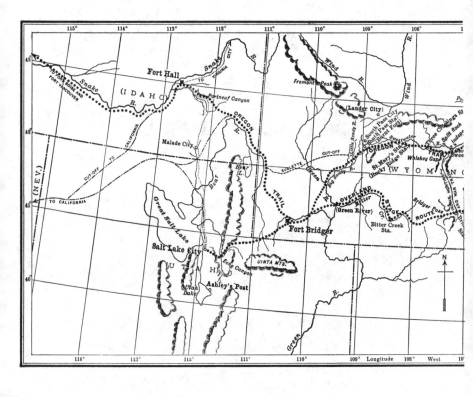

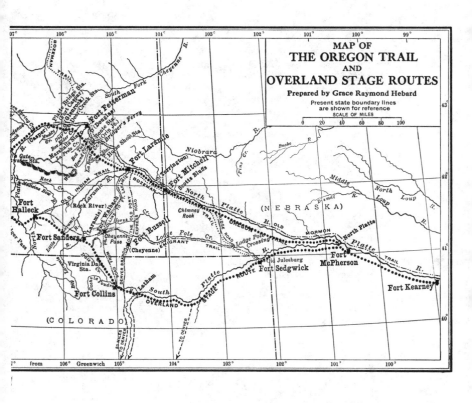

MAP OF
THE OREGON TRAIL
AND
OVERLAND STAGE ROUTES

Prepared by Grace Raymond Hebard

Present state boundary lines
are shown for reference

SCALE OF MILES

0 20 40 60 80 100

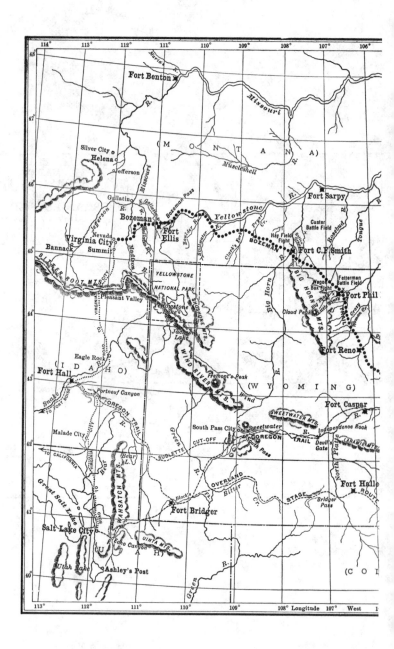

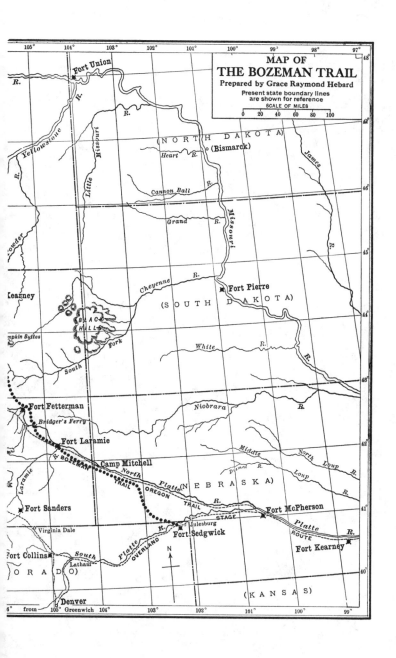

MAP OF
THE BOZEMAN TRAIL
Prepared by Grace Raymond Hebard
Present state boundary lines
are shown for reference
SCALE OF MILES
0   20   40   60   80   100

The Great Medicine Road of the Whites

For more than a century the Platte River has been the trail, each in turn, of the Indian, the fur man, the explorer, the gold seeker, the Mormon, the soldier, the pony express, the telegraph line, the stage station, the railroad and civilization. Along the banks of this fickle stream – sometimes only inches deep and yards wide, then, in a night, feet deep and miles wide, with an ever-shifting sandy bottom – more people have ventured to and beyond the Rocky Mountains than along any other of our streams. There is nothing unusual in this. The route was the one of least resistance; the one most easy of approach, and when once upon it, the least difficult to travel; the one the wild animals used; the one the Indians selected.

Before the Platte River route to the West was a generally used thoroughfare, the Santa Fé Trail, to the south, was being utilized as a road of commerce to the old interior city of Santa Fé. This road of commerce, (for it was not a homeseeker's trail) was in its most active existence from 1822 to 1843, though this path into Mexico had been used before 1822 by the occasional trader, and after 1843 it continued to be a merchant's road to a limited extent. During 1843 the trail was operated as a military road, and was a part of the trail for the emigrants on their way to California. On the Santa Fé Trail were encountered many hostile Indians, among them being the Osage, Arapahoe, Pawnee, Kiowa, Cheyenne, Comanche, and Apache tribes. As the trail was eight hundred miles in length, which was five times as long as any that had been put into use to that time in the United States, constant vigiliance and alertness both day and night became a necessary precaution to avoid hostile Indians.

In the earliest days of the traffic over the road, transportation was carried on exclusively by pack-train, wagons not being used until 1824, when a train, or caravan, as it was called, of twenty-five wagons drawn by horses, left Independence, at the bend of the Missouri, for the long, dusty, desert journey across the plains. The caravans started, in reality, from St. Louis, going from there to Independence,[1] Mo., by steamboat; but the actual beginning of the land journey was many miles west of St. Louis, near the mouth of the Kansas River. The washing away of the bank of the Missouri at Independence forced its abandonment as a shipping point, or starting point, on the trail, and Westport, a few miles distant, took its place in overland activities.

The method of transportation by oxen was inaugurated on the Santa Fé Trail in 1829, which proved to be more profitable than horses or mules, for the monotonous, dry journey seemed better fitted to the plodding oxen. From this date, oxen hauled more than half of the entire traffic over the Santa Fé Trail.

The transactions in merchandise were not all made at Santa Fé, for the caravan moved from that city down to Chihuahua, Mexico, a distance greater from Santa Fé than Santa Fé was from St. Louis. For a number of years the Santa Fé Trail was not definitely marked out, the train of pack horses or wagons going over no

---

[1] In the earlier days the starting point was from Franklin, about 205 miles west from St. Louis. The point of land departure was changed to Independence in 1827. Westport was established in 1833, Kansas City in 1838.

well-beaten path, but the wheels of commerce and the hoofs of the patient oxen had by 1834 cut into the sod a distinct trail, which from that time on was closely followed. Council Grove, one hundred and fifty miles from Independence and six hundred and fifty from Santa Fé, was the first noted camping ground along the trail, and the place where council was held with the Indians. Southwest of this place the trail went across the Cimarron Desert, the Rio Mora, the Rio Gallinas, past Wagon Mound, Las Vegas, San Miguel to Santa Fé city, an illimitable stretch of barren land, of sandstorms, and dangerous desert, without a white inhabitant from Independence to Las Vegas, fifty miles east of the sleepy city at the end of the trail. In order to escape sixty miles of the worst part of the desert lying between the ford of the Arkansas and Cimarron a cut off was made, which again took up the trail at the crossing of the Mora. It is this branch route that is today followed by the Atchison, Topeka & Santa Fé Railway.[2]

On May 15, 1831, a caravan conducted by Josiah Gregg started over the trail with a train of such magnitude and with such a variety and quantity of merchandise, that his venture marked a new era in the commerce of the plains. That he did not make just a single journey, but many of them, and most successfully, is witnessed from his journal, a classic for caravan travel over the Santa Fé Trail.[3] The collection of merchandise consisted of crapes, pelisse, cloths, shawls, handkerchiefs, cotton hose, looking glasses, ginghams, velvet, cutlery, firearms, and many other commodities, the majority of which were to be exchanged for Mexican gold and silver.[4] The oxen, raising clouds of chok-

---

[2] Completed to Santa Fé in February, 1880.

[3] Gregg (Josiah) *The Commerce of the Prairies*, 2 vols.

[4] In this caravan were many wagons of the Conestoga canvas top and

ing dust with their awkward hoofs, traveled from twelve to fifteen miles a day with the load, the return trip, with mostly empty wagons, making twenty miles daily, the caravan making a trip of two thousand miles between the months of April and November. A well-organized wagon train contained twenty-five to twenty-six large wagons to carry from three to three and a half tons each, with six yoke of oxen to each wagon, and about thirty additional oxen to take the places of disabled ones.[5]

In 1843 the trail was brought to its end through the raids by the Indians, the conspiracies of the Texas bandits and the hostility of the Mexican government through its president, Santa Anna, who prohibited commercial relations with our country because he believed that Mexico and the United States would soon be at war.

With the temporary abandonment of the Santa Fé Trail, the Oregon Trail along the Platte became a necessity. In 1846 Gen. Stephen W. Kearny, when the United States and Mexico had become involved in war, used the Santa Fé Trail as a military road, thus making it a road of national importance, not only to the government, but the country to which the trail extended. The successful issue of the war, in which the trail had played a conspicuous part in military transportation, was the initial step toward the annexation in 1848 of New

prairie schooner style, each drawn by four or five pairs of oxen, some drawn by mules; men walking, riding on horses, and a few in light vehicles. In 1822 the pack animals carried on their backs over the trail merchandise valued at $15,000; in 1824 wagons hauled $35,000 worth; in 1830 the valuation was increased to $250,000, and in 1843 half a million dollars were paid to the merchant caravan owners.

[5] Majors (Alexander) *Seventy Years on the Frontier.* Majors, at the arrival with one of his wagon trains at Santa Fé, received from the merchants for whom he freighted, the sum of $13,000, all paid in Mexican silver money.

Mexico and Arizona, parts of Kansas and Colorado, and all of California, Utah, and Nevada. When the embargo of 1843 was lifted, commerce over the old trail was renewed and greatly increased, until, during the late sixties and the early seventies, the trade going over the trail amounted to more than five millions of dollars. Not all of the merchandise, however, remained at Santa Fé, for a large portion was sent into California over another trail, the Gila, which was extensively used by the gold-seekers of 1849 to California. The Santa Fé Road became one of commerce, war, and homeseekers, all factors in the development of the territory on the Pacific.

There were many who went to Mexico who did not return to the States, but pushed toward the Pacific, going over what was known as the Gila Trail, which, after leaving Santa Fé, crossed the continental divide from the valleys of the Rio Grande and the Arkansas, south to the Gila River and west to the Gulf of California. There was also another trail to the west known as the Old Spanish Trail, which went north from Santa Fé by way of the Colorado River, northwest across the Sevier and Virginia Rivers, skirted Death Valley, and then west to California, ending at Los Angeles. Thus, there was now established, by the union of the Santa Fé and Gila Trails, a southern transcontinental road over which Kit Carson went, in 1846, to carry a message to Washington from General Fremont, telling of the uprising of the inhabitants of California, and along which General Kearny hurried to California to assume control of the Pacific coast. The conquest of Mexico and California created new problems for the United States, no one greater than the protecting and guarding of these large tracts of border territory, and the holding firmly to our government the Americans who lived in the lands newly acquired.

The stubborn determination of the Blackfoot Indians, their home being largely within those boundaries now embraced within the state of Montana, to avenge the killing, in 1806, of one of their chiefs, by Captain Meriwether Lewis, of the Lewis and Clark Expedition, made the invasion by the white man along the upper Missouri River one of unusual danger. It is to be remembered that Lewis and Clark had been sent by the United States government, in 1804 to explore the sources of the Missouri River, and to blaze a trail if possible to the Pacific Ocean. After reaching the headquarters of the Missouri, and crossing the Rocky Mountains, the expedition reached the Pacific coast and there spent the winter of 1805-6. The expedition finally returned to St. Louis, Captain Clark exploring down the Yellowstone, while Captain Lewis went north to search for the headwaters of the Marias River, a branch of the Missouri.

Captain Lewis, with his small escort of white men, was attacked while in his exploration of the sources of the Marias River, by the Blackfeet, when self-preservation demanded the life of the attacking chief. From the time of the killing of this chief by Lewis until the Indians were obliged to confine themselves within the boundaries of an Indian reservation, the Blackfeet looked upon the white man as their natural enemy and treated him as a hereditary foe.

The acts of hostility of this tribe drove many explorers and fur hunters to a safer and more southern route than that of the Missouri River. The Platte River afforded alluring possibilities, a shorter road, less Indian troubles, and, in earlier days, a new field for obtaining the precious beaver skins. When the Platte, particularly the northern branch, was explored, it became a thoroughfare for hundreds of thousands on their way to the west, seeking adventure, furs, fortunes, and homes.

It was the revengeful spirit of the Blackfoot Indians that prevented the Astoria Expedition, sent west by John Jacob Astor, under the leadership of Wilson Price Hunt, in 1811, from going to the sources of the Missouri River and then through the Rocky Mountain pass discovered by the little Shoshone Indian guide, Sacajawea[6] of the Lewis and Clark Expedition. Hunt and his men left St. Louis early that year to go to the mouth of the Columbia River to there establish a fur post that was to be headquarters for oriental trade. Warnings were given Hunt by friendly Indians when he and his party had reached, by the way of the Missouri, the country not far from the hunting grounds of the Blackfeet, that to push on farther up the river would be to invite immediate death, for the Blackfeet were remembering with intense hostility the death of their chief. Retreat was not to be considered, advance seemed unwise; variation from the scheduled route seemed a means of escape, and at the same time, a possible method of continuing toward the west, though no white man had ventured so far over this new route toward the setting sun as Hunt and his men now expected to go. To the southwest the company headed itself, in place of the northwest of the Lewis and Clark Expedition, in a few days reaching what is now the northeastern boundary of Wyoming. The party crossed the Powder River country, which, in a half-century was to become the bloody field of fierce and decisive Indian wars;

[6] Indian wife of Toussaint Charbouneau, interpreter for Lewis and Clark.

through or over the Big Horn Mountains to the Wind River and its eternally snow-capped mountains, to the passes south of the Yellowstone Park, not difficult of travel; in the shadow of the majestic Teton Peaks, which at that time were called the "Three Brothers" or "Pilot Knobs," and then to the Snake River the Astorian party journeyed toward the Pacific. Down the Snake the party now wended its way; down the Columbia to its mouth, where a site was selected on which was built the historic fur post or fort known as "Astoria."

On the return of the Astoria men under the leadership of Robert Stuart, in 1812, when they were east of the present boundary between Idaho and Wyoming, a well-beaten Indian trail was discovered and followed for a few days.[7] The fear of encountering Indians at the end of this trail caused the little depleted band of wearied men to deflect from the outgoing route and strike out for the south in place of returning through or in the neighborhood of Union Pass.[8] In the course of a few days the men arrived in the neighborhood of a rift in the Rocky Mountains which was in time to be known as South Pass, through which the trains of emigrants on the road to the west were obliged, in follow-

[7] Irving (Washington) *Astoria,* Vol. ii, ch. 18 ". . . where they came again upon the large trail of Crow Indians, which they had crossed three days previously, made, no doubt, by the marauding band. . . This trail kept on to the southeast and was so well beaten by horse and foot, that they supposed that at least a hundred lodges had passed along it. As it formed, therefore, a convenient highway, and ran in a proper direction, they turned into it. . ."

[8] Dale (H. C.) *The Ashley-Smith Explorations,* p. 34: "Pushing up the Wind River they (speaking of the Astorian on the way to the Pacific) reached the continental divide. The next day was occupied with crossing the range, apparently in, the neighborhood of Union Pass. . ." p. 35: "a new crossing of the continental divide had been found, though a difficult one over the Union Pass. . ." p. 284: "Pursuing the old route of the overland Astorians, he (Jedediah Smith) ascended Wind River, crossed the Union Pass to the Hoback."

ing years, to pass.   Striking the Sweetwater west of Devil's Gate, the Astorians followed down the North Platte to its junction with Poison Spider Creek (eighteen miles west by south of the present city of Casper, Wyoming). Here they constructed a log cabin, expecting to spend the winter (1812-13) in a secluded spot, but being discovered by Indians, the band of white men pushed down the North Platte, arriving at St. Louis in the spring of 1813. Thus, we now have the first organized party of white men to use the Indian road that was to become the trail to the west for the white men, and to be known as the Oregon Trail, which the Indians, in time, called "The Great Medicine Road of the Whites." This trail was also known by the name of "The Overland Trail," "The Mormon Road," "The Emigrant Road," "The Salt Lake Route," and "The California Trail."

These first explorers along the Platte River and their finding of a new overland way to the west, directly links them with the present narrative of the Indians' stubborn, persistent, and at some times, successful battles and raids against the white man, and his invasion into their hereditary hunting grounds.   It mattered not to the red man if his natural foe were headed toward the west for furs, a home in the Oregon country, gold in California and Montana, or silver in Nevada; it was invasion.

When in the early sixties gold was discovered in Colorado, Idaho, Montana, Nevada, and Wyoming, the stampede over the Oregon Trail to the new gold fields only added to the Indian's wrath and his war paint, for now the red man realized that the whites were not only to invade his cherished hunting grounds, but take possession of them.

To thoroughly appreciate the white man's motive
for trespass and to understand the bitter and persistent
fighting of the red man, necessitates some detailed descriptive material.

The earliest band of white men to trap in those
streams which run parallel with the Oregon Trail or
were crossed by that road, belonged to William Ashley's
fur company from St. Louis, that was formed to trade
in and to trap for beaver skins in the Rocky Mountains.
Under the management of General William Ashley of
St. Louis, in 1822, a fur company was organized to go
into the mountains to trap and trade.   This organization has commonly been called The Rocky Mountain
Fur Company, but this company did not *legally* exist
until 1830, though Ashley's company was frequently
called by the name.[9]   Among other members of Ashley's organization were Andrew Henry, Jedediah S.
Smith, William Sublette, Milton Sublette, David E.
Jackson, Robert Campbell, James Bridger, Etienne
Provost,[10] and many others, all of whom wrote their

[9] The license obtained by Ashley was known as "Licenses to trade with
Indian 1822" (U. S. Senate Documents, 18th Congress, 1st Session, No. 1).
Chittenden (H. M.) *The History of the American Fur Trade of the Far
West*, p. 262: "The beginning of the Rocky Mountain Fur Company may be
definitely traced to the following announcement, which appeared in the Missouri Republican of St. Louis, March 20, 1822: "To enterprising young men:
The subscriber wishes to engage young men to ascend the Missouri River to
its source, there to be employed for one, two or three years.   For particulars
enquire of Major Andrew Henry, near the lead mines in the county of Washington, who will ascend with, and command, the party; or of the subscriber
near St. Louis."   (Signed) "William H. Ashley."   The first recorded license
for Ashley to trade on the upper Missouri bears the date of April 11, 1822,
and "a license of precisely the same tenor and date was granted Major
Andrew Henry."

[10] Chittenden (H. M.) *The American Fur Trade of the Far West,* and
Thwaites, *Early Western Travels*, use this spelling; Dale, *The Ashley-Smith
Explorations* favors Provot; Dellenbaugh, *Romance of the Colorado River*
gives preference to Provo.   (See Harris, *The Catholic Church in America,*
p. 261 for discussion of spelling.)

The Green River at the site of William Ashley's rendezvous

Back of the trees is a meadow of 200 acres, known as Bridger's Flat. Here Ashley met his fur-trappers and those of the Hudson Bay Company. The first general rendezvous of the great Northwest, July 2, 1825.

names large in the early history of the West. Lakes, streams, mountain passes, peaks, forts, and cities bear testimony to their indomitable bravery. The men were sent by their leader into an unexplored region of the Yellowstone and Big Horn, reaching the country by the Missouri River route. From these upper valleys, in 1824, under the leadership of Fitzpatrick, the men went southward to explore the headwaters of the Big Horn and Wind Rivers. While on this journey over unbeaten paths, the white men discovered South Pass, a wide passageway between the lands drained by streams flowing toward the Atlantic and those that flowed toward the Pacific. This gateway was easy of passage, its ascent and descent so gradual as to be hardly perceptible, yet its significance on a road to the west was one of vital importance by unlocking the mountains that had been a barrier between the East and the West. The distinction of being the first white man to utilize South Pass seems to belong to Thomas Fitzpatrick who with his party in the spring of 1824 while seeking for an opening in the Rocky Mountains discovered that rift which gave easy passage to the country west of this ridge. From South Pass Ashley's little band of fearless fur men journeyed down the Big Sandy to its junction with the Green River, a site that soon, and also in years to come, was to witness strange scenes enacted by men of courage and daring, who had temporarily isolated themselves from civilization. The place became known as the "Green River Rendezvous." Ashley, in a technical way, was the first one to use the word "rendezvous" to indicate a definite locality where were to gather on a large scale the hardy fur men. On July 1, 1825, Ashley met his men who had been collecting beaver skins in an area

between the 34th and 44th degree of latitude on the
Big Horn, Sweetwater, Green, and Bear Rivers, on the
banks of the Green River about twenty miles north of
the present Utah-Wyoming boundary line. In this collected assemblage were twenty-nine fur trappers of the
Hudson Bay Company, who, with Ashley's trappers
made a gathering together of one hundred and twenty
men, divided into two camps. The site of this historic
meeting is today easy of identification, an area of two
hundred acres known as Bridger's Flat. The rendezvous was a selected site at which the yearly contracts
between fur traders and fur trappers were made and
former contracts settled. Every trapper knew, in the
years to follow, where the rendezvous would be held,
and about the first of July each year they began to
gather. "Here would come gaily attired gentlemen
from the mountains of the south, with a dash of the
Mexican about them, their bridles heavy with silver,
their hats rakishly pinned with gold nuggets, and with
Kit Carson or Dick Wooton in the lead. In strong
contrast would appear Jim Bridger and his band, careless of personal appearance, despising foppery, burnt
and seamed by the sun and wind of the western deserts,
powdered with alkali dust, fully conscious that clothes
mean nothing, and that, man to man, they could measure up with the best of the mountain men. At this
gathering you would find excitable Frenchmen looking
for guidance from Provost, the two Sublettes, and Fontenelle, the thoroughbred American, Kentuckian in
type, with his long, heavy rifle, his six feet of bone and
muscle, and his keen, determined, alert vigilance; the
canny Scot, the jolly Irishman, best represented by
Thomas Fitzpatrick, the man with the broken hand,
who knew more about the mountains than any other

man, except possibly Bridger; and mixed in the motley crowd an alloy of Indians – Snakes, Bannocks, Flatheads, Crows, Utes – come to trade furs for powder, lead, guns, knives, hatchets, fancy cloth, and, most coveted of all, whiskey, that made the meanest redskin feel like a great chief." [11]

Ashley in his expedition of 1825-26 had a two wheeled cannon taken through South Pass to one of his fur posts in the neighborhood of Great Salt Lake. The wheels of this engine of war made the first dim traces of vehicles along the Oregon Trail – the trail that was to lead to peaceful possession of the Oregon country in the years soon to follow.

In 1826 Ashley sold his interests in his fur company to Jedediah Smith, David Jackson, and William Sublette; when again in August, 1830, this newly-organized company passed into the control of Fitzpatrick, Bridger, Milton Sublette, Henry Fraeb, and Baptiste Gervais, who operated until 1834 under the name of the Rocky Mountain Fur Company. In 1835 contracts were made to transfer all of the company's possessions to Lucien Fontenelle, who represented a rival company known as the American Fur Company. This company used a recently-constructed fur post situated on the Laramie River as headquarters for trading in furs, which soon became known all along the trail as Fort Laramie.

Allured by the vast wealth accumulated by William Ashley from his fur expeditions, Captain Benjamin Bonneville, on a leave of absence from the United States Army, marched, in 1832, over the old trail which was then in its beginning, with an escort of one hundred

[11] Hebard (G. R.) *The Pathbreakers from River to Ocean,* p. 64. Many of the men mentioned belonged directly or indirectly to Ashley's fur expeditions.

and ten men, and twenty wagons drawn by oxen and mules. The clanking chains, the creaking wagons, the costly trappings for the horses, made a deep impression on the red men, who, waiting to see the train pass in review, wondered if the white men were invaders into their treasured hunting grounds, or if they were only passing on to other fields. To the perplexed Indians the deep marks made by hoof and wheel were ugly scars on the face of their traditional hunting ground. Bonneville, from 1832 to 1835, made many expeditions in the country north and south of the trail of Ashley's party, and followed along the entire length of the Oregon Trail, using the route to Fort Vancouver, Washington, which Jedediah Smith had discovered while exploring to the Pacific coast.[12] Though no fortunes were made, Bonneville, the scholarly fur trader, contributed, by his wonderful maps and surveys, a vast amount of valuable information to our government in regard to the geography of the country, and the sources of many important streams in the territory he had explored.

Nathaniel J. Wyeth, merchant, from Cambridge, Mass., became ambitious to establish fur posts on the Pacific. Though this plan was not as ambitions as that of John Jacob Astor, the purpose was the same – trading with the orient. Traveling over the entire length of the Oregon Trail from Independence to Vancouver, Wyeth, from 1832 to 1836, explored in many new places; but to his special credit was the erection in 1834 of Fort Hall, a fur post on the trail situated on the left bank of the Snake River near the mouth of the Portneuf (Idaho). As with Bonneville, Wyeth lacked an adequate preparation, which Ashley possessed to a marked de-

---

[12] See Dale (H. C.) *The Ashley-Smith Explorations,* for maps and description of Smith's routes to the Pacific Coast, 1826-27, and Fort Vancouver, 1828.

gree, for exploring in what was to him an unknown territory. His early training in no way qualified him for the financial adventure. His lack of success may also be attributed to the failure of our government to understand its own interests on the Pacific and to realize the methods being used by the Hudson Bay Company against any American who attempted to obtain a foothold in the Oregon country.

Accompanying Wyeth to the west in 1834 were many people, the most prominent of the group being Jason and Daniel Lee, Cyrus Shepard, C. M. Walker, and P. L. Edwards, missionaries, who had been sent into the wilderness to preach and teach the Indians living south of the Columbia River; Captain William Stewart, a veteran under Lord Wellington at Waterloo, who was traveling for pleasure; Thomas Nuttall, a botanist, and J. K. Townsend, an ornithologist. In the immediate years following, the missionaries and others of Wyeth's party settled in the Willamette valley, built homes, cultivated the soil and became the nucleus of Americans who were to wrest from the British authority the Oregon country.

Following the Lees in their religious zeal to help christianize the Indians, in 1835 Reverend Samuel Parker and Dr. Marcus Whitman, led through the mountains by the indominitable Fontenelle, went over the trail toward the Oregon country. When the party traveled through South Pass, Parker remarked that there would be no difficulty in constructing a railroad from the Atlantic to the Pacific, so gradual was the grade through the pass. Among those at a Green River rendezvous, many Indians from many tribes were congregated, all begging for the "Book of Heaven," as they called the white man's Bible. Finding a large number of savages desirous of obtaining religious instruction, Dr. Whitman decided that two men were insufficient to do the teaching, and sent Parker, the elder man, on into the wilderness, with Jim Bridger for a guide, while he, the younger man, retraced his steps back to the East to obtain recruits for the religious educational work. The next spring, Whitman, with his bride, and Reverend H. H. Spalding, with his bride, back to the East to obtain recruits for the religious work. When the little party, on July 4th, 1836, arrived at South Pass, Whitman went through the formality of taking that part of our country in the name of God and our government. Over the Oregon Trail their wagon journeyed, the wheels marking the road more indelible, but the great significance of these deeper ruts was that they were made by wheels that were carrying white women to the West—the first white women to go over the trail, an unmistakable sign of possession of the land on which were to be built homes by Americans in Oregon. As a result of the establishment of these homes, the Whitman party of 1836 was followed by another wagon-train in 1843, commanded by Dr. Marcus Whitman, who had once more returned to the Atlantic, the largest and most important train that had, to this time, ventured over the trail. In the train were over two hundred wagons, one thousand cattle, many men and women, but also numerous children, who were to be the future citizens of a free American commonwealth on the Pacific coast. The wagons of this long train traversing the entire length of the Oregon Trail, were loaded with farm implements, grain for seed, and the more choice pieces of household furniture that had been saved from the gradual lightening of the load along the road. In the Oregon country, through the efforts of the Americans, places of worship were constructed, schools were started, the soil cultivated, and a small printing press put to work to help mould public opinion. The American with his family had come to stay. The Hudson Bay Company now realized the seriousness of the problem as to which nation, England or the United States, was to possess the rich valleys of the Oregon country.

The first government expedition over the trail was conducted by John Charles Fremont in 1842, when he made a preliminary survey for a possible trans-continental railway. Fremont made five expeditions into the West in attempts to find passes in the mountains through which a railroad could be constructed, three of them for our government and two financed by private means. The first was the Wind River Mountain Expedition of 1842;[13] the second the Salt Lake, Columbia and California Expedition of 1843-44, in both journeys using a major portion of the Oregon Trail for the transportation of men and equipment. To bring the Pacific nearer to the Missouri, to hold the territory on the coast in close relation with our government by railway transportation, and to help keep the people west of the Rocky Mountains loyal citizens of our union – people who were to develop the rich land in the West, were the missions assigned to Fremont.

From Fremont's reports, which the government printed and distributed in great numbers, many emigrants gained a favorable impression of the West, and as a direct result, sought homes beyond the Rocky Mountains, their route to the coveted lands being largely over the Oregon Trail. Into the hands of

[13] On this expedition, after going through South Pass, Fremont pushed into the Wind River Mountains and ascended the Peak that now bears his name.

Brigham Young came this printed information, which was, in the main, responsible for his selection of Utah as a home for his followers. The Mormons, as well as those who sought homes beyond Utah, did their part in making this road more enduring and more easy of travel. Fremont also made a valuable set of topographical maps of the country over which he traveled, the data from which were used for distances along the trails in locating streams and mountains in the government pamphlet.

The Oregon Trail was in reality now a national road, though the government never contributed a cent to its construction or preservation. It was a national road of opportunity, and the longest single road in history. Siberia has a thoroughfare that is a longer highway, but at stated intervals along the way are buildings inhabited by men and women; on the Oregon Road, in 1842, there were but four buildings between Independence, Mo., and Vancouver, Wash., and these were not homes, but fur trading posts – Laramie, Bridger, Hall, and Boise. No engineer placed his transit or rod on this road; no grade was established; no bridge was built over the streams crossing its path; no fills were made; no mountain passes surveyed, yet Father De Smet pronounced the trail one of the finest highways in the world. Now the road which had been a path for the wild animal, the tepee footway for the Indian, the trail of the trapper and the road of the home-seeker, became so deep, so wide, so easy to travel that it might well have been called the Broad Highway to the West.

General W. F. Raynolds, although seeking the Oregon Trail on his way South in 1859, from the Yellowstone, traveling on the Northwest side of the Big Horn Mountains, feared that his expedition might cross the

MORMON EMIGRANTS ON THE OREGON TRAIL AT SOUTH PASS
From a photo taken in 1866.

old trail and not know of its existence! He acknowledges his error by saying: "Before starting, I had, in my ignorance, asked Bridger (his guide) if there was any danger of crossing the road without knowing it. I now understand fully his surprise, as it is as well marked as any turnpike at the East. It is hard, dry and dusty, and gave evidence of the immense amount of travel that passes over it. . . The Platte Road is truly a national thoroughfare. . . The Indians are perfectly peaceful, and it is not unusual to see men riding singly along the road, though for company more than for considerations of safety, they generally traveled in parties of two or three."[14]

No wonder the white man was eager to push on beyond the firing line of civilization by using this road. No wonder that the red man was ever persistent that his lands should not be utilized by dividing them up by the "Medicine Road." That the Indian frequently came into conflict with the white man as he drifted back and forth with the season, on either side of the trail on the annual hunt, was an inevitable consequence of frontier conflict for the control of land.

General John Charles Fremont, after his first expedition to the Rocky Mountains by way of the Oregon Trail, strongly recommended to our government that military forts should be established along the Oregon Trail. Not to protect the settlers in the regions of the forts, for there were no such hardy people along the road, but to assist and guard the Americans and their trains of wagons on their way to the West, who were to help in the development of the Oregon country. Of the four forts finally taken over by our gov-

[14] *The Yellowstone Expedition*, Congressional Document, 40th Congress, 1st Session, Senate *Executive Document*, No. 77, Serial number No. 1317, p. 70.

ernment and garrisoned by the regular soldiers who safeguarded the lives of those, venturesome and daring, on their way to the west, no one was so important and became so well known for its romance and tragedy, as Fort Laramie.

Largely upon the recommendation of Fremont, Congress established along the Oregon Trail to protect two thousand and twenty miles of road, four forts, viz: Fort Kearney (Nebraska), in use 1847, purchased 1849, three hundred and sixteen miles from Independence, on the Platte near Grand Island; Fort Laramie (Wyoming, three hundred and fifty-one miles from Fort Kearney, a fur post in 1834, purchased in 1849, situated near the junction of the Laramie with the Platte; Fort Bridger, four hundred and three miles from Fort Laramie, established by Jim Bridger in 1842 as a repair and blacksmith shop for the emigrants in the valley of the Black Fork, a tributary of the Green, (used as a military post 1858-1890); Fort Hall (Idaho), situated two hundred and eighteen miles from Fort Bridger, seven hundred and thirty-two miles from Fort Vancouver, on the right bank of the Snake, nine miles above the mouth of the Portneuf, built in 1834 by Wyeth as a fur post— four military stations, each hundreds of miles apart, in the heart of the tribes of hostile Indians. No wonder the Indian had small fear of the soldiers and little respect for a government that had such a limited knowledge of Indian warfare and unprotected trails into the undeveloped West.

Those daring white men who plied the first fur trade in the West along the Oregon Trail went up the Missouri as far north as where the river is joined by the Platte (Omaha, Nebraska). From here the route West was along the south side of the Platte to the junction of the north and south branches of the river. At an early date in fur trading over the Oregon Trail a more direct road was established by a cut-off which abandoned the Missouri not far from Independence and went to the northwest by crossing the Kansas, Big and Little Blue Rivers, reaching the Platte about twenty miles below Grand Island, the distance to this point from Independence being three hundred and sixteen miles.[15]

The Santa Fé and Oregon Trails were one and the same for forty-one miles west of Independence, at which point the two roads separated, one going southwest to Santa Fé, the other to the northwest to the Pacific. The directions on a sign-board at the point of deviation read: "This Road to Oregon"—not too-detailed instructions for one thousand nine hundred and seventy-nine miles of travel through many tribes of hostile Indians, across countless streams, over treeless prairies, and through numerous mountain passes!

From where the Oregon Trail met the Platte the road continued on the south side of the stream, and also along the south side of the North Platte, to the northwest, passing the two historic land marks, Chimney Rock and Scott's Bluffs, to Fort Laramie (667), a place of rest, protection, repairs, and supplies having been erected in 1834 by William L. Sublette as a fur store house rather than a fortification against hostile Indians. From Fort Laramie the trail went northwest to the big bend in the North Platte, near the present city of Caspar (794), down the west side of the Platte, but not following it, the road crossed the Sweetwater at Independ-

---

[15] Figures in parenthesis designate distance from Independence taken from Chittenden (H. M.) *History of the American Fur Trade in the Far West,* Chittenden's data was to a great degree obtained from General Fremont's surveys.

ence Rock (838) then directly west to Devil's Gate, a rift in the mountains through which all of the wagons had to go which traversed the Oregon Trail—to Split Rock and South Pass (947). This was the half-way point between Independence and Vancouver, the streams east of the pass flowing toward the Atlantic, those west toward the Pacific. In the earlier days, before Fort Bridger was built, the Oregon Trail went southwest to Pacific Springs, across the Little and Big Sandy to the Green River (1014) and then northwest to Snake River. Early in the using of the trail the road from Pacific Springs deflected its course to the southwest to Black's Fork near its junction with Ham's Fork where James Bridger had erected a blacksmith shop and repair station for the emigrants, known as Fort Bridger. In place of always stretching to the southwest, in order to save time and many miles, there was established a branch of the Oregon Trail known as the "Sublette Cut-off" which left the main trail at Little Sandy (969) taking a direct route to the west crossing Big Sandy and Green River thence to Bear River (1093) where it blended with the road coming from Fort Bridger. Though fifty-three miles were saved by this short cut, the emigrants missed Fort Bridger, where supplies could be obtained and repairs made. From the fort the trail went to Fort Hall (1288) whence it reached the waters of the Columbia, west to American and Salmon Falls, to Fort Boise (1585) and then directly northwest to the Columbia River (1835) thence it continued west on the south side of the river to the Dalles (1934) from the Cascades to Fort Vancouver [16] (2020) opposite the mouth of the Willamette River.

---

[16] Fort Vancouver was the headquarters of the Hudson Bay Company

EMIGRANT TRAIN ON THE OREGON TRAIL, CROSSING GREEN RIVER
From an original painting made in 1853.

The Oregon Trail, hazardous though not difficult of travel, did not have between Fort Laramie and Fort Bridger any intervening stations until the coming of the pony express and stage coaches. In the sixties these stations were constructed, not to house or protect the whites, but for the exchange of tired horses for fresh ones. In order to go to Oregon, California, Nevada, Idaho or Montana, this trail had to be used. The constant procession of emigrants over this road, coming from the country east of the Missouri, caused the Indians to wonder and ponder. Placing their hands upon their mouths they called the trail "The Great Medicine Road of the Whites," believing that the lands from whence the white man came must now be empty, so great was the exodus to the West. At first the Indian made no objection to this invasion over his traditional trail which he used when in quest of game or as a more permanent trail to places for water.

Ultimately a time came when protests from the red man became so forceful in the way of ambush, raids, and open conflict against the white man, that those who went over the "Medicine Road" now had to go in groups, and by force of firearms passed over the coveted trail.

Had it not been for the hostilities committed by the Indians along the Oregon Trail, and the frequent depredations upon parties of emigrants going West, this road would have been in use to the exclusion of any other until the advent of the Union Pacific Railroad. In order to avoid the hostilities of the Indians, a road along the South Platte was established and called the Overland Route, though contrary to expectations, the raids

on the Columbia for many years, Doctor John McLoughlin being in charge of the post.

were as numerous and depredations as serious as along
the old trail. The old road by the way of Fort Laramie,
the North Platte, Sweetwater, and Fort Bridger, with
the coming of the iron trail, was abandoned in 1869,
although the unnumbered feet, hoofs, and wheels have
made indelible this route; the road today being easily
traced and the furrows accurately followed for miles
along the North Platte and Sweetwater Rivers.

No specially accurate record has been kept of the
number of human souls trudging over this road during
the long years of its operation, though the record for
the year 1852 has been quite accurately estimated during that one year as amounting to over fifty-one thous-
and.

The Overland emigration on the Oregon Trail in
1846 was unending, though never outnumbering those
who, in 1849, scrambled in seeming madness over the
road to the gold fields of California.[17]

Many who sought health and wealth in the country
at the end of the trail failed to reach their destination;
the number of graves along the trail were silent witnesses in the testimony of the battle for territorial expansion. In 1849 four thousand two hundred died on
the plains, while cholera, in 1852, which followed in
the path of the emigrants, claimed five thousand as its
toll – enough graves to mark the entire trail every half
mile for over two thousand miles. To cover this two
thousand (2020) miles took four months under the most
favorable conditions of weather and method of transportation; six months if out of luck.

The tide of emigrants in 1843 to the Oregon country

---

[17] The emigrants who went to the gold fields of California in '49 followed
in the main the Oregon Trail, though many used the Santa Fé and Gila
Trails, the Panama route, and the long voyage around Cape Horn.

CROSSING THE NORTH PLATTE RIVER

On the Overland Stage Route, west of Fort Halleck, and east of Bridger Pass. Observe the method of making a corral to repel night attacks. In the foreground are the graves of emigrants

From an original drawing.

was so large that it was possible for the Americans to set up a provisional government, providing for joint occupancy of that country. The colony that had settled in the Willamette valley, drew up and adopted a code of action before our government had obtained title to the land.[18] That the question of possession of the Oregon country was peacefully settled by the pioneers of the trail, is evidenced by the fact that the Hudson Bay Company not only accepted the terms of the compact for a provisional government, but through taxation added to the financial support of the settlement. By the treaty of 1846 with England, the Oregon country was ceded to the United States, and in 1848 the territory of Oregon was organized, embracing the lands that now are in Washington, Oregon and Idaho, and parts of Montana and Wyoming.

Thus the Oregon Trail helped to win an empire for the United States. The ultimate possession of the Oregon country had been left to that race that should first occupy the territory. The Hudson Bay Company brought its people from the Red River of the North, but the Oregon Trail brought American wagons and homeseekers, which settled the Oregon question once and for all. The old trail had won.[19]

---

[18] In January, 1843, in the United States Senate, one of the members, in speaking of the Oregon country, piously thanked God for His mercy in placing the Rocky Mountains there "as an impossible barrier." Written accounts denounced the entire country as "incapable probably forever, of fixed settlement," while only a portion was susceptible of cultivation. Daniel Webster said, "What do we want with that vast worthless area, this region of savages and wild beasts, of desert, of shifting sands and whirlwinds, of dust, of cactus and prairie dogs? Mr. President, I will never vote one cent from the public treasury to place the Pacific coast one inch nearer to Boston than it is now."

[19] Hough (Emerson). *Traveling Old Trails.* "The Oregon Trail in its full development was not the trail of the trapper, but the big highway of the homeseeker. Its real fires were not tepee smoke, but hearth fires."

The egress to the West feverishly continued all through the sixties, until the Union Pacific Railroad was constructed, as the following extracts from the diary of Sergt. Isaac B. Pennick, 11th Kansas Cavalry,[20] written between May and September, 1865, while a member of the Wind River Expedition, will demonstrate:

"August 17, (1865) . . . arrived before sundown 5 miles below Julesburg, on bank of South Platte River. Camped for the night. Hundreds of wagons along the river – ox trains, mule trains, horse trains, and pony trains in abundance; everything looks lively and brisk.

"August 19 – March at 5 a.m. . . . meet 315 wagons today, making, since leaving crossing at Julesburg, 615 in number, and with what were camped around that post, about one thousand.

"August 20 – Sunday. Remain in camp today. About 175 wagons passed along today.

"August 21 – Reveille at two o'clock a.m. March a little before sunrise . . . met 280 wagons going west today.

"August 22 – Reveille at 3 a.m. Met General Dodge and staff. . . 250 wagons passed today.

"August 26 – Marched one half an hour before sunrise about ten miles . . . a large train of Mormon emigrants camped alongside us at noon."

Thus was the invasion of the West, and the paradise of the Indians continuing. Little wonder that the red man imagined the East was being rapidly depopulated!

---

[20] Used by courtesy of William E. Connelley, Esq., secretary of the Kansas Historical Society.

The Overland Stage and Telegraph Lines

As the Oregon Trail widened and became deeper in the soil of the mountains and plains, stretching its arms toward the West, the people eventually did not have the Pacific coast for their destination. Gradually, here and there, the man with his family unyoked his oxen, unharnessed his horses, and prepared to make a home in those sections most attractive in what was named and known as "The Great American Desert." Occasional streams, on the banks of which vegetation had been courageous enough to grow, lured the homeseeker. Land was free, unsurveyed and unclaimed. Even with these attractions the land called but a few of the more venturesome men, their brave wives and care-free children, who knew no danger.

Around these isolated families towns sprung up, sparsely inhabited, it is true, but enough to say that the firing-line of a newer civilization was now being pushed rapidly toward the setting sun. Chiefly, however, were the camps in the mining districts, for in many places not only were gold and silver yielding "pay dirt," but were found to be most profitable.

The necessity for safer and better means of transportation of supplies to these mining camps became most urgent. Sacramento, the end of the California branch of the Oregon Trail, and the center of the early gold excitement in California, for a number of years had demanded the attention of the hardy frontiersmen and risking miner, in their mad rush to California, in

those days of the '49er and following years. With the
advent of gold being found in those inland territories
of Idaho, Utah, Montana, and Colorado, new trails or
roads were put into operation. These were not constructed by the government, but side routes from the
main trails, made by the men seeking gold. Anything
to add to adventure and excitement was not considered
a hardship, not even the opening of a hazardous road in
and through the mountains or on the trackless prairie.
As a logical outcome of the constant need for food,
clothing and tools, an organized movement was started
to have supplies transferred from the Missouri River
to the wealth-bearing mountains.

Over the Oregon Trail these supply caravans or
wagon trains wended their way through the country
that had been pronounced as "only fit for prairie dogs
and Indians." Of course the population was more or
less of a floating nature – many today, few tomorrow;
the next day a ghost city, a characteristic feature of the
many mushroom towns made or ruined by gold or the
lack of it.

Those who came to the mountains in these earliest
days of the development of the West and the making
of a camp, did not go into agriculture or any other occupation that was productive of the commodities desired by them. To have things to eat and wear, tools
for digging the ore, horses and mules to operate the
heavy work of the mines, and food for these working
animals, made the commerce of freighting an absolute
necessity.

Wagon traffic was to supply not only necessities but
luxuries for the West, be it on the isolated portions of
the plains, or in the hidden passes in the mountains.

Before the establishment of the regular freight

THE VERY OCCASIONAL HOME ALONG THE OVERLAND ROAD
in Laramie Valley, north of Virginia Dale Station.

trains, individual families, on their way to the West, banded together for self-protection from the hostile Indians. Exactly as to how commerce could be extended to those who had pushed into the unoccupied lands, received not only the perplexing consideration of those who were to make the journey, but companies doing a transporting business took the matter under advisement. Our government attempted to offer a solution for this congested form of trade, the demand for supplies vastly outrunning the possibility of getting the commodities to the West. In the desire to solve the problem, the government, on the line of the Santa Fé Trail, advocated and actually introduced some eighty camels to be used as a means of transportation. These "ships of the desert," which were not climatically adapted to our country, and which frightened the horses and mules of the caravans, were finally released and allowed their freedom. The experiment in these long-necked, double-stomached, and cushion-footed animals extended as far north as Idaho and Montana. In 1865 camels were used for freighting to the mining camps, particularly from Helena, Montana, to Walla Walla, Washington. The animals were able to carry a load from eight hundred to one thousand two hundred pounds' weight. This camel train went by the way of the Coeur d'Alene Mountains and through Hell's Gate to the gold mines. These camels in the northwest were doubtless a part of the experiment carried on by our War Department in 1856 over the Gila and Santa Fé Trails. The animals, in the first instance, coming from the Levant, costing our government the sum of thirty thousand dollars for the experiment.

Finally the people of the Pacific coast demanded that the government take the necessary steps toward estab-

lishing a mail route across the mountains and the plains.
When Utah was created as a territory, the people had to
wait for official information of the Act of Congress,
from September, 1850, to January of the following
year, the informing letter going by the Panama route to
California and then east back to Utah.   In July, 1850,
the first mail route of monthly service was established
between Independence and Salt Lake, where it met an
extension line going to California, a very unsatisfactory
enterprise, which only continued for a short time.   In
1854 the government established a mail service, also
monthly, to Sacramento from the Missouri by the southern route, via Albuquerque, a service that also failed to
meet the demand.

It was not until the year 1858 that efficient mail service for the far West was established, when the Butter-
field Southern Overland Mail route was put into operation.   The mail was at first sent only semi-weekly, but
soon changed to a six days in the week service, the stages
not running on Sundays.   This route was two thousand
seven hundred and fifty-nine miles long, going by the
way of El Paso, Yuma, and California, making the journey, under favorable conditions, in twenty-three to twenty-five days, carrying letters for ten cents per half ounce,
a passenger fare of one hundred dollars being paid for
the trip.   The one great advantage of this route over
other routes was that it was so far south that it avoided
the snows to be found on northern trails.   This stage
line was forty per cent longer than any other of our
established stage lines, an expensive affair from the
mere fact of its unusual length.   The road's equipment
was also costly, for it contained one hundred Concord
coaches, one thousand horses, five hundred mules, seven
hundred and fifty men, and one hundred and fifty driv-

ers. The Civil War coming in 1861 forced our government to change the route into a more northern territory, selecting the Overland Trail for a new road, to run from St. Joseph (Mo.) to Placerville (Cal.), the road being known at the "Central Route."

A mail stage was started July 11, 1861, over the Oregon Trail, simultaneously east and west, at the ends of the line, each stage making the journey in eighteen days against that of twenty-five days over the southern route, a saving of one week's time. The fare for the trip across the plains from Atchison to Placerville, in the early sixties, was six hundred dollars, which included twenty-five pounds of baggage, any excess costing one dollar a pound.

But the stages, lumbering at best, were too slow in their transportation of mail to the impatient, news-hungry people of California, who were demanding that a more speedy method to carry the mail must be inaugurated. As a result of persistent demand, through the efforts of William H. Russell, the pony express was put on the Oregon Trail, which carried mail to California in ten days. The road for the pony express, from St. Joseph to Placerville, a distance of almost two thousand miles, followed frequently the Oregon and California Trails, though cut-offs were taken to avoid the Indians, or to find places where stations could be maintained near a stream of water.[21] The horses employed were all small, and of western breed. There were five hundred of them, and the riders were light of weight to match their mounts.

The company operating the pony express had two hundred station-keepers, and one hundred and ninety

---

[21] From Fort Laramie to Fort Bridger the pony express utilized the Oregon Trail to the exclusion of any other road.

stations at which the eighty riders were given only two minutes in which to change horses and transfer their saddlebags of mail. The stations were from nine to fifteen miles apart, depending upon the proximity to water. Letters, costing five dollars a half-ounce were limited to fifteen pounds for the average rider, the weight being equally divided into two flat leather securely locked mail pouches. During the years of operation of the pony express, from April 23, 1860, to October 22, 1861, the mail was lost but once, when it was stolen by the Indians. The best time made with this overland service by these relay riders was seven days and seventeen hours, when President Lincoln's inaugural message was whisked over the route. There is no more picturesque achievement of the plains than the operation of the pony express, which shortened the time for Pacific mail service, thus bringing the people of the coast many days nearer to their former homes and to the national government.

General Raynolds, when at his winter headquarters, in 1859-60, not far from the junction of Deer Creek with the North Platte, on the south side of the Oregon Trail, was one of the first west of Fort Laramie to receive mail by the means of the pony express. "The pony express was established while we were in winter quarters, and by it we several times received interesting news but three days old. . . The sight of a solitary horseman galloping along the road was in itself nothing remarkable, but when we remember that he was one of a series stretching across the continent, and forming a continuous chain for two thousand miles through an almost absolute wilderness, the undertaking was justly ranked among the events of the age, and the most striking triumph of American energy."

Alexander Majors, in 1858, when helping the government to fill its contracts to carry supplies to Utah, used three thousand five hundred wagons, four thousand men, one thousand mules, and more than forty thousand oxen.[22] During May, 1859, no less personages than Horace Greeley, Henry Villiard, and Albert D. Richardson rode into Denver on Majors' first stage coach, "Horsepower Pullman," making the distance of six hundred and sixty-five miles in six days, a distance that previously had been covered in twenty-two days. This first through stage coach made the trip of six hundred miles between Denver and Salt Lake "without a single town, hamlet or house being encountered on the way," there being, of course, a few necessary stage stations.

As the emigrants crowded the Oregon Trail, the question of transportation became one for solution by our government by cooperating with the regularly established freighting companies previously operating on the roads to the West. These regularly established trains materially reduced the cost of freight, and as a consequence immediately increased the sum total of emigration and the supplies incident to a larger western population. During the decade of 1859-1869 it has been estimated that at least two hundred and fifty thousand people went west by the route of the Oregon and Overland Trails. The greatest period of freighting was between the years 1863-1867, at the latter date the Union Pacific, in its extension to the west, reached Cheyenne, Wyoming.

Ben Holladay, between the years 1861-1866 operated

[22] Lummis (C. F.) *Pioneer Transportation in America.* "When estimating that oxen of the most enduring kind cost $1,000 a pair which with other expenses made a single wagon outfit cost in the neighborhood of $7,100, one has at least a faint idea of the enormous cost of a Conestoga wagon train."

daily about five thousand miles of stage coaches, having
an equipment of five hundred coaches and express
wagons, five hundred freight wagons, five thousand
horses and mules, and numerous oxen. The cost to take
care of the stock of this company averaged a million
dollars annually, while to equip and run the line for the
first year incurred the added expense of two million
four hundred and twenty-five thousand dollars. After
five years of freighting Holladay sold out his entire
business to the Wells Fargo Company, which remained
in active operation until 1869 in that particular line of
transportation, when the Union and Central Pacific
Railroads were completed. Holladay, in 1865, to
help out the overland route to the Montana gold fields,
established a branch line of his road, which went from
Fort Hall (Idaho) north to Virginia City (Montana).
In addition to freighting Holladay carried the mail for
the government during the period of the Civil War,
receiving annually one million dollars for the service.

Interesting statistics show that in 1861 over twenty-
one million pounds of freight went west from the shipping points of Atchison, which brought with it to the
plains four thousand nine hundred and seventeen wagons, six thousand one hundred and sixty-four mules,
twenty-seven thousand six hundred and eighty-five ox-
en, and one thousand two hundred and fifty-six men.

Russell, Majors and Waddell, for many years the
government contractors to transport military supplies to
the forts along the trails, used in their trail-freighting
train, six thousand two hundred and fifty oversized wagons, with a carrying capacity of six thousand pounds
each, and seventy-five thousand oxen. This array of
transportation facilities, if placed one in front of the
other, would have covered the trail for a stretch of

forty miles.   Charles F. Lummis states that there is a question if there were at this time as many oxen working in the United States as Russell, Majors and Waddell owned and used.   This mighty traffic scarred the face of the trail to the West so deep that in many places, for miles, there are still discernible traces of the heavy traffic of this period, even after more than half a century of disuse.

"It is doubtful if there was another section of the country on the face of the globe over which, in the sixties, passed so much traffic by ox, horse, and mule team.   A goodly portion of the travel, for two hundred to four hundred miles, was along the right, or south bank of the South Platte.   At times there was hardly an hour but what, as far as the eye could reach, there appeared to be almost a solid train of moving, white-covered wagons, or, as they were more familiarly termed, 'prairie schooners.'   Usually the most of these schooners were drawn by from four to six yoke of cattle, and the writer counted, from his seat on the stage coach, along the Platte, between Fort Kearney and old Julesburg, in one day during the Civil War, nearly nine hundred—to be exact, eight hundred and eighty-eight, destined westward on the great overland route. These wagons were drawn by no less than ten thousand six hundred and fifty animals—cattle, horses, and mules." [23]

Of course all of these did not belong to the Russell outfit, but the impetus given the trade by this well-organized company made itself immediately felt.   After the freighting system had been in intense operation, it was not an uncommon thing to see stretched across the plains each week over one thousand of these patient,

[23] *The Overland Stage to California*, by Root & Connelley.

plodding ox-teams, with wagons loaded many feet beyond the side-boards.

It was a collossal business to supply those things most
needed for the towns and cities that were springing into
existence in the West, and the Oregon Trail became
wider and deeper, until the snows and rains of many
years have not been able to obliterate the road made by
the feet of man, the hoofs of cattle and horses, and the
heavy, broad tires of the compactly loaded freight
wagons.

With the discovery of gold in Colorado and the con-
sequent growth of the city of Denver, the trail to the
West was somewhat changed by using the banks of the
South Platte, as well as those of the North Platte, for a
thoroughfare. The opening of the route up the south
branch of the Platte did not mean the abandonment of
the northern branch of this river, for the emigrants
used the old trail to the exclusion of the newer road,
over which went the stage coaches and teams of freighting.

The extending of the telegraph line across the continent, under the management of Edward Creighton,
in 1861, was the undoing of the pony express, which
had been inaugurated in order to have a better and
more rapid mail service from the Missouri River to
San Francisco. The through telegraph was put into
operation on October 24, 1861, when the first transcontinental message was flashed over the line. Thus, a
distinctive step was taken in the binding and uniting
of the Missouri with the Pacific Ocean. This telegraph line ran parallel with and over the Oregon Trail,
and soon became to the Indians a symbol of the white
man's despotism and his determination to finally possess the country through which the singing wires had

spun their way to the lands of the mining camps and new mountain homes.

There were established two stage and telegraph lines from the Missouri, one running from Fort Leavenworth to Fort Kearney, and the other going from Omaha to Fort Kearney. Here, at this last named post, the lines consolidated, going up the Platte valley as far as Julesburg, a conspicuous stage station near the mouth of Lodge Pole Creek, where it emptied into the Platte. At this characteristically-alive border town the lines again separated, the main telegraph line going northwestward to Fort Laramie and beyond to South Pass and Utah, while the stage line went southwestward to Denver, by the way of the South Platte. From Denver the coaches went north to Fort (or Camp) Collins, thence to Virginia Dale, across the Laramie Plains, Fort Halleck, Elk Mountain, Bridger's Pass, Bitter Creek, out to Fort Bridger, on to Utah, California, Oregon, and Montana. Just east of Fort Bridger the Oregon Trail and the Overland Trail united and became one.

The history of the experience of the men having in charge the stage and telegraph stations has been the tragedy of many a tome, for around these buildings was to be the battlefield of numerous Indian depredations and bloody conflicts – a contest between the white and red man, for the possession of the West.

The route of the stage lines crossing these savagely contested lands, had stage stations situated about every twelve miles along their length, while the government troops were posted along the route at specially constructed forts or stockades or blockhouses at intervals of about one hundred miles. The scarcity of soldiers, particularly during the Civil War, available for this dangerous duty, made the lives of the few who served one of extreme danger. Only a few armed and trained men were distributed at each station. In addition to these fortified buildings along the way, were the occasional farmer and ranchman, the relay stations for changing horses and the eating houses.

Julesburg, near the mouth of Lodge Pole Creek, has been described by General Grenville M. Dodge, soldier, engineer, and Indian fighter, as celebrated for its desperadoes. "No twenty-four hours passed without its contribution to Boot Hill (the cemetery where every occupant was buried in his boots) and homicide was performed in the most genial and whole souled way." At this station, which was built of logs hauled one hundred miles from a point down the Platte, were the express and telegraph stations, several stables and corrals, besides a log store or warehouse in which were stored the supplies belonging to the stage company. Just west, one mile up the South Platte, was located Fort Sedgwick, the beginning of a new road to Virginia City, Montana, called the Bozeman Trail. This fortification was at one time called Camp Rankin, established in August, 1864, becoming a fort the following year. Troops of cavalry were stationed here in order to prevent Indian depredations.

At this typical western town of Julesburg there was always a scene of excitement and tremendous activity, for here was located a large supply station where long strings of wagon-trains stopped and discharged their freight, which ultimately was to go to the camps and town both up the North and South Platte route. In the middle sixties the town consisted of a number of adobe houses, one story high. Shingles could not be obtained, the substitute being poles with sagebrush on top of them. On the top of the brush were gunny sacks, and then six inches of dirt. This was the style of roofing used on all of the buildings on the plains at this period of house construction. Not exactly rain proof; not perfectly stable, for the constant winds played havoc with the dirt; yet, for all of this, the covering to the house was adequate to keep out the hot sun, the snow and rain.

Our government ruled, as Indian warfare became more menacing, that additional posts must be established and maintained along the roads leading to the West. Many camps, forts and blockhouses, as a result of this mandate, were erected. Not too numerous were these buildings, as could be testified to by those who occupied them, and by those who had to defend the human freight and the commerce of the highway.

"A military necessity for the soldier's presence at a certain point arose, and orders were issued for a post to be built. A command was marched out, say on to the wide plain far from any one else, and halted beside a stream. It had been told to build a post, and a post was built. All of the labor of constructing it was done by the command, and with the few supplies procurable wonders were accomplished. There was not time to wait for the slow processes of Congress and appropriations bills. And so small frontier forts were created in this manner all over the West. These posts were badly needed, and needed at once, for many purposes. There were settlements to be protected until they were able to take care of themselves, roads to be opened, and travelers to be guarded. Indians had to be held in check and compelled to remain on their reserves, and depots maintained at favorable points. So these stations were constructed by the soldiers on the wind-swept plains, in lonely mountain passes, on desolate hillsides, in groves on the banks of swift-flowing rivers and in sunny valleys at the foot of snow clad mountain peaks." [24]

All through the history of this pioneer condition of our western uninhabited country are written, in supreme sacrifice, the stories of narrow escapes – of camps attacked, stock stolen, human suffering from sudden and continuous snow storms, extreme cold without adequate fire, the hardships of those who were separated by hundreds of miles from sufficient aid; of the heroic acts of those who were thrown on their resources for life and preservation. These were not the record of one brave sentinel, but that of hundreds of station men, telegraph operators, frontiersmen, and soldiers.

It would be difficult for the present day to realize the speed attained and maintained by one of the swaying and rocking stage coaches thundering along the dusty road. To go from one station to another no stops were made. There could not be, for there was no time to be lost, the stages being required to make the scheduled time of seven hundred miles in every seven days. Time lost on one day had to be added to the next. These roughly-built stations of sod, located in the most isolated places, would hold from twelve to twenty head of well-built, well-fed, and hard-worked horses. A detachment of infantry and cavalry guarded the stations, while, when danger was great, or even when it seemed there was no danger, the coaches were accompanied by from four to twenty mounted soldiers.

That the spirit of the Civil War extended to these plains is made manifest by the words used by the "Major-General of the Bullwhackers," as a leader of a caravan of oxen was called, who sang out, with oaths

[24] Forsyth (George A.) *The Story of the Soldier*, p. 105.

CAMP MITCHELL, NEBRASKA TERRITORY

HORSE-SHOE STATION, IDAHO TERRITORY

John Phillips arrived at Horse-shoe Station Dec. 25, 1866, whence he sent his
dispatches giving first official information of the Fetterman disaster.
Both reproduced from drawings made by Bugler C. Moellman, Co. G, Eleventh
Ohio Cavalry, in 1863.

most generally: "Come here, Grant! You Sheridan! g'long, Abe!" using the fierce, long and stinging whip with wonderful dexterity on the calloused backs of the oxen, all named for the favorite officers of the owner of the patient beasts, giving evidence of sympathy with the North or the South, as the animals responded to their high-sounding names.

The remains of these road stations have long since become a record of the past, though once in a while the more substantial foundations have left a bare outline, marking the site of their occupation. A mere mention only of some of these "isles of safety," is given, to be remembered, however, that to keep the plains from destruction by the Indians was to invite death — worse by torture and mutilation of the most horrible nature, revolting to an extreme.

The following military, stage, and telegraph stations along the trails to the West, each in turn protected the emigrants or the passengers in the stage coaches, through the watchfulness and bravery of the soldiers and civilians stationed along the route. A few landmarks along the trail are also included:

INDEPENDENCE, Mo. The starting point for those who were to go either by the Santa Fé Trail or the Oregon Trail to the far West.

FORT KEARNEY, Nebraska, three hundred and sixteen miles from Independence, two hundred and fifty-three miles from Fort Atchison, and four hundred miles from Denver. On the south side of the Platte River; a significant military post to which troops were first brought in 1847; the soldiers usually being assigned from here to all of the stations along the trails. From here went the North Platte route to the northwest, or the Oregon Trail.

CHIMNEY ROCK, five hundred and seventy-one miles from Independence, on the North Platte and Oregon Trail. A castle-like formation. No one going to the West in the early days over this trail failed to make mention of this famous landmark.

FORT MITCHELL, six hundred miles from Independence, (eighty-seven miles from the Lodge Pole Creek crossing) built in 1864, on the Oregon Trail, just east of the Wyoming-Nebraska boundary; used also as a telegraph station. Named for Brigadier-General Robert B. Mitchell, who, in 1865, was in command against the hostile Indians of the Overland Trail from Omaha to South Pass. This station had, in 1866, one company of sixty soldiers to hold back the stealthy hordes of warriors of the plains! It was but a feeble menace to the thousands of dissatisfied warriors who were then waiting to see what the soldiers could and would do with their ancient hunting ground.

FORT LARAMIE, about one hundred and eighty-four miles west of Julesburg. The most imposing and substantial of all the military posts on the Oregon Trail. Many of the Indian conferences with the whites were held here, and many treaties made and signed within its walls. All of the buildings were on the south side of the North Platte River at its confluence with the Laramie River. Between the years 1846 and 1869 Fort Laramie was in five territories, viz: Missouri, Nebraska, Idaho, Dakota, and Wyoming.

HORSESHOE STATION, thirty-six miles west of Fort Laramie; not on the North Platte, but on the Oregon Trail, which, from Fort Laramie to Deer Creek, did not follow the river, but went directly northwest, being several miles south of the river. In 1862 this station, also a telegraph station, was the headquarters of the

CAMP MARSHALL, IDAHO TERRITORY

DEER CREEK STATION, IDAHO TERRITORY

From a drawing made by Bugler C. Moellman, Co. G, Eleventh Ohio Cavalry, in 1863.

notorious John A. Slade. (About eight miles east of present Glendo, Wyoming.) It was to this telegraph station on December 25, 1866, that John ("Portugee") Phillips, the courier from Fort Phil Kearney, came to send word by wire to Fort Laramie conveying the news of the terrible Fetterman disaster.[25]

CAMP MARSHALL, also known as La Bonte; telegraph station about sixty-six miles west of Fort Laramie. Ten miles east of this old station, in 1857, Jim Bridger had a ferry which was in operation for the two following years. The site of the old ferry is a few miles east of Orin Junction of today, where the railroad bridge crosses the North Platte. From this point the old Bozeman Trail, on its way to the Powder River country, left the North Platte.

LA PRELE, about eighty-two miles west of Fort Laramie station; also a telegraph station. At this station, on April 15th, 1865, the telegraph message was received telling of the assassination of President Lincoln.

DEER CREEK STATION, one hundred and two miles from Fort Laramie, and thirty miles east of Platte Bridge. This fort and military station was on the largest tributary of the North Platte since leaving Fort Laramie. This was an important emigrant camping place, where a ferry was in operation. (Station where now is the town of Glenrock). Additional soldiers were frequently called to this station from Fort Caspar, as it was constantly being beseiged by Indians; not only on the Oregon Trail, but the Indian trails running north and south. In 1852 the emigrants crossed the North Platte at this point by a ferry. In Stans-

---

[25] The telegraph operator was John C. Friend, now of Rawlins, Wyoming, who sent the message also to Omaha from Colonel Carrington, advising the authorities of the Fetterman disaster.

bury's report appears the following: "(DEER CREEK, July 25, 1852): Just above the mouth of the stream there was a ferry over the north fork of the Platte, at which I determined to cross the train. The means employed for this purpose were of the rudest and simplest kind. The ferry boat was constructed of seven canoes, dug out from cottonwood logs, fastened side by side with poles, a couple of hewn logs being secured across the tops, upon which the wheels of the wagons rested. This rude raft was drawn back and forth by means of a rope stretched across the river, and secured at the ends to either bank."

PLATTE BRIDGE STATION, seven hundred and ninety-four miles from Independence and about one hundred and thirty miles from Fort Laramie; on the south side of the Platte; a strategic point for attack by the Indians. The station had a stockade, inside of which were accommodations for about one hundred men; about fifty rods from the station was the bridge of same name. A ferry was established here in 1847. From July 29, 1858, to April 20, 1859, a bridge in the meantime having been built by Louis Ganard over the Platte, United States troops were placed at this point on the Oregon Trail to keep open the communication with Salt Lake, and to aid in the prompt forwarding of supplies. From April 20th, 1859, there were no troops at the Platte Bridge until May, 1862, when the bridge was guarded by volunteer troops who were serving as escort for emigrants, and for the protection of the telegraph line. A year later this post at the bridge was reestablished, accommodating several companies of regulars.

SWEETWATER STATION, about fifty miles southwest from Platte Bridge Station, or Fort Caspar, as it in time was called, the first station after leaving the North

SWEETWATER STATION, IDAHO TERRITORY

Sweetwater was headquarters of Lieut. Caspar W. Collins, Eleventh Ohio
Cavalry.

THREE CROSSINGS STATION, IDAHO TERRITORY

Both reproduced from drawings made by Bugler C. Moellman, Co. G,
Eleventh Ohio Cavalry, in 1863.

Platte.   A telegraph station two miles east of Independence Rock.[26]

INDEPENDENCE ROCK, Wyoming.   A noted landmark composed of almost one solid rock one mile around its base.   Father De Smet, in 1852, called this "The Register of the Desert," for even by this time the faces of the rock were filled with names that had been carved indelibly on its surface.   Many of them, made even before the '60's, may be traced today.

THREE CROSSINGS STATION, one hundred and twenty miles southwet of Fort Caspar; a telegraph station. It received this name from the fact that, on account of the bends in the river within a few rods, it was necessary to ford the Sweetwater three times.   It was at this part of the route that Indians were encountered, and the road-agents made their headquarters in the mountains near here.   It was at this station, in 1866, Buffalo Bill (William F. Cody) while driving an overland express, was attacked by several hundred Sioux.   The experiences of this raid, Colonel Cody presented in a realistic manner in the early days of his Wild West Show.

ST. MARY'S STATION, also called Rocky Ridge Station; about three hundred miles from Fort Laramie; twelve miles below the old town of Lewiston, and eighteen miles from the old mining camp of South

---

[26] These stations were built to resist the Indian attacks and to house the animals as well as the men.   This station, characteristic of others, accommodating forty men, was surrounded by a log palisade fifteen feet high.   On the two opposite corners were block houses, affording the guards a sweeping view of the entire surrounding country.   Inside the enclosure were separate rooms for a hospital, telegraph office, dining room, mess room, surgeon's quarters, officers' quarters, parade ground, soldiers' quarters, laundress' quarters, four stables, warehouse, and granary.   This station was established in 1861 by the stage and telegraph company, and was the home station and division agents headquarters.

Pass City. This never became a station on account of its distance from the Trail. It was located over ten miles north of the Oregon Trail.

SOUTH PASS STATION, or Burnt Fort; nine hundred and forty-seven miles from Independence and half-way to Fort Vancouver. At this point the emigrants had great rejoicings, for then they were half over their long and dangerous journey. The wide rift of the Rocky Mountains at this point made the trail not only possible, but very easy of passage.

PACIFIC SPRINGS STATION, fourteen miles further to the west. Here, for the first time, the emigrants tasted the waters that flowed towards the Pacific Ocean.

FORT BRIDGER; in 1834 a small inferior trading post; built in a substantial way in 1843 by Jim Bridger; occupied by the United States Military forces from June 10, 1858, to October 6, 1890.

FORT HALL, one thousand, two hundred and eighty-eight miles from the starting point, built July, 1834, by Nathaniel J. Wyeth and his fifty men. The first important station on the waters that fed the Columbia River. Fort abandoned in 1855.[27] A road to California branched to the southwest from this fort, called the California Trail, which, after the finding of gold at Sacramento, became as much a thoroughfare as the road to Oregon.

FORT BOISE, built by the Hudson Bay Company on the Snake River, eight miles below the mouth of the Boise.

FORT VANCOUVER, the end of the original Oregon Trail, two thousand and twenty miles from Independence, one hundred and forty-four miles from the mouth

[27] Site on the Oregon Short Line Railroad, nine miles north of Pocatello, Idaho.

ST. MARY'S OR ROCKY RIDGE STATION,
IDAHO TERRITORY

SOUTH PASS STATION, OR BURNT FORT,
IDAHO TERRITORY

Both reproduced from drawings made by Bugler C. Moellman, Co. G., Eleventh Ohio Cavalry, in 1863.

of the Columbia, and one hundred and four miles from the site of old Astoria.[28]

By the South Platte Route, the following were some of the more important military, stage, and telegraph stations:

JULESBURG,[29] two hundred miles from Fort Kearney, one hundred and ninety-seven miles from Denver, one hundred and eighty-four miles from Fort Laramie and four hundred and fifty-six miles from Fort Atchison, on the south side of the South Platte River, near where Lodge Pole Creek enters the river.

FORT SEDGWICK, five miles west of Julesburg, named for Major-General John Sedgwick, also called Fort Rankin, established in the fall of 1864. This fort was the beginning of the Bozeman Trail, a road that caused Indian wars and most hostile feeling and demonstration against the whites.

LODGE POLE CREEK Crossing; about thirty-three miles from Julesburg; a telegraph station. The trail and telegraph line were on the south side of this stream for about thirty miles, when both turned to the northwest, leaving the stream, going directly to Chimney Rock on the Oregon Trail, and on to Fort Laramie.

CAMP WALBACH, directly west of the crossing at the head of Lodge Pole Creek; established to guard

[28] Nearly the entire length of the Oregon Trail today is traced by the iron trail. A strip of territory from the bend of the North Platte near the present city of Casper, Wyoming, to Independence Rock, fifty-six miles southwest, from thence to Bear River (Wyoming-Utah state line) is practically the only part of the Oregon Trail that has not been followed by a railway. However, it is true that cut-offs have been made on the old road, and curves have been shortened into straight lines.

[29] Owing to the intensity of the Indian warfare in 1862, the mail route was changed from the North Platte to the South Platte. In place of crossing the South Platte at Julesburg and then going to Fort Laramie, the new route ran along the South Platte to Latham, and Denver, and then north and west to Fort Bridger.

and protect the emigrants through Cheyenne Pass, a dangerous spot on this new trail. Established as a military post September 20, 1858; abandoned, April 19, 1859. Named for General J. B. Walbach, who said at the time the camp was constructed: "This was the route which should have been adopted when the road was changed from the Sweetwater and South Pass in 1862," meaning changing from the Oregon Trail to the Overland Route. After going through Cheyenne Pass, the emigrants were soon on the Laramie Plains, where this trail connected and became a part of the Overland Stage Route from the south. This road was never a mail route, but strictly and exclusively one for emigrants, who were driven from the Oregon Trail, unless in caravans, by the hostility of the Indians. From the plains the next station was Fort Halleck.

LATHAM, first known as "Cherokee City", was a mail and stage station at the junction of the Denver and California stage lines, one hundred and thirty-five miles west of Julesburg on the South Platte route, along the south side of the South Platte. The direct route from Latham to the Pacific was west to La Porte; the indirect route went southwest to Denver. From Latham thirty-five miles east of La Porte and sixty-one miles from Denver, and northwest from Denver went the Overland Stage Route to Virginia Dale, Fort Halleck, and then directly west to Utah.[30] Jack Slade also known as Joe Slade and occasionally called Alf Slade, figured quite prominently at this station, for it is here that he is alleged to have cut off the ears of "Old Jules" Reni, from whom the station was named,

---

[30] Latham was considered one of the most important stage stations on the Overland route, for here mail was not only transferred to the stage for Salt Lake, Montana, and California, but also for Denver.— Root & Connelly in *The Overland Stage to California.*

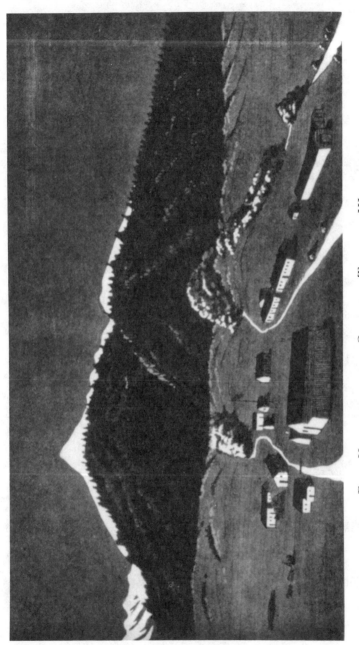

FORT HALLECK, ON THE OVERLAND TRAIL, IN WYOMING.

From a drawing made by Bugler C. Moellman, Co. G, Eleventh Ohio Cavalry, in 1863. Elk Mountain in background.

and wore them for a watch charm, because Jules had, on one occasion over a quarrel, filled Slade with shot.

CAMP COLLINS, also called Fort Collins, named for Colonel Wm. O. Collins, north of Denver, along the Cache La Poudre River. This section of the Overland Route was also called the Cache La Poudre Road.

VIRGINIA DALE STATION; forty miles north of Camp Collins; both a stage and telegraph station, just south of the Colorado-Wyoming boundary line, established in 1862; abandoned in 1867, when the Union Pacific Railroad was constructed. From here, not only did the road run to the northwest over the Laramie Plains to Fort Halleck, but struck off to the northeast to Camp Walbach and on to Fort Laramie. This station was known far and wide, largely for the holdups in the neighborhood and the depredations of Indians and desperadoes. Horace Greeley and Mark Twain stopped at this station in its earliest days on their way to the West. Jack Slade (Joseph A. Slade) was division agent at this station. The old station house yet stands, scarred by many a bullet in the days of dangerous travel.

LARAMIE PLAINS, not a station but a long stretch of country north of the Dale, which afforded an easy road for the Overland. The road ran west of the present city of Laramie, Wyoming, then north to Fort Halleck.

FORT HALLECK, at the foot of Elk Mountain, in the Medicine Bow Range (Carbon County, Wyoming), named for Major-General Henry W. Halleck; established in 1863. From here the stage route was directly west to Bridger's Pass[31] and Bridger's Pass Station to Bitter Creek Station, where the grass was

---

[31] The pass between the head waters of the streams making Sage and Muddy Creeks and twenty miles southwest of Rawlins, Wyoming.

poor and the water bitter and the alkali unbearable; to Green River, and then along the route adopted by the Union Pacific Railroad to old Fort Bridger, where the Oregon Trail and the Overland Route united, and thence to Utah. From Salt Lake City, the road went to Fort Hall, from here southwest to California, northwest to Oregon, and northeast to Virginia City, Montana. When the Overland Route for the mail was, in 1862, changed from the North Platte, the road came from Julesburg to Halleck by way of Latham, Collins, Lupton, etc. Fort Halleck was one of the centers of the Indian disturbances, being attacked from all the points of the compass. The red men came south from the Oregon Trail, north from the South Platte, east from the Camp Walbach road, and west from the Sweetwater.[32] The soldiers guarding this fort and the route to the fort in 1865 were from the Eleventh Ohio Cavalry. From Fort Halleck there ran an Indian trail, well-beaten, on the north side of the Laramie River, also used by the soldiers to go to Fort Laramie. Halleck was in operation from July 20th, 1862, to July 4th, 1866. Colonel Preston B. Plumb was in command of the fort in June, 1865, with five companies of soldiers, who were distributed on the road from Fort Collins to Green River, covering about four hundred miles of the Overland Route and the most dangerous part of the road. Over this road, at one time, and for two hundred miles, the Indians had driven off all the stage horses; Colonel Plumb having to use his cavalry

---

[32] It was at this fort in 1864, where the stage line from Camp Collins was frequently tied up on account of the stage horses being stampeded by Indians, that tons of mail piled up, destined for Salt Lake, Montana, Nevada, and the Pacific. It required, under cavalry escort, half a dozen large government wagons to transport even a portion of the accumulated matter to the Green River where the Indian depredations were less numerous.

horses to haul the coaches, and his soldiers being detailed as drivers. During this period on this section of the road the stages were only run at night, in order to better avoid the Indians.

While at Fort Halleck visiting his father, Colonel Collins, Lieutenant Caspar W. Collins sent home many letters and drawings telling of his life and adventures. The two following letters describe the conditions surrounding Fort Halleck, and his journey from there over a new trail to Fort Laramie. In transmitting these letters for publication, Mrs. Collins, mother of the young lieutenant, on May 12, 1897, from Hillsboro, Ohio, the family home, wrote in pencil on top of her son's letter to her: "I think the within account of James Bridger you will find interesting. My son was only a boy and went out with his father not as a soldier, but companion." (Signed) Mrs. Catherine Wever Collins.

"FORT HALLECK, September 30, 1862.

"DEAR MOTHER: We arrived at this point last night. Shipley's, Mackey's and one company of regulars are stationed here. We left Laramie six days ago and occupied the whole time making the trip. For the first few days we had nothing to eat but fat pork, etc., but at last we killed two antelope and some mountain grouse, sage hens and ducks. The party consisted of my father, Lieutenant Glenn, the wagon master, Sergeant Morris, two privates, one from the regular army and another from Captain Mackey's company, myself, a teamster, Major Bridger and cook. Captain Craig, with our old friend, Colonel Clark and John Reid of Hillsborough, were with us two days, but being in a hurry, left. Lieutenant Glenn was sick nearly the whole time, having dined on cheese and wild cherries one day when he got separated from the party. We found plenty of wild grapes and gathered a good quantity. The whole country back from here on the road is covered with lakes, both large and small, which are covered with ducks. We came through a pass in the mountains, the sides of which were, in some places, three hundred or four hundred feet high and perpendicular. The pass was in very few places more than thirty yards wide. When we were about ten miles from this place the ambulance met us and took Lieutenant Glenn, who is now quite well. We camped two nights in the rain and sleet without any tent, and had a rather disagreeable time, but by burrowing in the bed clothes we got along tolerably well. The first night we had hardly any wood, being camped in a barren prairie. We made out with roots, etc. We are invited to a feast given by John Esse, a French trapper with a Sioux wife and ten or twelve half-breed children. My father thinks it is going to be a dog feast and I do not think he will go. I may. This mountain above the fort is covered with new-fallen snow. It abounds in game, the boys having killed a good many elk and deer, and several times single hunters have been chased by grizzlys. Nine have been seen together almost within the fort. Only one has been killed around here, but a good many have been shot. We are going to explore another road across the Black Hills to Fort Laramie. The mail runs through here. Lieutenant Clark is at present in command of this place. They have a regular surgeon and a quartermaster, both from the Fourth U. S. Cavalry. We are occupying a tent heated by an underground furnace, which makes it very comfortable. There is plenty of wood almost within the fort. There is a boarding house here for the officers, kept by a married regular, the same that came over with us. Three clear streams run through the garrison. The men have their stables built, but have not got their houses done. Some of them are working for the sutler and get from him a dollar and a half a day. One of Shipley's men has died. Some Mexican teamsters have built themselves a house, partly under ground, which can be made as hot as a bake oven by a big fireplace in one corner. I would a great deal rather be on a tramp than in a fort, even for a single day. I rode a mule the whole trip and prefer them to horses to travel on. We had corn for our animals the whole trip and very good grass. This is the windiest place I ever saw – a hurricane blowing the whole time. It is a beautiful place, however. The tall mountains rising so abruptly that it does not look much farther to the top than it does to the foot. Sergeant Morris and four men will probably go back with us. We will probably take about seven or eight days going back. They have to haul their hay for this place about ten miles and their corn from seven hundred to nine hundred miles.

"Your affectionate son,   C. W. COLLINS."

"FORT LARAMIE, October 8, 1862.
"DEAR MOTHER: We arrived here from Fort Halleck yesterday. We had a very pleasant trip through the mountains. We came through on a new road never before traveled by anybody except Indians. We killed a great many antelope between that fort and this. In the mountains we did not see very much game, as the Indians have been hunting all through them and killed and scared all the game away. We had some pretty hard freezes and one snow storm that melted as it fell. We only put up the tent one night, but we always had good fires. The wagon master, Lieutenant Glenn, Sergeants Morris and Herman of Company C, four soldiers, including our hunting friend, Roberts, and the teamster and cook made up our party. I killed hares and rabbits, sage and prairie chickens, grouse and ducks and any other game in reach of duck-shot. My father killed two very large antelope. The dogs had the distemper on the march and had a rather hard time of it traveling. There is some of the grandest scenery you ever saw through the Black Hills. Immense piles of rock, covered with pines, and beautiful valleys of grass that is up to your waist. They are full of clear springs, which burst out and sink in the ground as soon as they reach the plains below. We had Major Bridger with us as a guide. He knows more of the Rocky Mountains than any living man. He came to this country about forty years ago in command of a party of thirty or forty trappers, and some time after, with some others, he organized the Rocky Mountain Fur Company, which drove the Hudson Bay Company from American soil. He is totally uneducated, but speaks English, Spanish, and French equally well, besides nearly a dozen Indian tongues, such as Snake, Bannock, Crow, Flathead, Nez Perce, Pen d'Orille, Ute and one or two others I cannot recollect. He has been in many Indian battles and has several arrow wounds, besides being hit so as almost to break his neck. Under him, Kit Carson first made his acquaintance with the Rocky Mountain region, and he traveled through them while Fremont

was a child. It is very dull to come here to this post. I always dread it when I am out on a march. Every day is the same except the changes of weather. The bugle commences blowing the first thing in the morning, and is tooting away when you are in bed at night. The same calls all the time. The weather here at the fort is warm enough, but in the mountains it is as cold as it is with us in November.

"Your affectionate son,   C. W. COLLINS."

It is to be noted that Lieutenant Collins mentions "a regular surgeon." In the diary of Dr. J. H. Finfrock,[33] assistant surgeon of the Eleventh Ohio Volunteer Cavalry, which bears the words on the title page, "Halleck, Idaho Territory," while he and young Collins were at Fort Laramie in 1862, the following notations were made:

"Out shooting with Lieutenant Collins. Plenty of ducks. Bought rifle of sutler, $15. Indian lodges on Laramie river. APRIL 10; pleasant and calm; went to Bordeaux with Stone and party. Had good dinner, eggs and milk. Bought shotgun and buckskins and moccasins. APRIL 11; mild and calm; spent day in post; bought bow and arrows. APRIL 12; cold, but milder; had a horse race; Idaho attached to District of Nebraska; headquarters, Omaha, under General R. B. Mitchell. Preparing to return to Halleck. Stone gave me a pointer pup—"Rap." APRIL 21; (after returning to Fort Halleck) mild and calm until evening when it began blowing and snowing, and continued throughout the night. Boys had a dance at Company C's quarters. Six ladies present; 65 wagons and 118 men passed the fort on way to west."

In this diary there were also recorded the events of

---

[33] For many years, until 1891, Dr. Finfrock and his family lived at Laramie City, southeast of Fort Halleck.

marriage, of children being born and of justice being administered by hanging.

The contest for the peaceful possession of these lands between the two Plattes and the safe travel over the roads along the two streams, called for the posts and fortifications described in the foregoing. To make this territory in any degree safe for stages, emigrant trains and freight wagons, involved the difficult and dangerous task of rounding up the hostile Indians and driving them over the North Platte River north into a country that had the Big Horn Mountains on its west, the Black Hills to the east and the Yellowstone River to the extreme north, driving them into a territory known as the Powder River country, the cherished and favorite hunting grounds of more than one tribe of Indians, and the land through which the white man was determined to construct and protect by forts, the hated Bozeman Trail or Road.

Fort Laramie

A combination of realism and romanticism have found their way into literature descriptive of old Fort Laramie. No fortification on the Oregon Trail had such a varied and prolonged history as this fur traders' post that ultimately expanded into a fort that served the purpose of a harbor of safety for the emigrant, a place where the red men exchanged pelts for beads, tobacco, and whisky, where the white man held councils with the Indian and signed treaties with their chiefs, and where the soldier, who was to battle with the hostile savage, made his headquarters. Fortunately many descriptions of the old fort from gifted pens have been given to posterity.

In 1834, Nathaniel J. Wyeth, on his way over the Oregon Trail to the Oregon country, recorded in his journal, under date of June 1st: "William L. Sublette has built such a fort as Fort Clark (at the Mandan villages) on Laramie Fork of the river of the Platte, and can make it a central place for the Sioux and Cheyenne trade." Thirteen of Sublette's men were working on this fur post on the date indicated.

This fort or post was originally constructed in 1834 and was known as Fort Williams, named for its builder, William Sublette. After this fur post was sold to Fontenelle, the name was changed to Fort John, named in honor of John B. Sarpy, bearing this name until 1846. Occasionally the fort was called, "Fort Laramie on the North Platte," or, at least, shipments were made for the fort marked with that address, but it was not known by the name of Laramie until the American Fur Company erected a new building on another nearby site. The original post was on the left bank of the Laramie River about one mile above its junction with the North Platte; the new site selected was still about another mile up the stream. At this last named site the fort was rechristened being called Fort Laramie, named for a French Canadian free trapper, Jacques Laramie, or La Ramée, La Ramie, de la Ramé—no one seems to know the exact spelling—for whom have been named the Laramie River, Laramie Peak, Laramie Plains, Laramie City, and Laramie County, all in the locality where this fearless fur trader before the year 1820 conducted his lucrative occupation of fur trapping. Fort John was torn down soon after the erection of Fort Laramie, the latter post being sold to the government in 1849 by the American Fur Company, and remained in our government's possession until it was sold in 1890 to private parties, the main purchaser being Mr. John Hunton,[34] who, since 1867, has lived

[34] Honorable John Hunton, has for so great a length of time identified himself with Fort Laramie, that no history of this old post could be written without the mention of this post trader, citizen of Wyoming Territory and State, and extensive cattle raiser and ranchman, and no biography of Mr. Hunton can be truthfully given without weaving into the narrative a part of the history of Fort Laramie, the two for over fifty years having been very closely associated. Mr. Hunton was born in Madison Courthouse, Va., spending his youth in the South, and serving all through the Civil War in Company A, Seventh Virginia Volunteers. Coming to the West in 1866, driving a mule team belonging to Seth Ward, he arrived at Fort Laramie in May of that year, intending to extend his journey to Nevada, but the inducements at Fort Laramie were attractive enough to persuade him that the fort was a place where there was a future for an ambitious young man. From that time until October, 1870, Mr. Hunton served as a clerk in the sutler's store, when he went into the cattle business, a part of his time being devoted then, as before, to the management of a freighting outfit, which carried government supplies to Fort Laramie and other forts. While Mr. Hunton has been a

in the vicinity of the fort, and who at this present time (1920) lives on this old site of the most noted and famous fort in the West. Mr. Hunton, in June, 1915, told one of the authors of this publication that when

successful stockman, from that time to this, he has engaged in other occupations, as well as being appointed post trader at Fort Laramie in 1888, holding the position until April, 1890, when the post was abandoned.

For a number of years Mr. and Mrs. Hunton have made their home in one of the officers' buildings at the fort, Mr. Hunton having purchased forty acres of the abandoned post, including the site and the buildings, particularly the site of the old sutler's store. This building, in a good state of preservation in 1920, was built in 1849, and has been the rendezvous of countless soldiers, Indians, and emigrants. In one end of the building was the officers' club, containing a large fireplace, around which congregated many who helped build the West, as well as many high in military affairs, and numerous Indian chiefs of prominence. Jim Bridger at one time made this store his headquarters, rooming with Mr. Hunton. Not only did the latter know the Reshaw (Richards) brothers, Bordeaux, Bissonett, "Little Bat," (Baptiste Gangnier) and "Big Bat" (Baptiste Pourier) and many other of the most noted scouts of the Oregon Trail, but he also knew personally Jim Baker, Robert Campbell, (who owned the fort as late as 1836, revisiting the post in 1868), Generals Sherman, Augur, Harney, Terry, and many other men prominent in military affairs, as well as various famous Indian chiefs against whom the white man had fought, such as Red Cloud, Spotted Tail, Otter Tail, Young-Man-Afraid-of-His-Horses, American Horse; these and many others attending the peace conferences, most of the chiefs signing the treaties with their cross or mark. Mr. Hunton was one of the witnesses of these signatures in the treaty of 1868, when the government abandoned the Bozeman Trail and the Powder River country, thus yielding to the claims of Red Cloud and other Sioux warriors.

While Mr. Hunton has lived many years at the old fort, he has not made the place his continual residence, for he resided in Cheyenne many years, and having several ranches, has lived on them, although during the past fifty-two years his homes have all been in Laramie County, not as it is now divided, but as it was originally organized. Many offices of trust and importance have been given to Mr. Hunton by the people, through election or by appointment of the state officials, or the government. Fidelity and competency have marked the carrying out of duties incident to all of the positions.

Mr. Hunton is a veritable mine of reliable information; his memory is accurate and the fund of information which he has always generously given to those asking historic data, has helped many who have written of Fort Laramie, Wyoming, and the West. No man has ever lived who was, or is, so well posted on the history of Fort Laramie and its vicinity, which has an extended radius. Of those who have been to Fort Laramie, whether in the days of the traders in fur, government officers, prominent officials, and those he went to Fort Laramie in 1867, there was an old half-breed Pawnee trapper around the place whose name was Antoine Ladeau, and who spoke English fluently. He was well posted on all early events that happened on the Platte in early days. Ladeau claimed that Fort Laramie never was known as Fort John, but that there was a Fort John nearer to the mouth of Laramie River, occupied at one time by Adams & Sybil.[35]

of recognized distinction, Mr. Hunton tells interesting tales, those most entertaining doubtless being of Jim Bridger, greatest of all frontiersmen, who was his tried friend.

As early as 1836, Seth E. Ward came to the West, establishing himself in the Indian supply trade at Fort Lupton (Colorado) where he carried on a lucrative business until early in the forties, then coming to the North Platte River, where he established, with William Guerrier, another store, rather substantially constructed of stone, nine miles west of Fort Laramie, which by this time had become a noted fur post along the Oregon Trail. In the early fifties Ward formed a partnership with Fitzhugh to conduct the sutler's store building, built of adobe in 1852, at Fort Laramie, succeeding the firm of Tutt & Daugherty at that place, who had the first sutler's store at the fort. Upon the dissolution of the firm of Ward & Fitzhugh, William G. Bullock became the agent for the firm, appointing Ward as the sutler, a position which he held until 1871, when he gave up the post tradership. The long years of training received in the several supply stores of the West, made Mr. Ward a specially qualified person to deal with soldiers, Indians, trappers, and emigrants who daily stopped at the sutler's store to replenish their depleted stock of supplies.

Commission of Seth E. Ward, as post sutler at Fort Laramie, 1857: Department of War, To all whom it may concern: Know ye, That reposing special trust and confidence in the patriotism, fidelity, and abilities of Seth E. Ward I do hereby constitute and appoint him sutler to Fort Laramie, Nebraska Territory, in the service of the United States, with all the privileges and immunities appertaining to said situation. He is therefore carefully and diligently to discharge the duties of Sutler, in conformity with the rules established for the government of Armies of the United States; and he is to be subject to such laws and regulations having reference to Sutlers, as now are, or hereafter may be, established. This warrant to continue in force; and to be valid until the fourth day of March in the year one thousand eight hundred and sixty, unless sooner revoked by competent authority. Given under my hand at the City of Washington, this thirtieth day of April, 1857. – John B. Floyd, Secretary of War.

[35] Also spelled Sybylle, Sibyl, Saville, Sibylee.

It is interesting to note how different authors were impressed with this historic landmark on the Oregon Trail. In this way one obtains a very complete idea of the general appearance of this noted fort. A few of their notations are cited.

In 1839 F. E. Wislizenus wrote *A Journal to the Rocky Mountains* (English translation), in which Fort Laramie is described as follows:

"At a distance it resembled a great blockhouse, and lies in a narrow valley, enclosed by grassy hills, near by the left bank of the Laramie, which empties into the North Platte about a mile below. Toward the west a fine background is formed by the Black Hills, a dark chain of mountains covered with evergreen trees. The fort lies on a slight elevation, and is built in a rectangle of about 80 x 100 feet. The outside is made of cottonwood logs, about fifteen feet high, hewn off and wedged closely together. On three sides there are little towers on the wall that seem designed for watch and defense. In the middle a strong gate, built of blocks, constitutes the entrance. Within are little buildings, with flat roofs, plastered all around against the wall, like swallows' nests. One is a storehouse, another a smithy; the others are dwellings not unlike monks' cells. A special portion of the courtyard is occupied by the so-called horse pen, in which the horses are confined at night. The middle space is free, with a tall tree in it, on which the flag is raised on occasions of state. The whole garrison of the fort consists of only five men – four Frenchmen and a German. These (forts) are often thought of as military forts, occupied by regular troops, and under military rule, when they are mere trading forts, built by single trading companies and occupied by a handful of hired men, to have a safe point for storing their goods, from which barter may be carried on with the Indians."

General John Charles Fremont, who had been sent to the West by our government to investigate the possibility and the practicability of establishing posts along the Oregon Trail, recorded on July 15, 1842:

"Built of clay, after the fashion of the Mexicans, who are generally employed in building them . . . every apartment has its doors and windows, all, of course, opening on the inside . . . over the great entrance is a square tower with loopholes, and, like the rest of the work, built of earth. At two of the angles, and diagonally opposite each other, are large square bastions, so arranged as to sweep the four faces and the walls. . . It is on the left bank, on rising ground some twenty-five feet above water, and its lofty walls, whitewashed and picketed, with the large bastions at the angles, give it quite an imposing appearance in the uncertain light of evening. A cluster of lodges, which the language told us belonged to the Sioux Indians, was pitched under the walls, and with the fine background of the Black Hills and the prominent peaks of Laramie Mountain, strongly drawn in the clear light of the western sky, when the sun already had set, the whole formed, at the moment, a strikingly beautiful picture."

While at Fort Laramie, General Fremont was warned by Chiefs Otter Hat, Breaker-of-Arrows, Black Night and Bull's Trail that to proceed further on the Oregon Trail would be not only his death, but the extermination of his entire company. Fremont then made this speech to the assembled Indians in the main building of Fort Laramie:

"You say you love the whites, why have you killed so many this spring? You say you love the whites and are full of many expressions of friendship to us, but you are not willing to undergo the fatigue of a few days' ride to save our lives. We do not believe what you said, and will not listen to you. Whatever a chief· among us tells his soldiers to do, is done. We are the soldiers of the great chief, your father. He has told us to come here and see this country and all the Indians, his children. Why should we not go? Before we came we heard that you had killed his people and ceased to be 'his children; but we came among you peaceably, holding out our hands. Now we find that the stories that we heard are not lies, and that you no longer are his friends and children. We have thrown away our bodies and will not turn back. When you told us that your young men would kill us, you did not know that our hearts were strong, and you did not see the rifles which my young men carry in their hands. We are few, and you are many, and may kill us all; but there will be much crying in your villages, for many of your young men will stay behind, and forget to return with your warriors from the mountains. Do you think that our great chief will let his soldiers die and forget to cover their graves? Before the snow melts again, his warriors will sweep away your villages as the fire does the prairies in the autumn. See! I have pulled down my white houses and my people are ready; when the sun is ten paces higher, we will be on the march. If you have anything to tell us, you will say it soon."

In Thwaites's *Early Western Travels*, there is also

a statement as to Fort Laramie, in connection with Joel
Palmer's journal of 1845:

"At Fort Laramie they rested, and feasted the Indians, who, in wonderment, and not unnatural con-
sternation, swarmed about them in the guise of beg-
gars. Palmer afterward harangued the aboriginal
visitors, telling them frankly that their entertainers
were no traders; they were going to 'plow and plant
the ground,' that their relations were coming behind
them, and these he hoped the red men would treat kind-
ly and allow free passage – a thinly veiled suggestion
that the white army of occupation had come to stay and
would not be interfered with by the native population,
or vengeance would follow.

"Here are two forts. Fort Laramie, situated upon
the west side of Laramie's Fork, two miles from Platte
River, belonging to the American Fur Company. The
fort is built of adobe. The walls are about two feet
thick and twelve or fourteen feet high, the tops being
picketed or spiked. Posts are planted in these walls,
which support the timber for the roof. They are then
covered with mud. In the center is an open square,
perhaps twenty-five yards each way, along the sides of
which are ranged the dwellings, store-rooms, smith
shop, carpenter's shop, offices, etc., all fronting upon
the inner area. There are two principal entrances –
one at the north, the other at the south. On the eastern
side is an additional wall, connected at its extremities
with the first, enclosing ground for stables and corral.
This enclosure has a gateway upon its south side, and a
passage into the square for the principal enclosure. At

FORT JOHN, 1844. From a drawing made by Alexander H. Murray.

At the junction of the Laramie and North Platte Rivers.

a short distance from the fort is a field of about four acres, in which, by way of experiment, corn is planted; but from its present appearance it will probably prove a failure. Fort John stands a mile below Fort Laramie, and is built of the same material as the latter, but is not so extensive. . . In the summer of 1845 Colonel Stephen W. Kearney took five companies of dragoons and proceeded from Fort Leavenworth via the Oregon Trail, to South Pass, returning by way of the Arkansas River and the Santa Fé Trail. The object was to impress the Indians, and to report upon the feasibility of an advanced military post near Fort Laramie. . . This was the first regular military campaign into the land of the Great West, and strongly impressed the Indians of that region. Kearney's recommendations were against the establishment of a post, because of the difficulty of supplying it; advising instead, a biennial or triennial campaign to this country."

General Philip St. George Cooke, in *Scenes and Adventures in the Army*, thus describes Fort Laramie:

"JUNE 15, 1845: Fort Laramie is about 200 feet square, with walls of adobes, made of the clay and sand soil, just as it is found; the dwellings line the walls, which is a part of them, and have flat adobe roofs and wooden galleries. The fort swarmed with women and children, whose language, like their complexions, is various and mixed – Indian, French, English and Spanish. . . The struggle is at close quarters; civilization furnishing house and clothing; barbarism, children and fleas."

On June 23, 1846, Edwin Bryant, in *What I Saw in California*, said, regarding his stop at Fort Laramie:

"Fort Laramie, or 'Fort John,' as it is otherwise called, has been the principal trading-post of the American Fur Company. It is surrounded by an extensive plain. Timber in the vicinity is scarce. Not a foot of ground around the fort is under cultivation. Experiments have been made with corn, wheat, and potatoes, but they have either resulted in complete failure or were not so successful as to authorize a renewal. The Indians, who claim the soil as their property, and regard the fur company as occupants by sufferance, are adverse to all agricultural experiments, and on one or two occasions they entered the small enclosures and destroyed the young corn and other vegetables as soon as they made their appearance above ground.

"The area of the fort enclosed about half to three-fourths of an acre of ground. The walls are surrounded by watch towers, and the gate is defended by two brass swivels. On three sides of the court, next to the walls, are various offices, store-rooms and mechanical shops. The other side is occupied by the main building of the fort, two stories in height. The Indians have permission to enter the fort during the day; at night they camp in their lodges on the plain."

Francis Parkman, in 1846, came to the West hunting for material for his literary works, and as the result of this exploration wrote his classic, *The Oregon Trail*, from which is the following extract regarding Fort Laramie:

"Fort Laramie is one of the posts established by the American Fur Company, which well-nigh monopolizes the Indian trade of this region. Here its officials rule with an absolute sway; the arm of the United States has little force, for when we were there, the extreme outposts of her troops was about seven hundred miles to the eastward. The little fort is built of bricks dried in the sun, and externally is of an oblong form, with bastions

FORT LARAMIE IN 1863

From an early drawing made by Bugler C. Moellman, Co. G, Eleventh Ohio Cavalry. Laramie River in foreground. Picket fence in right rear is enclosure for the old cemetery, where the new hospital was built when the old one was dismantled. This is to be seen just back of the three gabled building (the post sutler's home). The cavalry stables are to the extreme right center. In the center of the picture, and to the extreme rear (low roofs and tops of windows just showing) is the sutler's store. All of the roofs at this date were made of dirt. "Bedlam" stands at the right of the flagstaff, directly behind the four cannon. Laramie Peak in the background.

of clay, in the form of ordinary blockhouses, at two of the corners. The walls are about fifteen feet high, and surmounted by a splendid palisade. The roof of the apartments within, which are built close against the wall, serve the purpose of a banquette. Within, the fort is divided by partitions; on one side is the square area, surrounded by the store-rooms, offices and apartments of the inmates; on the other side is the corral, a narrow place encompassed by high clay walls, where at night, or in the presence of dangerous Indians, the horses and mules of the fort are crowded for safe-keeping. The main entrance has two gates, with an arched passage intervening. A little square window, high above the ground, opens laterally from an adjoining chamber into this passage; so that when the door is closed and barred, a person without may still hold communication with those within, through this narrow aperature. This obviated the necessity of admitting suspicious Indians, for the purpose of trading, into the body of the fort; for when danger is apprehended, the inner gate is shut fast, and all traffic is carried on by means of this window."

In 1849, in accordance with the recommendations made by General Fremont, our government purchased Fort Laramie under an act of Congress, dated May 19, 1846, the government keeping control of the fort until 1890, when it was sold, and on May 20th of that year the last military troops left the fort. On March 30, 1849, a general order was issued, stating in part: "To carry out the provisions of the sixth section of the Act of May 19, 1846, relative to establishing military posts on the Oregon Route, and to afford protection to the numerous emigrants to that country and California the first station has been established. . . and is known as Fort Kearney . . . under the same instructions of the Secretary of War, it now becomes necessary to establish the second station at or near Fort Laramie, a trading post belonging to the American Fur Company. The garrison at this post will be two companies of the mounted riflemen to be halted on the route, and one company of the Sixth Infantry." On April 6, 1849, additional instructions were given: "Recent instructions from the War Department makes it necessary that supplies for one year shall be forwarded for two military posts to be established on the route to Oregon – one at or near Fort Laramie, and the other in the vicinity of Fort Hall. The garrison at Fort Laramie will consist of two companies of mounted riflemen and one company of infantry. It will be supplied with provisions for one year and the full ration of forage (grain) for six months."

Then again came an order of December 1, 1849: "In compliance with your letter of instructions of the 11th of September, 1849, requiring more definite information concerning the purchase of this fort, I have the honor to report that the sum of four thousand dollars was paid to the agent of the American Fur Company for the buildings and improvements. There was no ground included in this purchase. The four thousand dollars was paid by Lieutenant Woodbury of the Engineers' Department, who is charged with the construction of this post out of the amount appropriated by the Act of Congress, August 14, 1848. This section of the country, from Horseshoe Creek, forty-three miles above the post, to the forks of the Platte, is claimed by the Sioux, the Arapahoes, and the Cheyenne Indians. Each of these tribes is divided into several bands and are scattered over the country from the Kansas to the

Missouri. The chiefs of the several bands are to assemble at this post in the spring, at which time it is proposed to purchase the ground."

By the year 1851 the government entered into a treaty with the Ogalalla and Brule Sioux, the Arapahoes, and Cheyennes, representing about six thousand Indians, the terms of the treaty being to donate to the red men the sum of fifty thousand dollars, the amount to be distributed in supplies and goods; added to this, the government was to set aside a tract of land in the way of a reserve on which the Indians might hunt and live, the tract of land between the one hundredth and one hundred and seventh meridians of longitude and the thirty-ninth and forty-fourth parallels of latitude, which included lands in western Kansas, nearly one-half of Colorado, a portion of southwestern South Dakota, half of the western part of Nebraska and a large part of what is now the eastern part of Wyoming. In consideration for setting apart these some one hundred and twenty-three thousand square miles, the Indians agreed not to fight the soldiers located at stations along the Overland Trail, and to cease killing the emigrants going over the Oregon Trail. This was the beginning of the real trouble with the Indians, for the annuities were not paid; and when the government, in its mistaken policy, reduced the force of soldiers at the Laramie fort, the Indians saw their opportunity, and took advantage of the limited guard at the garrison. Raids, killing and capturing of the emigrants, and fighting, became of frequent occurrence, and the bitterness of the future Indian wars was now having its birth.

Fighting the Indians on both sides of the Platte

In order to reach the gold-fields of Montana, there was no direct route from the Missouri River. There were several roads which might be followed which would eventually land the prospector, miner, and merchant into the rich gold-fields of both Montana and northern Idaho. The first road, the river route, was along the Missouri River by the way of Dakota, following the route taken by Lewis and Clark on their way to the sources of this branch of the Mississippi, and also up the Yellowstone, the route taken by Clark on his return trip from the Pacific. These lines of travel involved many unnecessary miles, for it was a very roundabout way, and consumed more time than men, rushing for riches, were willing to devote to travel.

In the second place, there was the Oregon Trail, following the Platte, the North Platte, and the Sweetwater Rivers, by the forts of Kearney (Nebraska), Laramie, Bridger (Wyoming), and Hall (Idaho). From old Fort Hall a branch road ran directly northeast to Virginia City, Montana. This road, while not difficult of travel, although in places harrassed by Indians, was too long, for many of the miles to the west had to be doubled back after Fort Hall was reached.

The third route, the Overland, and the one that was at this time extensively used, was the South Platte Road, by the way of Denver, with stage stations at La Porte, Cherokee, Virginia Dale (Colorado), Rock Creek, Medicine Bow, Fort Halleck (also called Elk Mountain), across the North Platte, Sage Creek, Bridger

Pass (thirty-five miles west of the North Platte), and Sulphur Springs. The road now on the west side of the continental divide, went to the Bitter Creek region across Green River to Fort Bridger (Wyoming), Echo Canyon, Weber and Salt Lake City (Utah). Leaving Salt Lake City the journey was directly north and west toward the Snake River, across Bear River, through its valleys (Utah) to Malade City, Robbers' Retreat (in Portneuf Canyon),[36] Desert Wells, to a point just east of old Fort Hall; along the Snake River to Eagle Rock, where the road crossed the Snake, Pleasant Valley (Idaho), Black Tail Deer (fifty miles from Virginia City), Beaver Head and Virginia City, Montana. From Virginia City, branches of the stage road went, west to Bannack, northwest to Deer Lodge, north to Helena, northeast to Gallatin. This long roundabout road offered, through Colorado and Wyoming, the same difficulties from the Indians, and the dangerous travel, as experienced over the North Platte and Sweet-water.

The fourth possible line of transportation to the gold-fields of Montana and Idaho, the Bozeman Trail, was from Fort Sedgwick on the South Platte to Fort Laramie on the North Platte, and then northwest into the Powder River country, along the east side of the Big Horn Mountains, across the Powder, Crazy Woman's Fork, and Tongue River to the Big Horn. From here a road was to be used going west over Dubois Creek, Pryor's River, Clark's Fork, the Stillwater, and the Boulder to the Yellowstone, where, some few miles

---

[36] Langford (N. P.) *Vigilante Days and Ways,* p. 427. The Canyon of Port Neuf, memorable in the early days and for two decades later for murder, robbery, and disaster, was about forty miles east of Fort Hall. Attacks upon the downward bound coach became so frequent that for several years before the completion of the railroad the stage company provided for each treasure coach a guard, whose business it was to defend both treasure and passengers by all means in his power.

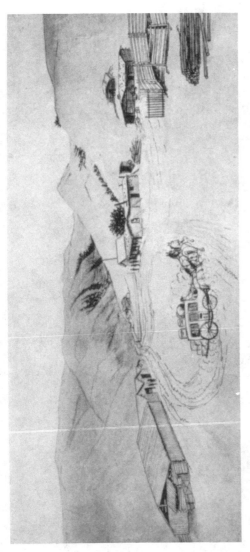

BRIDGER PASS STATION, ON THE OVERLAND STAGE ROUTE
From an original drawing.

northeast of Bozeman Pass, a ferry was crossed. The road continued through the Pass to Bozeman City and up the Madison, thence west to Virginia City. From Bozeman there were branch roads to Gallatin, Jefferson City, Helena, and other mining camps; from Virginia City branch roads reached Bannack, Summit, Nevada, and other gold-fields.

At this time (1864) this fourth trail was the road of the occasional freighter and prospector, blazed by John W. Bozeman in the winter of 1862-1863, while seeking a shorter route over which the emigrants were to migrate from the eastern states to Montana. The difficulty in using this fourth route was that it led into the heart of the Indian territory, the invasion of which the white race had been forbidden by a treaty made by our government with Sioux chiefs at Fort Laramie in 1851, and renewed and amended in 1865, allotting special land for the exclusive use of the Indians. The violation of these treaties on the part of our government, and the using of the Indians' choice hunting grounds, by ultimately establishing a military road across this favorite piece of country, precipitated a series of wars, the savageness and bitterness of which have not been equaled by any of our Indian wars. The contests for the possession of these lands to be used as a passageway to the mines in the north, were characterized by the fierceness of the battles, the great loss of life by both contesting parties, and a general distrust and deep hatred between the red and white man that had not before been made manifest on our western plains.

The beginning of the contest for territorial possession was in the raids by the Indians; the results were the Platte Bridge fight, the Powder River Indian Expedition, the Fetterman disaster, and the Wagon Box and

Hayfield fights. The finale was Custer's battle of the Little Big Horn.

It seemed impossible to convince our government that the only way to subdue the Indians was to go after them in sufficiently large numbers, drive them away from the scenes of depredations into a part of the country not traversed or occupied by the whites, and then overwhelm them by vastly superior forces. In place of sacrificing a limited number of soldiers here and there through lack of adequate numbers and sufficient battle equipment, with occasional fights, overwhelming forces of trained soldiers should have been put into the field, with the most modern army equipment and plenty of ammunition, when a decisive blow might have been struck. However, when one now realizes the numerical strength of the Indians, and the banding of the tribes, with their determination not to yield to the white man's demand for more domain, the solution seems easier than it was then possible to execute. At that time the Civil War had not ended, the available fighting men were actively engaged in conflict, the supplies of modern firearms were needed in the regular armies, and the amount of ammunition (all too limited) at the command of the government, was being utilized in the struggle between the North and the South. The Indian problem, in comparison with the war, was a minor affair which the authorities believed might be easily adjusted. In the meantime, the Indians were clever enough to take advantage of the mobilization of the fighting men on the regular battlefield, and openly made their boasts that now was the time for them to strike a blow and drive the white man back off their hunting grounds. Hence, before our government fully realized the true condition of Indian warfare in the

West, the red man was taking a stand, assembling warriors and inducing unfriendly tribes to now join forces against a common foe. Every success of the Indian in a conflict with the small fighting force in the West and on the borders, and along the trails and stage roads (and these successes were becoming all too numerous) incited more intense activity and more horrible depredations. Something had to be done. Drastic measures seemed to be the only solution.

The gold-fields became more and more alluring, those of Montana promising the greatest and quickest returns for the investment of money and the labor given to the adventure. The shortest route to these fields was by the Bozeman Trail, which, when utilized, enraged the Indians to such a point of fury that they realized that if anything could be done, it must be done at once to stop the invasion of their precious and loved territory in the region of the Powder, Tongue, Big Horn, and Yellowstone Rivers. To destroy those who attempted to pass through this territory was not entirely satisfying to the red man; anyone who dared to appear on the trails to the south, particularly between Julesburg and South Pass, also became a marked man upon whom the hand of hate and vengeance descended, resulting in torture, mutilation and death.

General Alfred Sully, in the spring of 1864, took an expedition by the way of the Missouri into the Bad Lands of the Little Missouri, where he battled with the combined tribes of the Sioux. The expedition was one of the most costly, powerful, and best equipped sent out to fight the Indians. The war party contained four thousand cavalry, eight hundred mounted infantry, twelve pieces of artillery and three thousand teams, requiring the services of fifteen steamboats to carry the

supplies. The expedition went to the head of Cannon-
ball River, thence across the country to the Heart River, in which country the soldiers and red men entered
into a marching battle that lasted for three days. The
fierceness of the Indian fighting was due to the fact
that they were trying to prevent the soldiers from entering their home camp, which was on the main route of
the white men. The Sioux, with heavy losses, finally
disappeared south toward the Black Hills; the soldiers
entering the village found everything destroyed.

The Indians were driven west into the region north
of the Platte, south of the Yellowstone, and east of the
Big Horn Mountains. It has been estimated that there
were at least eight thousand warriors engaged in the
fights against General Sully, three hundred and eleven
of whom were killed and seven hundred wounded, the
casualties among the soldiers being nine killed and
one hundred wounded.

While this campaign, from a military standpoint,
was considered a success, the expedition was directly
responsible for the massing of hostile Indians in the
North Platte country, making the conditions on the
Overland Route and the Oregon Trail even more serious and intolerable than before "the war of extermination."

During the Indians' raids of 1864, the depredations
were so numerous that Ben Holladay, the noted stage
magnate, who in 1862, had practically assumed control
of the entire transportation to the mines in Colorado,
narrowly avoided having to suspend operations on the
plains. Toward the middle of August, 1864, the Indians made simultaneous attack on the stage stations
and isolated farms and ranches, as well as small emigrant trains, from the Little Blue to the country just

east of Denver. One of Holladay's agents stated that for a distance of three hundred and seventy miles along their line "every ranch was abandoned and the property deserted to the Indians."

Denver, fearing an attack by the Indians early in June, 1864, following the killing of a farmer and his entire family, twenty miles from the city, appealed to Governor John Evans for more adequate protection. At once Governor Evans organized his militia and called for help from the regular army. The appeal for government aid received no favorable response, for the troops were occupied in attempting to subdue Indian uprisings elsewhere on the plains. Governor Evans, thus being forced to handle the somewhat local situation, asked the Indian Department to permit him to issue a proclamation calling for a conference with the Indians. Only "friendly" ones were to be invited to the councils, which were to be held at Forts Collins, Laramie, Larned, and Lyons. The outcome of the proposed assembly justified Governor Evans in believing that there were no Indians who "intended to be friendly with the whites." He reported to the government that the proposed peace meeting "met no response from any of the Indians of the plains."

With the first signs of winter, the Indians made overtures for peace; their hunting season was over; peace meant food, clothes and shelter from the government. Chief Black Kettle, a Cheyenne, and White Antelope, with other warriors, came to Fort Lyons on Sand Creek for a conference with Governor Evans, to plead for an immediate peace before the cold weather. Fully appreciating the insincerity of the petitioning chiefs, Governor Evans stated his position. "So far as making a treaty now is concerned we are in no condition to do it . . . you, so far, have had the advantage; but the time is near at hand when the plains will swarm with United States soldiers. I have learned that you understand that as the whites are at war among themselves, you think that you can drive the whites from this country; but this reliance is false. The Great Father at Washington has enough men to drive all the Indians off the plains and whip the rebels at the same time. Now that the war with the whites is nearly through, the Great Father will not know what to do with all the soldiers, except to send them after the Indians on the plains. My proposition to the friendly Indians has gone out. I shall be glad to have them all come under it. I have no new proposition to make. Another reason that I am not in a condition to make a treaty is, that war has begun, and the power to make a treaty of peace has passed to the great war chief."

The direct outcome of the conference was that many of the Cheyenne and Arapahoe Indians made a partial surrender to the authorities. They went to Fort Lyons and established their lodges near the fortification. Questions of authority and jurisdiction of those in command of the fort ultimately caused the Indians to be driven forty miles away from the fort to Sand Creek, where they made camp. Late in November, Colonel J. M. Chivington with Colorado troops left Denver, believing that the Indians were still on the warpath, while the red men claimed that peace had been made or would soon be made with the whites, in conformity with the contents of the recent proclamation of Governor Evans. On November 29, 1864, Chivington attacked the Cheyenne village on Sand Creek, destroyed the lodges and killed many of the Indians, in a relentless battle that lasted for at least four hours. Colonel Chivington reported five hundred killed, while others estimated the number at one hundred and fifty, and some at one hundred and sixty; in any event the dead were mostly women and children.[37]

An attempt was made to have Colonel Chivington court-martialed, but his term of service had expired and he could not be tried by a military court. An investigation was held in March, 1865, the committee reporting that the Indians were rapidly increasing and that "the committee are of the opinion that in a large majority of cases, Indian wars are to be traced to the aggressiveness of lawless white men, always to be found upon the frontier or boundary lines between savage and civilized life."

The government now had a new problem of war. Where, before the Sully expedition and the Sand Creek massacre, the war for extermination was against a few thousand Indians in several localities, now, the centralizing of tribes with many grievances made Indian warfare a critical operation. Concentration of military forces was demanded to cope with this new condition of Indian mobilization.

After the Sand Creek trouble, the Cheyennes, without a home, and enraged with our government, sent a pipe of peace to the Sioux and the Northern Arapahoes, inviting them to enter into a joint war to exterminate the white men on the plains. The proposition of a united war was, in December, 1864, accept-

[37] Coutant, *History of Wyoming*, p. 418: "Sand Creek was the cause of much severe comment through the entire country. The subject was thoroughly discussed at the time in all newspapers of the country and much said for and against the officer commanding the troops on this occasion. The matter, even to this day, remains in dispute as to whether it was honorable warfare, such as the government was urging against the Indians, or a 'horrible massacre.'"

ed by the leaders of both the Sioux and Arapahoes. Thus the three tribes joined forces in depredations along the Platte and swept the Oregon Trail for two hundred miles, the first point of attack being the Julesburg station. Here, on January 7, 1865, when a band of one thousand Cheyennes, Sioux, and Arapahoes united their forces and raided this stage station, Captain Nicholas J. O'Brien, and his command at Julesburg, had a brisk encounter with the Indians, sustaining a loss of eighteen men killed, of whom fourteen were soldiers and four citizens. The storehouses of the station were raided, plunder being carried on more for the excitement of stealing than the value of the article taken. A passenger coach arrived at Julesburg while the depredations were being committed, one passenger being the United States paymaster having the money to pay the troops on the plains. Dropping his box of money, he fled to the protection of the station building. "The Indians found the box and knocked it open with tomahawks. They were greatly disappointed to find that it contained nothing but bundles of green paper. None of them knew what it was, and they emptied the paper on the ground. Bent secured as much of the property as he could comfortably carry. He saw a warrior take a thick bundle of money, chop it into three or four pieces with his tomahawk, and then throw it into the air. He shouted with glee as the bits of paper were whirled away and scattered by the wind. After the Indians had gone, the paymaster ordered out the garrison and had the men search the whole valley for the money. They found bills scattered all along the valley, but did not recover half of what the box had held." [38]

By December, 1864, all the roads along the trails of

---

[38] Grinnell (G. B.) *The Fighting Cheyennes.*

the West became so infested with the fighting Indians that passage became blocked, the wagon trains could not carry their freight, telegraph lines were down and the stations along the road were burned or had fallen into the possession of the red men. At this period of congested traffic, General Grenville M. Dodge was assigned to take charge of the Indian Department of the Missouri, a territory embracing all the land south of the Yellowstone River and including all of the overland mail route and telegraph lines to the Pacific Ocean. At this time the Indians were in complete possession of the country crossed by these lines, placing the territories in a panic of fear; for the troops, all too meager in numbers, stationed along these lines of travel, had been driven into their stockades. As a result, the Indians were having their war dances over their almost universal victories.

General Dodge declared at the time he assumed control of the Platte Indians, as they were called, that the two thousand red men had destroyed over a hundred miles of telegraph line, and were in possession of the land on both sides of the Platte River.

The Oregon Trail, or the Platte Route, by 1864, was as heavily used as the road in the days of the forty-niners, when the rush to California was at its height. Over this road went all of the supplies in the commodious freight wagons. On the road were the wagon trains headed for the gold-fields of Montana, emigrants bound for Oregon, landseekers for California and Mormons hurrying for Utah. In this eager and restless procession were many men who were seeking the vastness of the West in which to be lost, in order to escape the draft for war service.

To this great overland highway (the finest natural

road in the world), crowded with mail coaches, freight wagons, and emigrant trains, the Cheyenne and Sioux Indians sent their raiding parties. The combined attack, commencing in the summer of 1864, was soon felt all along the great trail when the rifle, tomahawk, arrow, and scalping knife did their relentless slaughter. These depredations along the highway of the Platte were principally made by warring tribes of Sioux and Northern Cheyennes, who scalped the white men, destroyed coaches, killed the stage drivers, burned ranches, captured whole wagon trains, took into captivity women and children, destroying, rather than utilizing, the merchandise which filled the wagons. The spirit of plunder was rampant; the desire for battle spurred the warriors into deadly combat; the mail routes were abandoned, forcing the stage companies to carry the mail for Denver by the way of Panama, to San Francisco and thence back to Denver. Such were the conditions for five weeks when General Dodge assumed control.

As a matter of amusement, the Indians took great delight in robbing the freight trains loaded with every conceivable class of goods, not for the advantage or use to be derived from the merchandise, but for the satisfaction of wanton destruction. Repeatedly a bolt of bright colored calico would be taken; the Indian, mounting a pony, took one end of the cloth, letting the bolt bob up and down on the prairie as the pony was put under the whip, and as yards upon yards unwound and floated in the air, the Indians howled with mad delight. The goods taken from the wagons filled every Indian camp along the trail. "Warriors were strutting about with ladies' silk cloaks and bonnets on, and the Indian women were making shirts for the young men out of the finest silk." Flour, then selling at Julesburg for $30 a hundred, was stolen by the ton, not to be used for bread, but to obtain the sacks out of which to make shirts and breech-clouts, the bags of flour being emptied along the road as the ponies hurried back to camp, leaving a white trail along the route. Shelled corn, selling at this time for $6 a sack in Julesburg, was no temptation for the Indian ponies, as they were never fed on this grain; but the corn proved to be useful to the red men, who were prompt in its utilization by generously sprinkling the kernels on the frozen streams, serving as ashes, to prevent the ponies from slipping as they pulled their heavy loads on poles over the ice.

To have the forts or camps kept in close communication with each other was an impossibility during the periods of extended depredations, for not only were telegraph wires torn down, but the poles were hacked to slivers with tomahawks. The Indian soon learned that the "talk-a-heap," as they called the humming wires, were, in some strange way, the cause of relief to the isolated travelers. Hence, the wires were continually being cut, thus shutting off communication with the outside world.

When these singing wires were first strung, the Indian was taught to respect them, but the quick response by the soldiers to the sounding line, taught the Indian to connect the rumbling noise of the poles with help, and the whole system of wires, poles, and insulators became a mysterious and detested sign of civilization. It was useless to try to teach the red man that the wire, stretching from station to station was "great medicine," for to him it was an evil genius, an ally of the white man. General Dodge endeavored to establish a respect among the chiefs for this modern method of communication by wires and poles, but when the novelty wore away, destruction along the road went on as it had before. After the line was opened to Fort Laramie, some of the more intelligent chiefs were stationed at the fort and others at Fort Kearney, the two forts being over three hundred miles apart, when messages were dictated by the chiefs to the operators. The time of sending the message and also of receiving it at the other end of the line was noted. Then the red men mounted their swiftest ponies and came toward each other, meeting at Julesburg, or Old Jules' ranch, being half-way between the forts; the message and answer being given as the chiefs met. The difference in the time of wire message and pony express astonished and mystified the Indians. It was not unusual to see Indians with their ears to the poles, as if by chance to catch some secret which the white men were sending over the wires.

The Indians, finding the chopping down of the telegraph poles too laborious, would spread along the line. One buck would squat near each pole, which he would set afire, waiting, as he smoked his pipe, for the poles to topple over when the base was burned. These poles when cut or burned down would be rescued as soon as the Indians moved on, the burning end being extinguished when placed in a newly dug hole. These poles were used again and again until they were so short that the wires could be hung by line repairers while standing on the ground. Many of the repairs were made in the darkness of the night, horses having their hoofs muffled in folded blankets, and hammers wrapped in cloth to prevent the noise made by the driving of spikes on which the wires were to be hung, from being heard for any distance.[39]

These telegraph stations were not always buildings regularly constructed for sending messages. Many of them were the old stage stations, which were no longer used after the South Platte Road was in operation. On Lodge Pole Creek, a telegraph station had been put in working order by being located in a dog-tent, with the telegraph instrument fastened to the movable end of the wagon box and placed on the ground in the tent. In order to send a message, the operator had to crawl in the tent, which was not man high, on his hands and knees, send or receive his message and back out by the same means of locomotion.

All the operators at the stations in the West were enlisted soldiers. The private citizen had "lost no Indians," hence, he was not hunting them, and could not be induced to volunteer his services in such hazardous places as along the Platte. Once a soldier learned the art of telegraphy, he was not released until he could find a substitute. Many men had, as a result, to serve in this dangerous occupation for a long time. One operator at Platte Bridge station on the North Platte, had been a prisoner in that office for five years. His term of enlistment had long since expired, but he was still held, partly by force and partly by increased pay, and the many opportunities for "making a million." At another station "we were cut off from the outside world as much so as if we were completely

---

[39] A favorite and effective way of destroying the line was by throwing their lariats over the wire and then putting their ponies on the run, pulling the line from its holdings and destroying all connections. This destruction was the frequent reason for the defeat of many of the soldiers during a raid, for, not being called, there seemed to be no need of assistance, when, in fact, immediate help was seriously needed. The outside world, receiving no appeal, concluded that all was well in the mountains and on the plains of the West.

frozen up in icebergs in the region of the North Pole."[40]

In the diary of Sergeant Isaac B. Pennick, who was fighting the redskins all along the Oregon Trail from Fort Laramie to South Pass, he writes from Fort Caspar on July 3d, 1865: " . . . ordered to send ten men to Sweetwater to escort operator and repair the line. Boys refused to go in so small a party. Ten more then detailed; still they refused to go. Ten more volunteered to go with them, in all, thirty-four men. JULY 4: Can hear nothing from the boys who went above (meaning up the Platte River) last evening; fear that they have not wire enough or that something is wrong. JULY 7: All safe. Found a good deal of line destroyed, four hundred yards cut; the Indians carried off about seven hundred yards of the wire . . . at Devil's Backbone found wire down, about seven hundred yards of it, but not carried off . . . at Poison Creek found four hundred yards of wire cut and down . . . arrived at Horse Creek. Found eight hundred yards of wire down, two or three hundred yards carried away . . . exhausted all our wire on this cut. Crossed creek, found one thousand yards of wire cut and carried off entirely . . . the cut end was tied to a post with a buckskin string, a sharp trick of the Indians . . . at the point where the Virginia City (Montana) road leaves for the northwest, find four hundred yards of wire down and the insulators carried off; several poles down and burned partly up." Thus, we find the same disheartening reports all along the North Platte—wires down, poles destroyed, Indians burning camps, the killing of emi-

---

[40] Holliday (G. H.) *On the Plains in '65.* (Pamphlet, pub. 1883).

grants, the scalping of enlisted men, the stampeding of horses, and the capturing of livestock.

These were the conditions found along the Platte, confronting General Grenville M. Dodge, when he was sent into the heart of the territory where the Indians were most fierce and determined in their concerted efforts to exterminate the intruders upon their soil. It was a position that required hardihood, courage, and physical prowess–all the qualities richly possessed by this officer, who was assigned the difficult task of subduing the Indians and opening up the road for transportation toward the western gold-fields.

Having had experience in fights and fighting in the Civil War and on the plains, General Dodge was exceptionally well qualified for his new duties, into which he entered with the imagination that lures brave men to great deeds. This military experience, and an extensive knowledge of the West, were now to be put to the extreme test, a sharp punishment was to be inflicted and extermination of the red man was a possibility, if he were not subdued. Quite typical of a general who handled men and soldiers was his first order to all of his district commanders: "Place every mounted man in your command on the South Platte Route at once. Repair telegraphs. Attack any body of Indians you meet, large or small. Stay with them and pound them until they move north of the Platte or south of the Arkansas."

From now on, all trains on the trails, which for weeks had been closed to traffic–be those trains freight, coach or emigrant, were ordered to concentrate, and thus avoid massacres, due to isolation. Soldiers were sent to guard and patrol the whole main overland road; scouting parties were sent out in every direction;

positive measures of restraining and punishing the blood-thirsty Indians were taken; the immediate country of the trail was combed for invaders; a general round-up was inaugurated.

To assist in this method of driving the Indians into a definite territory, and away from the Oregon Trail, Major Frank North, a plainsman and interpreter for the Pawnee Indians (who also were pressed into service) accepted the dangerous task of attempting to locate the hostile Indians. In 1860, North, then twenty years of age, was employed on the Pawnee reservation. Here he acquired such fluency of the Pawnee tongue that the next year he was employed as interpreter. It was at the breaking out of the Sioux War that North was commissioned to organize the Pawnee Scouts, who were not only friendly to the government, but were also the hated foes of the Sioux. Seventy-seven young warriors were selected by North. This system of enlistment of Indians for regular government service proved an invaluable addition to the soldiers of the plains.

That the hostile Indians were the Cheyennes, Arapahoes, Ogallalla Sioux, Brules, and Blackfeet,[41] all well supplied with ammunition and the best modern firearms, were well established facts, but the exact locality where a stubborn stand was to be made, perplexed even those who were versed in Indian movements.

The concentration of the Indians along the Platte and Sweetwater was a direct result of the union of the tribes of the north with the Sand Creek and Black Hills fighters, which made a formidable hostile array. At the end of the year 1864, the Indians held sway over stage stations from Julesburg to Valley Junction

---

[41] A tribe of the Sioux – the Sihasapa.

and to Mud Springs. West of Fort Laramie, the telegraph lines were under their control, thousands of stolen cattle were in their possession, wagon trains were daily overhauled, ranches and farms destroyed, men killed and mutilated, and women and children taken to a fate worse than death. These women and their children were captured from the stage stations, wagon trains and lonely ranches, and were taken from the trails to the country north of the Platte. Slight information was received from the captives by friendly Indians or an occasional note stealthily dropped along the road. While the information was not all that might be wished, it gave the soldiers a knowledge of the country in which the women had been taken, and also of the horrible condition under which the captives were living. It was to be the work of the Pawnees, under the efficient guidance of Major North, to locate the camps and restore the captives to civilization. Finally, it was learned that the women had been taken to the Indian villages to the north of the Platte; that the villages were unprotected in any way, because the warriors had gone on the warpath before renewed activities. The squaws with their children had disappeared from the trails, leaving the field of combat to the warriors, their trail being toward the Powder River country.

The soldiers of the plains, owing to the small number sent to fight the Indians, and the repeated successes of the Indians in their raids and depredations, became discouraged, and in many instances, in place of exposing themselves to certain death simply as a target for the red men, stayed in their stockades. The general condition on the plains seemed to them an impossible one; that there was no solution for the difficulty, and that it was useless to add sacrifice to a helpless and hopeless cause.

From the officers under the command of General Dodge, who had been detailed to ascertain exact conditions along the trails, came most discouraging reports in regard to Indian affairs in the territory through which the roads of travel and commerce extended. From the section of travel represented by the road between Omaha and Julesburg, General Robert Mitchell reported that he could obtain no communication with Fort Laramie or Denver; that the lines were all down; that telegraph poles were cut down and destroyed on the Denver line for fifty miles beyond Julesburg; that from Lodge Pole Creek on the Fort Laramie route, fifteen of the twenty-five miles of wire had been taken down and carried away. To attempt to repair the lines would necessitate the hauling of poles a distance of one hundred and forty miles, every mile being watched by hotsile Indians. The report further declared that the Indian villages could not be located, though the belief was that they were somewhere south of the Yellowstone; that many of the Indians were those against whom General Sully had made his campaign the previous summer. Furthermore, Julesburg Station had been surrounded, the telegraph and stage station burned, the supplies destroyed belonging to both the telegraph and stage companies, to citizens, and to the government. Fears were entertained that the Indians on Running Water, in the northern part of General Mitchell's district, might, any day, unite with the Indians on the trails.

From Colonel R. R. Livingston came a similar report of depredations and destruction of property. The statement was made that large parties of Indians were moving westward on the Republican River, and that their families were traveling with them "forming a camp of four hundred lodges containing eight warriors each, many lodges being thirty robes in size;" that in a recent skirmish two thousand Indians had fought, well armed with breech-loading carbines and rifles, and were utterly indifferent to what the small handful of soldiers might be trying to do, and when last seen by the Indians were slowly moving toward Fort Laramie. The country at this time was so well guarded by Indians that no white man's spies could be sent out of the station. The prediction was made by Colonel Livingston that unless vastly more soldiers were sent at once to the Platte, the trails would be devasted tracts without men or ranches.

General Moonlight, then commanding the Eleventh Kansas Cavalry, with headquarters at Denver, confirmed the opinion of other officers when he stated that "the Indians are now determined to make it a war of extermination and nothing short of five thousand men can make it extermination for them."

The testimony of another officer was, that at Mud Springs there had been a fight in which there were two thousand Indians charging the soldiers "in the face of artillery and were nearly successful." The stock belonging to the freighting company of Beauer and Creighton was captured and driven northward, the Indians with seven hundred lodges going beyond Pole Creek. Again came the report reaffirming other messages, that telegraph poles were carried away and burned and wires "were so inextricably tangled as to be useless."

In addition to having control over the Oregon and Overland Trails, the Santa Fé Trail was also being constantly harrassed by the red men. This southern road was the line of transportation for supplies for all of New Mexico and Southern California, as well as the intervening territory. The fear was expressed that if conditions grew worse on this trail, and the Santa Fé Road were closed, then "all would be lost."

This serious and complicated crisis, presented a condition that challenged the keenest, strategic, military ability of our army. The dangers, known and unknown, confronting the stage stations and their faithful men, might have staggered a commander less familiar with Indian warfare than General Dodge when he took control of the Department of the Missouri, consisting of Missouri, the Indian Territory, Kansas, Colorado, Utah, and Wyoming. Not only did he have command over this large tract of territory, but his authority extended to the overland mail routes and telegraph lines to the Pacific. The importance of taking mail, passengers and supplies, and sending telegrams from the Missouri River to outlying districts, and to the coast, carried with it a more vital significance than mere food, supplies, men, and information; it helped to preserve the nation which was then in the final struggles of a civil war.

That a grave problem was awaiting solution is evidenced by the report that was given General Dodge at the time he assumed control of the department containing the trails. General Curtis, the former commander, had reported to General Grant "against any winter campaign; that the Indians had possession of the entire country crossed by the stage lines, having destroyed the telegraph lines; and that the people living in Colorado, western Nebraska and western Kansas were without mail, and in a state of panic; that the troops distributed along the routes of travel were inside their stockades;

that the Indians in nearly every fight defeated them. This success had brought into hostility with the United States nearly every tribe of Indians from Texas on the south to the Yellowstone on the north. It was a formidable combination, and the friendly Indians were daily leaving the reservations to join their hostile brethren."[42]

Early in 1865, the Seventh Iowa Cavalry was stationed at Fort Laramie; the Eleventh Ohio and the Eleventh Kansas Cavalry were stationed on the Sweetwater and at Platte Bridge Station. The first order, before reaching the far West, was to have the troops march to Fort Kearney from Fort Riley. This the soldiers refused to do, because the snow was on the ground and the thermometer registered below zero. An order for immediate arrest convinced the men that Indian fighting was a serious undertaking. The results arising from mutiny being made known to the soldiers, the companies moved on toward the country of the hostile Indians.

The final command at Kearney, before the troops separated to take different stations along the road, was for aggressive war, no matter how large the Indian band might be, or how small the number of soldiers; hereafter they "must stand and fight; that if they did, the Indians would run. If they did not, the Indians would catch and scalp them, and even if they had to retreat, they must do so with their faces to the enemy."

An attempt was made to overtake the Indians before they crossed the North Platte and escaped into the Powder River territory, the tribal home and hunting ground of many of the fleeing Indians. This land was a veritable paradise for hunters and the out-of-doors

[42] Dodge (G. M.) *The Indian Campaign of the Winter of 1864-65.* (Written in 1877, published 1907).

man, be he white or red. But the Indians could not be followed into their lair, for by this time General Dodge and his men were out of supplies, food, clothing, and ammunition – a condition which would not justify a chase into a region from which nothing could be obtained to carry on the warfare. The late winter added serious difficulties to the new situation, for the snow was now two feet deep on the level, and a hard freeze made a heavy crust, which prohibited travel, either by men or horses.

After two weeks of intense and aggressive warfare and the loss of many soldiers, General Dodge and his men had driven the Indians north, where they were intercepted by the soldiers from Fort Laramie, who drove them across the Platte, from where they traveled toward the Powder River and the Black Hills, seeming to realize that a new era of warfare against the Indians had been inaugurated. General Dodge, after being in command for two weeks, had six hundred miles of wire restrung and poles replaced between Omaha and Denver. The speed of this construction can be better understood when the report is read of the soldiers' activity: "We ran twelve miles of wire and set eight miles of poles; had two severe fights and marched fifty-five miles in fifty-two hours. Operators furnished valuable services."

Following the reconstruction of communication by wire, the next important work was to open up the stage lines, in order to keep in closer communication at this vital period of our nation's growth, with conditions along the road and public affairs at each end of the trail. In the incredibly short period of seventeen days after the opening of the telegraph line, during a siege of extreme weather, with the thermometer registering thirty degrees below zero, the roads were freed from Indians and the trails open for travel. The wonderful fortitude of the soldiers, their great personal bravery, and their skillful work, received favorable comment from all of those who were familiar with this critical and dangerous period on the plains.

Reviewing the results obtained from the aggressive campaign of less than six weeks, General Dodge, eager to rob the plains of their terrors, sent an earnest plea to General Grant to make extensive preparations during the coming summer to thoroughly chastise those Indians; for if this were not done, and done effectively, the Indians would successfully attack the overland stages and undo all the work which had just been completed.

The theory advanced by General Dodge, based on experience "to be just as watchful and just as vigilant when I knew the Indians were not near me as I was when I knew they were in sight," was taught to him and instilled into him by his friend and scout, Jim Bridger, who always gave the warning, "whar' ye don't see no Injuns, thar's whar they're sartin to be thickest."

By March 1, 1865, when the overland routes were regularly carrying traffic, and troops had been stationed to guard and protect the stations and the stage coaches, General Dodge returned to headquarters at St. Louis, not only reporting what had been accomplished but sounding words of alarm as to what he believed the Indians would attempt in their renewed attacks along the trails with the coming of spring and new grass.

While General Dodge, by dynamic force was whipping the Indians off the overland trails, and was establishing at least temporary subjection, the authorities at Washington, with their static ideals of treaties, had many theories to advocate, even demanding that these ideals be put into immediate operation. About the time that General Connor was to be sent into the Powder River country to crush the retreating Indians forced there by General Dodge, orders came from Washington that the armies of the plains must be materially reduced, in order to diminish the expenses of Indian warfare.

At this critical period of attempting to subject the red man, General Pope, having a thorough understanding of the real conditions confronting those who had been, and were, battling for the freedom of the plains, dispatched a reply to the order for a reduction of soldiers, stating that only the continuation of the fighting force now stationed along the lines of travel, plus additional aid, could possibly finish the work that, in its beginning had cost so many lives; that all of the tribes of the Rocky Mountains were in open hostility; that the uninhabited land for three thousand five hundred miles had to be protected from the savages, not only for the United States mail, but for saving human lives, particularly the large number of emigrants, who not only used the main roads, but "every route supposed to be practicable," making highways in every direction across the great plains, and driving off or destroying the game. No part of the region along the trails escaped the prying eyes of the gold-seekers. No route which promised discoveries of value, or in any manner shortened the route of travel, was neglected. "Of course neither the movements nor the conduct of these parties can be controlled." It was further argued that a policy to settle the Indian question by treaties was one that could not be fulfilled, for promises had been made that could not be carried out.

The first and great demand coming from the Indians was that white men should not invade their territory. How could this be done unless the government stopped emigration of the whites from the East to the West? As a matter of fact, our government was encouraging in every way possible a larger and more numerous exodus to the West; furthermore, this self-same government sent protecting soldiers (it is true, often in insufficient numbers) with all of these trains of gold, land and home seekers. When these people were to take possession of the territory which belonged to the Indians, where was the red man to find an abode or a hunting ground? Logically, thus reasoned the Indian. To gradually allow encroachments into his country would ultimately leave him without a home. From the red man's standpoint there was nothing to do to protect his territory but to fight. The same alternative was open to our government, but this could not be successfully done with a diminished force of trained men. The Indians were concentrating all their tribes for a final and decisive battle, not only to protect their country but to sweep clean the overland roads and emigrant trails, ridding forever, as they thought, their territory of the pestiferous whites. How little they knew! How little the government understood!

At this time (1865) General Dodge knew that twenty-five thousand savages were on the warpath on the roads that were in, or were leading to, the country that is now embraced within the eastern half of the state of Wyoming. The experience through which he had just gone to establish order and open traffic on the trails, satisfied him that every tribe of importance, from Canada to our extreme southern boundaries, was preparing to engage in open hostilities. Not only was the extent of the fighting of the warriors known to General Dodge, but he realized the fighting ability of his foes. Repeated were his requests to the Washington authorities that in place of depleting the plains' army, a large increase was a necessity, or the West be abandoned to the Indians. The government, however, had "eyes that see not and ears that hear not." Stupidly the government insisted in its policy of diminishing expenses by reducing the military force, thus increasing the depredations and the slaughter of emigrants.

Thus, is found the condition of affairs on both sides of the Platte when General Connor, with an army of invasion, was taken from the Overland and Oregon Trails, which he and his men had been guarding for hundreds of miles, and ordered to hunt the Indians, subdue or annihilate them and drive them off the Bozeman Trail and out of the Powder River hunting grounds.

Before following the Powder River Indian Expedition there should be recorded some extraordinary events which transpired at Fort Laramie, showing how the bitter feeling existing between the soldiers and the Indians had grown to a spirit of acute hostility. Colonel Thomas Moonlight[43] was in command of the Eleventh Kansas Cavalry, which had reached Fort Laramie early in the spring of 1865. Upon the arrival of the regiment at the fort, the soldiers had been distributed at the various stations of the northern sub-districts of the Division of the Plains. A greater part of these stations were simply stockades, with logs twenty feet in length set in the ground, with a number of port-holes in each side. Such were some of the fortifications extending

---

[43] Of the Eleventh Kansas Cavalry, commander of the district of Colorado. (Governor of the Territory of Wyoming, 1886-1889).

from Fort Laramie to South Pass, each about thirty-five miles apart, the buildings being able to accommodate a company of men and their horses. These soldiers not only protected the stations and telegraph lines, but acted also as escorts to the emigrants on the trail.

On the 27th of May, Colonel Thomas Moonlight and his men captured Two Face, Black Foot, and other Sioux chiefs, with their respective bands. These chiefs had taken a conspicuous part on August 7, 1864, in the killing of some white people. A stage driver and stage keeper, Joseph Eubanks and family, were killed, except Mrs. Eubanks and her daughter, one and a half years of age. The scalping of her husband, the killing of ten stage men and ten settlers, all occurred before Mrs. Eubanks' eyes, she and her daughter escaping with their lives to experience something worse than death. The two were kept in captivity fourteen months. After the capture of the Indians, Colonel Moonlight transmitted from Fort Laramie on May 27, 1865, to Captain George F. Price, the following report:

"I have the honor to submit the following report of the capture of Two Face and Black Foot, Sioux chiefs of the Ogallala tribe, along with their bands, and the execution of the two chiefs. About the 18th inst., some Indians were discovered on the north side of the Platte, near the Indian Village, encamped 10 miles east of Laramie. Mr. Elston, in charge of the Indian village, took a party of Indian soldiers and captured what was found to be Two Face, having a white woman prisoner (Mrs. Eubanks) and her little daughter, whom he had purchased from the Cheyennes. During the same evening and the next morning early, the other Indians who were with Two Face, and who had fled on the approach of Elston's party, were also captured and lodged in the guard house here. Mrs. Eubanks gave information of the whereabouts of Black Foot and the village, and a party of Indian soldiers started to bring them in, dead or alive.　The village was found about 100 miles northeast of here, on Snake Fork, and compelled to surrender without being able to make any fight.　Black Foot and his companions were placed in the guard house with the others, making six men in confinement.　Both of the chiefs openly boasted that they had killed white men, and that they would do it again if let loose; so I concluded to tie them up by the neck with a trace-chain, suspended from a beam of wood, and leave them there without any foothold.　The property captured was as follows: six United States mules, three United States horses, five mules not branded, but I believe claimed by some party down the river, and fifteen ponies, in miserable condition, which I left in charge of Mr. Elston for the use of the Indian soldiers in scouting. The other animals were turned in to the acting assistant quartermaster, to be taken up on his return.　On the person of Two Face was found $220 in greenbacks, which I gave to Mrs. Eubanks, also $50 taken from another of the band.　This lady was captured by the Cheyennes on the Little Blue last fall, where her husband was killed, along with several others.　She was treated in a beastly manner by the Cheyennes, and purchased from them during the winter by Two Face and Black Foot, who compelled her to toil and labor as their squaw, resorting, in some instances, to lashing.　She was in a wretched condition when she was brought in, having been dragged across the river Platte with a rope.　She was almost naked, and told some horrible tales of the barbarity and cruelty of the Indians."

Another recital of these facts has been dramatically recorded, showing that a report was sent to General Connor that the chiefs had been captured.　A telegram came back to Fort Laramie, "Where are those villains now?"　The answer was sent back, "In chains."　The next wire from General Connor gave the command, "Hang them in chains."　Shortly after this last message was sent, General Connor regretted the severity of the order, and forwarded another wire, "I was a little hasty; bring them to Julesburg and give the wretches a trial."　Again a message was wired General Connor:

"Dear General: I obeyed your first order before I received the second."

F. G. Burnett,[44] under date of March 6, 1919, writes the authors:

"In the spring of 1865 I was at old Fort Laramie and saw hung on a scaffold, by order of General Connor who was in command at that time, Two Face and another chief who had captured a train of emigrants and murdered all but two women. . . After hearing the story from the captives of the terrible torture and abuse they had been under, the chiefs were ordered hung, which order was executed at nine o'clock in the morning, when a volley of twelve pieces was also fired at the Indians, and then they were left to hang until further orders. I passed through the fort again in October, and the bones were still hanging on the scaffold. If you could have heard the story of these poor women — how they had been starved and abused, and of the horrible torture and mutilations the Indians had caused the poor emigrants to suffer, you would have thought any death too good for the redskins."

The scaffold was constructed of two upright posts and a cross-beam, on a military road below the fort, on which the chiefs hung "until they resembled well preserved Egyptian mummies." The platform was made from two drygoods boxes placed in two government wagons, drawn by six-mule teams. On the boxes the doomed chiefs stood while the chains were being adjusted around their necks. At this point the teamsters cracked their whips, the mules jumped forward, while the band played "Yankee Doodle." One of the Indians

[44] Mr. Burnett, now a resident of Fort Washakie, Wyoming, was at one time in the employ of Sutler A. C. Leighton, who had stores at Forts Reno, Phil Kearney, and C. F. Smith.

died game by jumping backward before the mules started, but the other chief held on to the box with his feet until the last moment.

Among those to accompany Colonel Moonlight to arrest the chiefs was John C. Friend of the Eleventh Ohio Cavalry, who had come to the West as far as Fort Laramie, October 10, 1863. In the summer of 1864, Friend was one of the members of a detachment that was sent to the relief of the Larimer party, an overland emigrant train which had been brutally attacked by the Sioux July 12th on Little Box Elder. Several of the emigrants had been killed, though a worse fate meeting Mrs. Larimer, Mrs. Fanny Kelly and her adopted daughter, about twelve years of age, who were all taken into captivity by the Indians. In November of the same year, after serving at Deer Creek Station, Friend was transferred to Sweetwater Station, near Independence Rock, fifty-five miles southwest of Platte Bridge Station, at which place he was, by chance, on the day Lieutenant Caspar Collins was killed, in which fight Friend took an active part. During the summer of that year (1865) John Friend was again transferred to detached service and employed by the Pacific Telegraph Company in repairing and keeping up the line between Platte Bridge and St. Mary's Station on the upper Sweetwater, carrying the news in June, 1865, to the Platte Bridge Station of the burning of St. Mary's. When Mr. Friend's company was again transferred to Fort Laramie, early in September of that year, he was detailed on escort duty, making two trips to Fort Connor (Reno), being one of the twenty soldiers refusing to drive government mule teams, when detached. General Frank Wheaton, in command, summoned before him Friend and his companions, telling them they were mutineers and were liable to be shot. The reply was that they were not mule drivers, but soldiers, pointing to their records. Mr. Friend writes: "He evidently accepted our view of the question, as he ordered us to quarters with the admonition to report to the quarter-master in the morning. Those who failed to report were at once detailed to escort the paymaster to Powder River, I being among the number."

The Naming of Fort Caspar

The Crow Indians originally owned and roamed over that part of the West along the Yellowstone, Big Horn, and Wind Rivers, claiming the land that was embraced in the Powder River country. The land this tribe had selected over which to roam and hunt, was not only ideal as to location, but abounded in rich grass, fruits, and game. Because of the wondrous abundance of food for man and animals, the Crows experienced serious difficulty in holding from their enemies this choice country. For seventy-five years the Blackfoot Indians were determined to control the territory which extended to the North Platte River in Wyoming and north to the Missouri River in Montana. From here, they were annually driven north, beyond the Yellowstone, by the Crows. During the middle of the nineteenth century, the Arapahoes, Cheyennes, and Sioux made repeated raids upon the Crows, in their determination to gain and live upon the land which had been the loved possession of their enemies. Finally, the fiercest and most savage of the plains' warriors, the Sioux, were successful in their prolonged and continuous raids, and became the ruling tribe on the Crows' hunting grounds. From that time, the Crows allied themselves, more or less, with the whites; the enemies of the Crows becoming enemies of the whites. Unfortunately, our government never allied itself with the Crows in warfare to subdue the Sioux. Had this been done in the early sixties, many hundreds of soldiers would not have

suffered death, and doubtless the Sioux would have
been exterminated or driven back out of the Powder
River country, a condition of affairs desired by the
peaceful Crows.

Old Crow, the greatest chief of the Crows, once said,
in a military council held on the eastern side of the Big
Horn Mountains, along the Bozeman Trail:

"The great white chief will hear his Indian brother.
These are our lands by inheritance. The Great Spirit
gave them to our fathers but the Sioux stole them from
us. They hunt upon our mountains. They fish in our
streams. They have stolen our horses. They have
murdered our squaws, our children. What white man
has done these things to us? The face of the Sioux is
red, but his heart is black. But the heart of the paleface has ever been red to the Crows. The scalp of no
white man hangs in our lodges. They are as thick as
grass in the wigwams of the Sioux. The great white
chief will lead us against no other tribe of red men.
Our war is with the Sioux and only them. We want
back our lands. We want their women for slaves to
work for us, as our women have had to work for them.
We want their horses for our young men, and their
mules for our squaws. The Sioux have trampled upon
our hearts. The great white chief sees that my young
men have come to fight. No Sioux shall see their
backs. Where the white warrior goes, there shall we
be also."

The Sioux, who were harrassing the people on the
Oregon Trail, had their home in the country between
the Big Horn Mountains and the Black Hills. These
Indians, in 1851, at Fort Laramie, made a treaty with
the government which granted to the white man, the
right to pass through, but not to occupy, the lands of the

Sioux. For a number of years the Indians observed the terms of the treaty, with occasional violations, it is true, until early in the sixties, when an additional treaty was needed and was made in 1865. At the gathering of the chiefs at that historic treaty-making fortification, Fort Laramie, not all of the Sioux tribes were represented, many of the leading chiefs making no effort to be present at the conference. Thus, entered into in a half-hearted way, this treaty did little more than renew the oft-forgotten treaty of 1851, granting to the whites only rights of transit through the Sioux territory.

West of South Pass, on the Oregon Trail, the Indians did not materially disturb the telegraph stations and destroy the wagon trains, for this territory was not included in the treaty which prohibited the white man from using the Sioux country. East of South Pass, to Fort Laramie and beyond, there was a determined effort to raid and kill those who dared to use the Oregon Trail. At the bend in the North Platte, just as it comes from the south, abruptly turning to the east,[45] there had been constructed a permanent bridge made of cedar logs, built on cribs, filled in with stones. Just how substantial the bridge was may be indicated from the fact that there were twenty-eight piers, all made of hewn pine logs, with piles about thirty feet from center to center. As was written in the diary of Sergeant Isaac B. Pennick, stationed at this place May 27, 1865: "It is a very substantial structure for this wooden country. Price for crossing six mule team, from one dollar to five dollars each, according to the stage of the river." It was estimated at the time of the Fort Caspar fight that the bridge had cost in the neighborhood of sixty thousand dollars. Privately constructed by Louis

---

[45] Near the present site of Casper, Wyo.

Ganard, a French-Canadian squaw-man, toll bridge charges were being exacted from the emigrants and. stage lines as they went over the Oregon Trail; the scale of charges being regulated by the water in the stream. Stationed near this bridge were the soldiers of Camp Dodge. They had been sent in the spring of 1865 from Kansas to the west to engage in an aggressive campaign against the Indians who were then fighting both north and south of the Oregon and Overland Roads, one of their chief delights being to destroy the telegraph lines. These special troops of Camp Dodge were to help guard the North Platte Trail from Fort Laramie to South Pass, a distance of three hundred odd miles.

Both of these routes, the Oregon Trail (used mostly by emigrants) and the Overland, or Bridger Road (largely used by stage and express lines), by the way of Fort Collins (Colorado), Virginia Dale, Fort Halleck, Bridger's Pass and Fort Bridger, continued to be harrassed by the Indians, with daily destruction and savage warfare. It was no rare occasion for the stage to run through this dangerous division on the plains at night, the soldiers being so few in numbers and the distances to be covered so great; the maximum at any station being ten men.

With headquarters on the North Platte, near the bridge, Colonel Plumb hurried his soldiers east and west along the Platte and Sweetwater, stopping a raid here, preventing a surprise there, driving the Indians north at other places, repulsing attacks on stages to the south in the direction of Fort Halleck, or protecting the emigrants as they went West on the Oregon Trail.

When the warm days of the spring of 1865 came, the Southern Cheyennes joined forces with the Northern

Cheyennes, who had a camp just north of the Platte River bridge. Banded with the Northern Cheyennes were the Sioux, who now realized that with this new addition of warriors there was a chance of keeping the white man out of the country of the Powder River, as well as to drive the soldiers and emigrants off of the Oregon Trail. Not only were the Indian villages stretched for miles along the Powder River to the north, but corrals and stables had been built to hold and safe-guard the most valuable of their ponies; for the Sioux (natural enemy of the Crow) was in that part of the country, waiting an opportunity to steal horses for the spring hunt. When the spring came, giving the ponies plenty of food, all of the banded tribes moved further south, in the immediate country about the Platte Bridge and toward the emigrant trail, with a determination to raid the road from South Pass to Fort Laramie, and, in addition to drive the stage coaches from the road of the South Platte. The most strategic point along this road of the Platte was at this bridge, at the bend in the river. On the hills north of the bridge came the Sioux, headed by Chief Young-Man-Afraid-Of-His-Horses, the two tribes of Cheyennes, Arapahoes and members of other tribes in less numbers, until the allied host numbered over three thousand fighting warriors and hundreds of their women.

It now became a daily occurrence for the Indians to try and draw the soldiers out into the open and entice them across the bridge, thus attempting to decoy them into a favorable position for a united attack. Hundreds of the Indians would suddenly appear from un-looked-for positions and sweep down upon the unsuspicious soldiers. Elaborate preparations were made to provoke an ambuscade; mirror signals were flashed from hill to hill; Indians were seen using field glasses; runners were skurrying from group to group, and at every possible vantage point the Indians were massed for an exterminating blow. While the red men near the bridge were challenging the soldiers to cross the structure, special war preparations were taking place back of the Indian lines. Ceremonies and prayers were being made in supplication to the Great Spirit for success in battle and for protection for the warriors, and numerous incantations were indulged in by the savages, tending to place the white despoilers of their country within their power.

Notwithstanding these elaborate efforts to draw the soldiers into an open conflict, no great depredations were committed until July 26, (1865), when Lieutenant Caspar Wever Collins, with many soldiers, paid the supreme sacrifice during a raid. The manner of his sacrifice received recognition and soon after Platte Bridge Station became known as Fort Caspar.

First Sergeant Isaac B. Pennick, Company I, Eleventh Kansas Cavalry furnishes new material from his diary that serves not only as an introduction to the fight near the Platte Bridge, but gives an eye-witness account of the tragedies enacted at the telegraph stations on the Oregon Trail. Pennick had his headquarters at the Platte Bridge:[46]

"May 14, 1865–Arrived at Sweetwater at one p.m. All right at station. Bridger, the old pioneer, our guide, took supper with us. His life has been a romantic one in this country since he was 13 years old, when he came here. He has been roaming and tramping for

---

[46] Used through the courtesy of William E. Connelley, secretary Kansas State Historical Society.

42 years over this country. General Moonlight took supper with us. Snow all afternoon. Letters.

"May 19 – Warm. Strong wind. Thermometer 86 deg. Fahrenheit. News of Indians. "H" Company had a skirmish with them.

May 20 – Took a walk to Independence Rock, two miles west of station. It is on the north side of Sweetwater. The stream washes the southwestern base of it. It is about 700 paces long and 1900 paces in circumference around the base. While there I heard recall. Hastened to camp. The Indians have attacked the Three Crossings Station from 500 to 600 strong. Station surrounded. They have cut the telegraph wires. Some fighting about 5 P.M.

"May 21 – Sixteen men cross Sweetwater and follow trail of Indians until satisfied that they went to Wind River. Sweetwater very deep and rapid. About 150 to 200 Indians; war or hunting party.

"May 22 – Start from Three Crossing for Sweetwater; travel 15 miles to Split Rock; passed Castle Rock on right of road, 10 miles east of Three Crossings. Passed Whisky Gap south of road about 6 miles. Came to Devil's Gate before sundown. After sundown arrived at Sweetwater. Colonel Plumb has been fighting Indians across the Platte at Deer Station; 200 Indians; one killed on each side; several Indians wounded.

"May 26 – (Being now west of the Platte Bridge), Pass over the Devil's Backbone; south of Willow Springs is an oil spring said to run 50 barrels of petroleum per day; hear that Indians tried to stampede stock at Sweetwater yesterday afternoon; 30 or 40 of them. They did not succeed.

"May 27 – Have news that the Indians attacked

Rocky Ridge[47] today in strong force. The fight is still going on; don't know what the result will be. The operator says there is an immense number of the enemy.

"May 28 – Hear that the Indians crossed the Platte River in front of our provision train. Moonlight has sent reinforcements to the train and a dispatch to Colonel Plumb to send a detachment also from this end of the road. No telegraphic communication further east than Deer Creek, nor west of Sweetwater.

"May 29 – Talk of another expedition to go north to Powder River after the Indians in a few days.

"May 30 – Train attacked twice between here and Laramie. One man killed.

"June 1 – Hear that Rocky Ridge Station was burned by the Indians. Don't know whether the garrison escaped or not. Some anxiety on that account. Two companies of galvanized troops (rebel soldiers sent on the plains to fight Indians) started for there escorted by a detail from our regiment.

"June 3 – At 3 p.m. received dispatch from Colonel Plumb that Indians have attacked station at upper bridge; ordered to cross lower bridge with 20 men and attack them in the rear. Capt. Greer and 20 men started, but the Indians were gone when we got there, but plenty of fresh tracks. Colonel Plumb is in close pursuit, and was in fighting distance at two hours before sundown. We have heard from the fight; two of our men killed and one Indian and several ponies. One of our men had ten arrows shot into him; scalped and fingers cut off and terribly mangled.

"June 7 – No telegraphic communication east of Laramie for five days. Indians have cut wires between there and Julesburg.

---

[47] Rocky Ridge and St. Mary's Station were the same.

"June 14 – Mail came today. Indians have burned all ranches west of Cache la Poudre to Platte River on Denver side.

"June 15 – Indians and our forces fighting at Fort Mitchel; 4 killed on our side; 7 wounded; 15 Indians killed.

"June 16 – Twenty-one of Company "I" refuse to do duty. All put under arrest; mutineers acknowledge they were wrong and are relieved from arrest.

"June 17 – Snowing like forty thousand devils; ground covered with snow.

"June 21 – Operator at Sweetwater killed and one wounded; three Indians killed by our men.

"June 23 – 300 wagons, emigrant train, near Laramie, coming out to gold region.

"June 24 – Our boys back from Sweetwater. The Indians in the fight were Arapahoes; about 40 of them and 9 of our troop. Three Indians supposed to have been killed; one of our men was killed and one wounded. Colonel Moonlight is relieved of this district. Powder River expedition about to start.

"June 28 – Emigrant train of 180 wagons went up on the other side of the river yesterday, bound for Utah, Oregon, Idaho, and California.

"July 2 – Just as we were falling in for inspection, three shots were heard in quick succession, which was the signal in case Indians were seen. All except a small party to keep camp started to save the horses, which were grazing some ¾ mile from the camp. When the horses were safely started for camp, we pressed a little on beyond to the brow of the bluffs on the west and down in the valley ½ mile distant were the Indians. We fired a few shots and returned to camp. Sent out a few mounted men to ascertain their strength. Horsemen soon returned. Indians came nearer, within range of camp, shooting from ravines. Sent out 5 or 6 men to engage them; fought them for awhile from one ravine to another. Didn't pay. Sent 12 to 14 men under Captain Greer and charged them. Drove them, shooting one; captured a great many of their trinkets – bows, shields, etc. Indians then drew off on the hills to the east. Captain Greer and 9 or 10 mounted men pursued, endeavoring to cut off some of their stragglers. Proceeded ½ mile when the Indians were discovered to be in force just beyond a hill we were about to ascend. After some hesitation we fell back slowly, which we had no sooner begun than they charged on us in greatly superior numbers, endeavoring to cut us off from camp. We put in what shots we could to the best of our ability, but in spite of our efforts to repel them, they drove us a few hundred yards. Sergeant Holding was wounded in this engagement; ball entered back of the neck and passed out through the lower part of the left ear. The man who shot him was supposed to be a white man; was shot himself by one of our boys (Hammond) through the breast, just after he had shot Holding. Could not ascertain anything about how many Indians were killed, only by the blood which marks the field, and which proves that quite a large number of men or ponies were killed or wounded. This fight on Reshaw (Richard) Creek, 4 miles from lower bridge.

"July 3 – Lieutenant Drew with 20 men ordered on a scout to Deer Creek, 28 miles west; started at noon.

"July 7 – Trip on scout to Sweetwater Bridge. Major Mackay telegraphed Captain Greer to send 10 men to Sweetwater, 55 miles, to repair telegraph line and meet Colonel George of California, which order was almost equivalent to an order to march that number of men to shoot them down, scalp them, cut off their hands and feet, cut out their hearts, livers, sinews, and send them to the savages. The boys refused to go unless 30 men were sent. I volunteered to take command of the party. Marched continuously with scout in advance as far as Devil's Backbone or near it. Found wire cut 400 yards; carried it off about 700 yards off the poles. It being dark, it took two hours to repair it. Indian camp south of road some distance. Heard their dogs barking distinctly. Went on west side of Devil's Backbone; found wire down, about 700 yards of it, but not carried off; daybreak against we repaired it. . . Went to lower Willow Springs some two or three miles, turned horses loose to graze. Near Horse Creek struck a large Indian trail of ponies and lodge poles, 100 yards in width, going north. Scouts saw one Indian two miles north of road. Trail very fresh; crossed one hour in advance of our arrival. Fortunate for us we were detained so long on the road. From the trail suppose about 300 to 500 warriors in the party. Made rapid time into Sweetwater Station. Found about 400 yards of wire there. Telegraphed west—none nearer than Rocky Ridge. A party went down and put up line, but no communication east. The cut west was tied to a post with a buckskin string. Sharp trick of Indians.

"July 8 – Started with a new supply of wire for Platte Bridge . . . proceeded to Devil's Backbone. Find wire cut badly; about 700 yards cut; some carried off. Repaired and started on.

"July 12 – The Indians yesterday did not number more than 30 warriors. A large train of emigrants passed the bridge today; 75 wagons bound for Montana, Idaho, and the gold regions. Wire cut beyond Sweetwater; 20 or 30 men ordered to start with wire to fix it on tomorrow morning; 1300 yards gone; they lack 300 to repair the line.

"July 14– . . . A dispatch from General Gus Henry ordering Captain Greer to take command of the post at Platte Bridge and all troops stationed there; Major Anderson of our regiment ordered to take command of all troops from Laramie to South Pass; headquarters, Platte Bridge.

"July 15 – Major Anderson and the Eleventh brass band will be here tomorrow evening. We are to be relieved as soon as the Sixth Michigan Cavalry arrive.

"July 17 – Fifty-five of our company, 24 from "K," and some of the infantry at the station, start at one o'clock to Horse Creek with 8 of the Ohio Eleventh, and one howitzer, to surprise an Indian camp that was seen there about the 25th of June, and which I was satisfied left for the north, Powder or Wind Rivers, about the 4th of July, from personal knowledge. But now, 15 days after, 'old fogie' commanders send a party to surprise a camp that the rank and file know to have been clear out of the country for at least twelve or fifteen days, from having seen their trail at the time they were leaving, and also their rear men as they were going off.

"July 23 – Five of our horses stolen from near camp last night by a party of Indians. Captain Greer with a detachment of 26 men pursued Indians, but unable to overhaul them. Indians crossed mountains about 14 miles southeast of our old camp, about 10 of them; one white man with them. Captain Greer's party found where the war party that fought us three weeks ago to-day first stopped after the fight; found where they had dressed the wounds of their party, received in the fight.

A great many bloody rags were discovered. One of their warriors was found hidden under a rock; supposed to be a great warrior or chief, from the trappings found with him; silver ornaments, etc.

"July 25 – Fine breeze this morning. Considerable noise among the horses last night. The guards think Indians were prowling around; too dark to see well. Immediately after dinner the cry of 'Here comes the Indians!' rang through the camp. I ran out of the tent, where sure enough, they were coming up the opposite side of the river. The boys commenced shooting and made some good shots. Fifteen of them rode along the bank, yelling and hooting like madmen. We crossed the bridge, 10 mounted, following them a couple of miles. We killed two if not three of them. They were gradually reinforced until we feared we would be taken. We fell back to camp. They commenced crossing the river two miles below and ran into the cattle herd. Twelve or fourteen of the boys went after them and we had a severe fight, killing one, a head chief, who was scalped; also two or three others mortally wounded. We finally drove them back across the river. They killed one steer, but we stuck to it and hauled it into camp. We fought them across the river until after dark, when we returned to camp; they did not disturb us during the night. About 50 to 100 in sight.

"July 26 – Terrible day for our command, and no knowing how it will end. At daybreak a few Indians were seen in the hills north of the river. Lieutenant Britney and 10 men arrived from Sweetwater before daybreak. Detachments of Company "H" and "D" to be here by 12 or 1 o'clock. They camped three miles this side of Willow Springs. Captain Greer received an order to send a detachment to meet "H" and "D" Companies. I took charge of it by request of the Captain. On reporting to Major Anderson I found that Lieutenant Collins, of "G" Company, Eleventh Ohio, was going out alone, but the captain, thinking it would be best, I went along, 20 to 25 in all. We crossed the bridge and got about one mile from camp, when from northeast and southwest, and every point of the compass, the savages came. It appeared as though they sprung up out of the ground. They completely surrounded us. There was no other alternative. Death was approaching on every side in its most horrible form – that of the tomahawk and scalping knife of the Indians. We turned and charged into the thickest of 'them, drawing our pistols and doing the best we could. It was a terrible ordeal to go through. It was really running the gauntlet for dear life. After a terrible break-neck race of ¾ of a mile, we arrived at the bridge, where the boys had run out to our support. In the charge we lost five killed and about twelve wounded. Lieutenant Collins was killed. Everything was in full view from the station. Over 1500 Indians were around our little party. The Indians suffered dreadfully, as our pistols were pushed right against their bodies and fired, doing great execution. We were forced to come back. Every horse nearly was wounded in one or more places; 4 were killed. They now cut the wires both east and west. Twenty men under Lieutenant Walker went two miles east to repair it. The enemy attacked him, killing one and wounding two of our company. He had to retreat, not getting the wire fixed. At one-half past eleven o'clock, "H" and "D" companies detachment came in sight west of us. The savages surrounded them. Five of the boys crossed the river three miles below; two were killed, three came into camp afoot, their horses being killed. One, on horseback was near the mountains, but several Indians were in close pursuit. All this we could plainly see from the station, but could do nothing for them. "H" and "D" detachments corraled, or tried to corral their wagons, but did not succeed very well. We could see the Indians in swarms charge down upon our boys, when they would roll volley after volley into them. It seemed to us as though the boys were in a strong position, 20 in all being the number. At about 4 o'clock p.m. the firing ceased, and the smoke, that of the burning wagons, commenced ascending. The enemy commenced going off north by twos and threes, till at sundown not a living being was to be seen. We are certain that all of the boys were killed, but from the length of time they had held out and the immense numbers of Indians charging in solid masses upon them, they must have suffered terribly in killed and wounded. Two Snake scouts started at half-past nine p.m., with dispatches to Deer Creek. Would they get there before day?

"July 27 – Up at daybreak. Went on top of the post with glass. Soon the Indians commenced appearing on the ridge just opposite, on the north side of the river; first one and then two, until by sunrise hundreds were in sight on all the hills. Some of them halloed across in the Cheyenne language, telling the women to leave, as they were going to burn us out and kill all the soldiers and men here. They are now going southwest on the high ground, toward Red Buttes, but few in sight at 8 a.m. The Indians are very mad. They told the Indians (Snakes, friendly) that they had killed all the men of "H" and "D" yesterday, and were going to kill more white men today, and that our men had killed and wounded heaps of Indians. Copy of papers found on battle ground yesterday, viz: "Blackfeet, Cheyennes, Arapahoes, Sioux and a few Comanches are here now. They want to fight four days more. I was taken prisoner down on the Platte River. You killed a chief yesterday evening. They say they do not want to have peace. There is over one thousand (1000). They want your stock and want to fight. They are moving to battle on the place." A party of us crossed this afternoon to try and bring in some of the dead. We found Lieutenant Collins and McDonald and one other man in a dreadfully-mangled and cut-up condition. Our scout at the west discovered the Indians in force about 2 miles off, dancing, encircled by their horses. Think that body is 600 strong. Another body from the east came in sight, when we were recalled. They proved to be a reinforcement from Deer Creek, 50 strong. Our Indian scouts got there after daylight. Lieutenants Hubbard and Greer started immediately. Another party is just starting to try and bring in the dead bodies nearest the river. The boys are all in safe (sundown) and brought in the three dead bodies left nearest; 58 arrows are found in one body; 24 in the body of Lieutenant Collins and several in McDonald's body. Two Indians showed themselves in the west on the hills. The three boys that escaped from the train on yesterday fought their way for 7 miles. Sixty Indians crossed the river and followed them, killing all their horses, and two out of the original five that were cut off from the train at the first charge of the Indians. Four of the Indians were killed and several wounded. The fighting was distinctly seen by all at the station. The three boys got into the bed of a brushy creek; when the band of Indians pursued, nearly all left them, only 14 Indians continuing the pursuit of them; they disabled two or three, when they also gave up the pursuit.

"July 28– . . . No Indians appeared up to 2 o'clock p.m. A detachment started to find our boys above. About five miles out west of the station 20 of the dead bodies were found; the wagons burned. The Indians had a great many killed and wounded. They had cut up a good many telegraph poles and split them to drag off their killed and wounded. The Indian scouts (Snake) say there were 3000 Indians at least north of the trail.

"July 29–A strong party went out to bury the dead. Twenty-one bodies were buried on the battleground, a horrible sight; all scalped but one, who was nearly burned up. The savages set the wagons on fire and heated the irons and bolts and burned the men with them, and turned their feet into the fire, torturing them if alive in every possible manner. They were buried in two graves, 7 in one and 13 in another. One body was buried in the other side of the river from where the train was taken. Wire cut east.

"July 31– . . . Nothing of note took place last night. No telegraphic communications east or west yet. Sixth Michigan not up yet, and some alarm on their account. Our rations are out today. The messes have had no meat for three days, and are out of flour this morning; things begin to look serious. If nothing turns up we will have to commence butchering and jerking beef for our subsistence. . . Saw two Indians below camp a couple of miles. The herd was brought in immediately. . . Succor must come soon; this suspense is terrible.

"August 1 – Pleasant morning; no news whatever from below. We cannot imagine what can be the matter. General Connor telegraphed when line was up that Sixth Michigan Cavalry would reach here by Saturday night. It is now Tuesday and not a word of any kind from below, and Indians between here and Deer Creek. . . Our ammunition is very short; but a few rounds . . . We can hold the fort for two hours if assaulted by the enemy in force, by firing 10 shots each from our carbines, but our pistol ammunition is plenty for close quarters. . . At 4 o'clock the joyful word came "The line is working." The joyful tick, tick, tick put a glad smile on every face. Soon heard the Sixth Michigan Cavalry would be here tomorrow.

"August 3 – Homeward bound."

Caspar W. Collins came to the West in 1862, not as a soldier, but as a companion to his father, Colonel Willam O. Collins, of the Eleventh Ohio Cavalry, who at different times was stationed at Fort Collins (Colorado; named for him); at Fort Halleck and Fort Laramie. Lieutenant Collins arrived at the Platte Bridge Station on his way to the Sweetwater, where he was stationed, the day before the battle, having just received at Fort Laramie his commission as first lieutenant. He was a young man, not yet 21 years of age, boyish in appearance – so much so that, it is reported, during the day he had been accused of being afraid to fight the Indians. This accusation, still ringing in his ears, made him determined to lead the men against the Indians, though these men were not of his command, but to prove conclusively that he was no coward, even when he knew the odds were greatly against him. The borrowed horse he rode was a massive, willful

PLATTE BRIDGE STATION, IDAHO TERRITORY

Lieut. Caspar W. Collins arrived at Platte Bridge Station, en route from Fort Laramie to his own station (Sweet-water) but two or three days before the fight of July 26, in which he was killed. From a drawing made by Bug-ler C. Moellman, Co. G, Eleventh Ohio Cavalry, in 1863.

gray, which, excited by the noise of the battle – the rifle and revolver shots and the whoops and yells of the savages, became unmanageable, took the bit and ran away, in spite of all Lieutenant Collins could do to subdue the crazed animal. The horse ran, not from the Indians, but right into their midst, giving the enemy every advantage, which was, of course, the destruction of the young officer. Young Collins had a close comrade at the station, John C. Friend, who was urged to prevent Collins taking charge of the command, but all arguments were without avail. It was an opportunity to show that he was not afraid; he would do his duty. Mr. Friend was one of the thirty enlisted men and citizens who organized to go on foot, following Lieutenant Collins and his mounted men. It was also this companion who was a member of the party that found the young officer's body on the battlefield the next day and brought it into camp. Lieutenant Collins might have saved himself if he had not attempted to rescue one of his fallen men. Collins not only had charge of the Sweetwater Station, but also Three Crossings, Rocky Ridge, and South Pass, the most western military station in the Platte River department, situated on the Sweetwater River in the center of the pass bearing the name of the station.

Major-General Pope, on November 21, 1865, issued the following order:

> "The military post situated at Platte Bridge, between Deer and Rock Creeks, on the Platte River, will be hereafter known as Fort Caspar, in honor of Lieutenant Caspar Collins, Eleventh Ohio Cavalry, who lost his life while gallantly attacking a superior force of Indians at this place."

From this time on, the recital of one day was but the repetition of the day before, and a statement of what was to happen tomorrow–scrimmages, combats, raiding, stampeding horses and mules, cutting the wires and burning the stations. At times, ammunition was insufficient and rations would be late in arriving from the East. Tobacco was $10 a pound, when it could be purchased, but when the supply was exhausted, tea and coffee were smoked, and when there was no longer a supply of these, the soldiers had to resort to smoking sagebrush. Messes were without meat for days, and flour was not to be had.

With combinations of warriors of many tribes concentrating on the North Platte, and now suddenly withdrawing toward the Powder River country, the East could not understand about the true conditions of the West, with its killing, fighting, slaughtering, and mutilating, nor could the East comprehend the seriousness of the conditions and sacrifices of the soldiers. The war between the North and South being at an end, the eastern papers concentrated their attention on the Indians of the plains and mountains. Criticism was freely given of the methods used by the government in the war of "extermination" of the "noble red man." Sympathy was all for the Indian. Petitions were sent to the President of the United States and protests offered against any campaign against the warriors who were doing the bloody and ruthless work along the Oregon and Overland Trails.

Brevet-General Guy V. Henry had said that "So little is known of the hardships and sufferings undergone by our officers and soldiers in Indian campaigning–of all warfares most dangerous, the most trying, the most thankless; the first, because our foe is under cover; the second, because you are often on reduced rations, exposed to intense cold, fires being often forbidden. If wounded, there is no transportation or possible cure; left on the battlefield wounded, torture of the worst kind awaits you, or, if buried, your body is exhumed for desecration."

General Charles King, one of the best known of the army officers who fought the red man – from the Apaches of Arizona to the Sioux in the campaign of 1876, and who has undergone the rigors of many a severe experience on the plains, says, in his admirable work, *Campaigning with Crook,* in mention of the government's way of handling Indian affairs:

> . . . but it is so exquisitely characteristic of the Indian Bureau's way of doing things that, now that the peace commissioners have triumphantly announced that the attack on Thornburg's command was all an accident, and have allowed the Indians to bully, temporize and hoodwink them into weeks of fruitless delay (the rascals never meant to surrender the Meeker murderers as long as they had only Peace Commissioners to deal with), and now that, after all, the army has probably got to do over again what it started to do last October, and could readily have accomplished long ere this, had they not been hauled off by the Bureau, the question naturally suggests itself, how often is this sort of thing to be repeated? Year after year it has been done. A small force of soldiers sent to punish a large band of Indian murderers or marauders. The small band has been well-nigh annihilated in many instances. Then the country wakes up; a large force concentrates at vast expense, and the day of retribution has come, when, sure as shooting, the Bureau has stepped in with a restraining hand. No end of silk-hatted functionaries have hurried out from Washington, shaken hands and smoked a pipe with a score of big Indians; there has been a vast amount of cheap oratory, and buncombe talk about the Great Father and guileless red men; at the end of which we are told to go back to camp and bury our dead; and our late antagonists, laughing in their sleeves, link arms with their aldermanic friends, are 'dead-headed' off to Washington, where they are lionized at the White House, and

sent the rounds of the great cities, and finally return to their reservations laden down with new and improved rifles and ammunition, stove-pipe hats and Saratoga trunks, more than ever convinced that the one way to get what they want out of Uncle Sam is to slap his face every spring and shake hands in the fall. The apparent theory of the Bureau is that the soldier is made to be killed, the Indian to be coddled.

The public, reading the newspapers, and knowing only what the press printed, was in a frame of mind to make a scape-goat of any commander sent into the West to try and solve the problem and subdue the Indians. "It was plain to be seen that General Connor was to be a sacrifice, whether he succeeded or failed in the Powder River Expedition." The recall of General Connor from the fort located in the heart of the lands of the Sioux, was inevitable before the expedition started from Fort Laramie.

It is easy and safe to criticize a campaign (and particularly an Indian campaign) when the critic is located a thousand miles from the battlefield!

The Indian Fight at Platte Bridge Station[48]

Old Platte Bridge was located on the south side of the North Platte River, about one hundred and thirty miles west of Fort Laramie. The station was a stockade, inside of which were accommodations for a garrison of about one hundred men. About fifteen rods northwest from the station was a bridge about one hundred feet long. Nearly half a mile west of the bridge, on the north side of the river, a deep gulch came down from the north to the river. After crossing the bridge the road took a northwesterly course over the bottom land up to the bluff, along the edge of which it ran for a mile or two in plain sight of the river and station. The telegraph line ran along on the side of the road. The country north of the road was covered with sand hills and deep ravines.

At the time of the attack (July 26, 1865) the place was garrisoned by Company I of the Eleventh Kansas Cavalry, two of the Eleventh Ohio and about twelve of the U.S. Infantry (rebel prisoners who enlisted in the United States service to fight Indians in preference to staying in the military prisons). The headquarters of the Eleventh Kansas regiment were also at the station, making about one hundred and ten men, all under the command of Major M. Anderson of the Eleventh Kansas. Of these, about seventy or eighty had guns, the rest being armed with revolvers. Company I was

---

[48] From Diary of Lieutenant William Y. Drew, Company I, Eleventh Kansas Cavalry. Courtesy of William E. Connelley.

armed with Smith breech-loading carbines. The Eleventh Ohio boys had Spencer repeating carbines, and the U.S. Infantry ("galvanized troops," the boys called them) used the Springfield musket.

Just after dinner on the 25th of July, 1865, someone called out, "Indians!" and all hands, seizing their arms, ran out to see where they were, their number, etc. On the north side of the river about fifteen or twenty Indians on horseback were moving leisurely along. In a few minutes about a dozen men were mounted, and crossing the bridge they commenced skirmishing with the enemy. As fast as our men moved on, the Indians fell back, until our men had gone about three miles from the bridge. All this time the Indians were increasing in numbers, until there were about forty in plain sight. Our boys had been using their carbines with good effect, and had shot several Indians off their ponies without any particular loss or damage on our side. At this time an order was received from the station for the men to come back, as the Indians were showing themselves on the south side of the river, east of the station. As our men fell back toward the bridge, Indians kept coming out of the ravine, until there were about fifty in sight, showing that their maneuvering had been for the purpose of leading our men as far away from all support as possible, and to then wipe them out by superior numbers. Our men reached the station without any loss. On the south side of the river the boys were having about the same experience as their comrades on the north side; the Indians falling back as they were charged, and gradually increasing in numbers. In one of the charges the boys shot a Cheyenne chief through the bowels. He threw his arm over the neck of his pony, which wheeled to the left and went into a thicket of brush, where the chief fell off.

At this time, the Indians charged desperately on our men to drive them back. But at this juncture a reinforcement of about a dozen men came up from the station and the Indians were repulsed. The intention had been to hold our men back long enough to give them an opportunity to carry off their fallen chief. Two of the boys rode into the thicket and found the chief lying apparently dead. One man jumped off his horse and stabbed the Indian about the heart. He did not give the least sign of life. Then the trooper commenced to scalp him. As soon as the knife touched his head, the Indian began to beg, when another man shot him through the brain. The Indian's belief is that if a warrior loses his scalp, he cannot go to the happy hunting ground. Indians will lose their lives without the least sign of fear, but want to save their scalps. The boys took the chief's arms and a buckskin jacket he had on. The jacket was trimmed with about thirty-five different kinds of hair—white men's, woman's, and children's, Indians' and squaw's, which he had taken at different times in his battles and forays.

A word right here in regard to the action of the men in stabbing and shooting the wounded Indian. About ten days before this, the Indians had captured one of our men, and had tortured and mangled his body in a shocking manner. Our boys swore that if they ever got hold of an Indian they would cut him all to pieces, and they did as stated.

The fight on the 25th of July, 1865, at Platte Bridge, had resulted in the killing and wounding of several of the Indians, but with very little damage to our side. Several of our men had received slight wounds, but everyone reported for duty on their return to the stockade that evening, and all hands felt elated over the action. On making an inspection that evening of the arms and ammuntion, it was found that there was less than twenty rounds per man for the Smith carbines, and but very little more for the other arms. Owing to the oversight, or neglect, of someone whose business it was to attend to the ordnance supply, there had not been any cartridges for the Smith carbines sent out on the plains, save what the Eleventh Kansas Cavalry had on hand at the time of their departure from Fort Riley the preceding winter. Requisition had been made on the ordnance official at Fort Laramie, without success, and I presume he sent on our requisition to Fort Leavenworth, for a few days before we had been notified by telegraph that supplies had been received, and that we should send an escort to Laramie, with a requisition, and we would be provided for. At this time, Sergeant H. Todd and Corporal W. H. Smith, with some others, were on their way from Fort Laramie with commissary and ordnance supplies – but that did not help us out in the present crisis.

Some of the boys commenced running bullets and making cartridges; Private James E. Bush being one, I remember, who was very proficient in that line of work. During the night an alarm was given by the sound of horses crossing the bridge, but on being challenged, we were agreeably surprised to find that it was caused by five or six of Company G, Eleventh Ohio Cavalry, under command of Lieutenant Britney of the same company, from Sweetwater Station, about fifty miles west of Platte Bridge. They reported having left Sweetwater on the preceding morning in company with three wagons and twenty-five men of the Eleventh

Kansas, under command of Sergeant Amos J. Custard, Company H. The train, with its escort, had halted about eighteen or twenty miles from the bridge and purposed coming in as soon as possible the next day. They had seen no signs of Indians, either while with the train or since leaving it, and were surprised to find that they had not been attacked after we told them of the fighting during the afternoon.

The next morning, July 26th, as soon as we could distinguish objects, we scanned the surrounding country to see if we could find any of our previous day's opponents. We did not make out any on our side of the river, but on the north side there were some moving about, with others scattered on the hills. Altogether there seemed to be about ninety in sight—just about the number we had been fighting the day before. They looked as if they were out of a job and did not know just where to find one. We breakfasted, and then Major Anderson ordered Lieutenant Caspar Collins of the Eleventh Ohio Cavalry, to take command of a detail of twenty-five men and reinforce the train to prevent their being surprised by the savages. Lieutenant Collins had been at Fort Laramie and was on his way back to his command at Sweetwater, and had reached the Platte Bridge about three days before, with an escort of four or five men of Company K, Eleventh Kansas Cavalry, from Deer Creek, the next station east of us about thirty miles. Lieutenant Collins was a son of ex-Governor Collins of Ohio, and had been out on the plains with his regiment for two or three years. He was a brave young fellow, and was considered to be pretty well posted in Indian tactics.

The detail moved out in fine spirits, crossed the bridge and then rode leisurely along the bottom-land up on to the bluff. Quite a number of the boys had gone on foot over the bridge at the same time with the detail, and others were straggling along over. Among others, Lieutenant Britney of the Eleventh Ohio, with about a dozen men, had gone straight north up on to the bluff, and were waiting to see what action the Indians would take with the detail. Strict orders had been given by Major Anderson that no shot was to be fired by our men without it was actually necessary, on account of the shortage of ammunition.

On reaching the top of the bluff, two Indians were seen by the detail at the top of the telegraph poles a little over a quarter of a mile away, cutting the wires. As soon as they saw our men, they slid down the poles, mounted their ponies and started for the back country as fast as the animals could carry them. Their mounts appeared to be very lame, and they did not appear to make much headway. It looked like a soft snap to "take them in," and Lieutenant Collins ordered the boys to go for them before the Indians could reach their friends. This charge, of course, took them off the road and away from the sight of the river. The instant the last man disappeared from view, from behind the screen of willows west of the bridge, about four hundred Cheyennes, on horseback, appeared, and with loud yells charged over the bottom-land and up on to the bluff in the direction in which our men had gone. The instant they reached the top of the bluff, from behind every sandhill and out of every hollow, Indians appeared, and all with the one object of charging on our detail and annihilating them before they could get back to the bridge and friends again. As soon as the detail realized the situation, they retraced their steps with all possible speed. It was not more than a couple of minutes before the Indians were all around them as thick as bees. In fact, so many of them were on all sides, that they did not dare to use their firearms and bows and arrows for fear of shooting their own men, but used their lances, tomahawks, and spears, and even tried to pull the boys off their horses by main force. The boys kept together in two ranks, discharging their carbines with deadly effect into the crowd on their right and left; then not having time to reload, took their revolvers and kept up the shooting. A boy of about seventeen belonging to Company I of the Eleventh Kansas, had what we call a "muley" or "pepper-box" revolver, the hammer being on the under side of the weapon, and by pulling the trigger the hammer would raise the piece, revolve to the next charge, and then the hammer would fall on the cap and fire it. A big Indian struck the boy over the head with his spear, trying to stun him, but the horses were moving so rapidly that it did not injure the boy very much. The youngster pointed his pepper-box at the Indian; the Indian, with a sardonic grin on his swarthy face, exclaimed, "Ugh! no good!" and tried to grab the boy by the arm and pull him off his horse. Just at that instant the revolver went off and shot the Indian through the breast. His grin changed to a look of painful astonishment, as he fell forward on his pony's neck and wheeled out of the fight.

It did not take long for the detail to reach the edge of the bluff, and as soon as they got there the Indians on the right and left wheeled out of the way, and from the rear they poured out such a volley from their guns and revolvers that for a little while it reminded me of Wilson Creek or Prairie Grove battlefields. But our men were going very rapidly down hill and the Indians, in their alarm, fired so high that they hurt our men but very little, but did considerable harm to a lot of Sioux who were charging up to take the bridge. Lieutenant Collins and four men were killed in this fight, and nearly all of the balance were more or less wounded, though none mortally. The escape of any of them was little short of miraculous.

As soon as the Cheyennes came out of their ambush, all the men upon or near the bridge had run as fast as they could to help their comrades, whom they knew would soon be striving to get back to the station. They had gotten about half way over the bottom-land, when the detail came rushing down the hill, and the Indians, seeing the footmen coming, were deterred from further pursuit. Lieutenant Britney and the party with him, as soon as they saw the Cheyennes charge, turned from the bluff and ran to the bridge as fast as they could, and they were just in time. From the deep gulch east of the bridge, about five hundred Sioux had been lying in ambush, and as soon as the Cheyennes reached the top of the bluff, they came charging out to take the bridge, but seeing Britney and the men with him, and some reinforcements that came over the bridge, pouring in the shot so lively from carbine and revolver, and the other Indians firing so high when shooting at our men who were coming over the bluff, and having the Sioux in exact range, a good many of the latter were hit, and it got so hot for them that they could not stand the pressure, but turned tail and fell back into the gulch again about as fast as they had come out. If they had succeeded in their object of taking the bridge, they would have probably killed all of the balance of Collins' party and about fifteen or twenty others on the bottom-land going to their relief and would then, very likely have captured the station also. As soon as the Sioux were driven back from the bridge, the wounded men were sent to the station to have their wounds dressed and such other care as they required. The Indians were moving about on the bluff where the fighting was going on with Collins' party, threatening our men who had fallen, if there was any life left in any of them; and if dead, in scalping and otherwise mangling their bodies in every conceivable manner. One of our men had fallen on the edge of the bluff, just as the boys were coming down the hill, fully a thousand yards from the bridge. An Indian rode up to his body and commenced shooting arrows into it. After firing four or five arrows the Indian dismounted, took his tomahawk and commenced to hack him with it. The boys at the bridge were very much excited about this, and some of them wanted to rush up and save the body from further mutilation, but under the circumstances it probably would have resulted in the killing and wounding of several more of our men, without doing any good, they were forbidden to undertake it. One of the boys put his gun to his shoulder and fired at the Indian, but the shot did not seem to disturb his equanimity in the least. Then Hank Lard remarked: "I believe I will take a whack at him." Elevating his sight to a thousand yards, he took deliberate aim and fired. The Indian had his hatchet raised at the time, and was just about to strike it into the head of the dead soldier; but the bullet was too quick for him. It struck him in some vital part, for the hatchet dropped from his hand and he fell over on the ground. Pretty soon he managed to stagger to his feet, and succeeded in getting on his pony and started away, but he was badly hurt and swayed from side to side on his pony. He was just about to fall off, when two of the Indians noticing his condition, rode up, one on each side, and supported him off the field.

Very shortly after this we heard much loud talking among the Indians, who were gathered together in a large body on the bluffs about three-quarters of a mile from us. They seemed very much excited, and we expected they were making arrangements for another charge on the bridge, and we prepared ourselves for the onset, feeling very anxious as to what the result would be, but determined, that should we be overwhelmed to sell our lives as dearly as possible. At this time, a half-breed Snake Indian, who lived in a teepee between the station and the bridge, and who had crawled up on the bluff to find out, if possible, what the trouble was, the number of Indians there, etc., returned and reported that the Sioux and Cheyennes were having a big quarrel among themselves. The Cheyennes had charged the Sioux with being great cowards for not taking the bridge when they attempted it, thus failing to carry out the part of the program assigned to them. The Sioux retaliated by charging the Cheyennes with shooting a good many of their warriors when they fired down the hill at Lieutenant Collins' retreating party. The half-breed stated that it might have the effect of breaking up the whole party, as each tribe declared they would not coalesce with the other in the future, and were, moreover, just about ready to turn their weapons against each other. The half-breed's report relieved our anxiety, and we would have been very glad to have seen them commence hostilities against each other. It would have been a clear case of "dog eat dog," and we would have agreed to act in an impartial manner and not aid either side if they had consulted us in regard to it.

For about an hour there were no new developments, except that the Indians, by one means or another, tried to decoy some of us away from the bridge. One Indian on horseback moved along a little beyond the edge of the bluff, leading the gray horse which Lieutenant Collins had ridden. The gray acted very unwilling to be led, and pulled back. Two of the Indians rode up to him and commenced whipping him, but the animal only curvetted about and did not get ahead very fast. Some of the boys took a few shots at the Indian, but the instant the flash from a gun was seen, the Indian would lean over on the opposite side of his pony, and all one could see would be his hand grasping the animal's mane, and his foot over its back. The instant the shot had passed, the Indian would straighten up again. The shots struck a pony or two, but we had no ammunition to spare for that sort of business, and orders were given to cease firing, save in case of an attack.

As soon as the Indians saw they could not draw us out in that manner, they commenced to call us all the vile names they could think of, using language they had picked up among the whites previous to the breaking out of the war, or had learned from the renegrade whites among them. Just at this time, one of the boys sang out: "There comes the train!" And sure enough, there it was in sight, coming over the hills about four miles from the station. The Indians had perceived it about the same time, and in a minute every one of them was on his pony and urging his animal at its fastest pace in that direction. There was a small howitzer at the station, and a few rounds of ammunition for it. A fuse was cut for about three seconds' time and the piece aimed at the largest body of Indians and discharged; but the shell had not left the howitzer more than one second before it exploded in the air, doing no damage to anyone. Another shell was inserted with a longer fuse, but it exploded about the same time as the other. All the good that was accomplished was in warning the train that there was trouble ahead and giving them time to prepare for it.

We noticed that the train moved a great deal faster toward us for a few minutes, but the advance of the Indians soon appeared. Sergeant Custard, in command of the train, had sent five of his escort about a quarter of a mile ahead of the others as an advance guard. Quite a body of Indians came suddenly up a ravine between this advance guard and the train. The corporal in charge of the advance at first attempted to get back to the train, but seeing the large force he had to contend with, and many others augmenting it every second, he ordered his men to turn to the right and gallop as fast as possible to the river, about a quarter of a mile south of them. Some of the Indians pursued, but the boys fought them back to the best of their ability. Just as they reached the river, one of the soldiers fell, shot through the heart. The rest plunged into the stream. When about four rods from the opposite shore, another man was shot and fell from his horse into the river. The others reached the shore in safety and headed toward the station. Quite a number of Indians had been concealed on the south side of the river, probably in ambush, waiting for some party to go out on that side and reconnoiter, or else hoping to seize a favorable moment to rush in and surprise the station, but as soon as the train appeared, they came out of their hiding places and made for the train, most of them crossing the river below the station, but about fifteen or twenty of them going south of the station towards the train.

When the three men escaping across the river were about half-way to the station, they struck the advance of the Indians on the south side. There were only four or five of the redskins, and the boys shot two before the others appeared in sight. They then turned their horses toward the mountains to the southeast, riding as rapidly as possible until they came to a deep ravine with some brush along the banks. Here they abandoned their horses and wound their way among the brush down into the ravine. After working down this ravine about a quarter of a mile or more, they stopped to reconnoiter a bit. The corporal crawled up to the edge of the ravine and raised his head for a peep of the surrounding country. Just the minute his head was exposed a bullet plowed along the top of it, just close enough to stun him for a second or two. He dropped, and the other boys pulled him back and bathed his head. This brought him to. Then they concluded to move down a little further and make another investigation. The next time they looked they could not see any Indians on that side of the river, except two or three who were stationed on points of ground about three-quarters of a mile distant, evidently as lookouts. The boys then discovered another ravine about half mile away that ran down to the river, and within about half a mile of the station. They concluded to make a run for this ravine. They started, and it did not take them long to get to it. No more Indians had appeared in sight and they began to feel safe. While they were running to the last ravine, some of us at the station had noticed them, and the instant we realized what it meant, about fifteen or twenty of us started on foot to meet them and to help, if necessary. About the same time fifteen or twenty Indians came out of the ravine into which the boys had first gone, and came charging out toward the ravine into which they had just disappeared. We all ran as fast as we could, shouting to the boys to work down the ravine and toward us as fast as possible. Soon we saw them emerge from the ravine into the open and make for us at top speed. They had advanced about half-way to us when the Indians reached the open, but we were now close enough for our rifle balls to reach the Indians, and after they had fired a few shots at us they fell back toward the train. The three men proved to be a corporal and two privates from Company H, Eleventh Kansas Cavalry. These were the only men who escaped from that wagon train, and it was a very close call for them. All that saved them was the desire of the Indians to be in at the plundering of the train, and the good sense they showed in abandoning their horses when they did. You may be sure they received a hearty welcome from all at the station.

At the time the party from the station sallied forth to the relief of these three men, about a dozen others, mounted, started from the station, crossed the bridge and went up to the bluff where the fight with Collins' party had taken place, to bring in the bodies of the slain soldiers. They found them mangled in a shocking manner, the noble red men taking a fiendish delight in mutilating the dead bodies of their fallen foes in a way too horrible to be described. Near one of the bodies a piece of paper was lying, which one of the men picked up. From its appearance it was torn out of a pocket diary or account book. It was written about as follows:

> I was taken prisoner about seven months ago at LaBonte station. You must be careful or you will all be killed. There are between three and four thousand Indians here, and about another thousand expected here in a day or two. They belong to the Cheyennes, Sioux, and Arapahoe, with a few Comanches and Blackfeet. You killed one of their principal chiefs belonging to the Cheyennes yesterday, and they swear they will have a terrible revenge on you for it. The intentions are to clean out all the stations on this road and then go onto the Fort Collins road and clean that out. I shall escape from them if I can.

I do not remember the name signed to it, but it was evidently some person with the Indians who was feeling friendly toward us. Some of the Eleventh Ohio men thought it was a man who had belonged to one of their companies and who was supposed to have deserted at the time he mentioned at LaBonte Station. A good many of the Eleventh Ohio Cavalry had been recruited from the rebel soldiers who had gone into Ohio on the celebrated Morgan raid, and after their capture preferred enlistment in the United States army to fight Indians in preference to remaining in military prisons in the north until the war should end, or until they could be exchanged. Most of them made good, faithful soldiers, but some of them were exceptionally hard cases, deserting and joining the Indians, and helping them in their warfare against the whites; and what the Indians didn't know of devilment, these renegades taught them.

From the roof of the station, and with the aid of a large spyglass, we had a pretty good view of what was going on at the train. It had stopped on a side hill, and with the three wagons the men had formed three sides of a square, with one front facing up the hill to the north, one east, one south, but the west side open. The first Indians who came to the scene of action charged right onto the train, but they were repulsed. As others arrived they again made a charge, but were again driven back. After this, for a long time there did not seem to be much action going on. Every once in a while we could see a cloud of smoke from the wagons, or from the side hill below the wagons, which showed that the fight was still in progress, but we could not tell with what result, though we noticed that the puffs of smoke from the hillside on the south were gradually getting closer and closer, and we felt that the end could not be far off. Never in all our service as soldiers had we experienced anything like this before. To know that about twenty of our comrades, with whom for nearly three years we had been soldiering in the south, were now within two and one-half miles of us, surrounded by an overwhelming number of savage enemies determined on their destruction, and we not able to do anything for their relief, was heart-rending. Some of us went to Major Anderson and requested that forty or fifty of us be allowed to volunteer and go out on foot to attempt a rescue, but the major, while feeling deeply for the brave fellows who were making such a heroic fight against such terrible odds, realized that an attempt at relief by any who started from the bridge force would doubtless means the destruction of the entire party, in which event it would have been an easy matter for the Indians to have taken the station and massacred all who were left. At that time we thought the major too cautious, but since then, knowing what the Indians did to the Fetterman party the next year near Fort Phil Kearney, and later to the gallant Custer and his brave men at Little Big Horn, we are satisfied that the major's decision was a wise one, and that by it alone are any of us left alive today.

About three o'clock in the afternoon the major ordered a party of twenty mounted men, under Lieutenant Walker, to proceed about two miles east of the station and repair the telegraph wire that was cut at that point, so that we could wire to Deer Creek and other stations below, and have them send reinforcements and ammunition enought to enable us to cope with the Indians. At the same time Walker's party left, the ten or twelve "galvanized soldiers," under command of their officer, were to go out about a half-mile from the station and support the cavalry under Walker on their return to the station, if the Indians should develop any force that would interfere with the repairs on the telegraph wires. A set of signals had been arranged by which Lieutenant Walker was to be notified if the Indians from the west were moving back from the train and interfering with carrying out his orders. The flag at the station was to be waved if the Indians were moving toward him, and should it develop that sufficient Indians were coming to frustrate his plans, the howitzer was to be fired, and at that, Lieutenant Walker was to bring his command back to the support of the others, and all would fall back to the station.

Walker arrived at the break in the telegraph wire, and then sent four men, Sergeant McDougal and Privates Porter, Hilty and Chappel, all of Company I, Eleventh Kansas Cavalry, about a quarter of a mile to the east to watch for Indians. The others went to work joining the wire, which was broken in several places.

Very soon after Walker's command left the station it was noticed that a large number of Indians, who were

on their ponies between the station and the train, had
commenced moving north, and it was but a short time
before they were crossing a divide about a mile northeast of the station. We then knew they had observed
the party leaving the station and were on their way to
intercept them. The signal was thereupon given with
the flag as soon as it was positive that enough of the
the savages had passed to be certain it would not do to
delay longer. The howitzer was also fired as a signal
for the party to come in. As soon as the report was
heard, the men dropped the wires, mounted their
horses, and then Walker, without waiting for the four
men whom he had thrown out in advance, ordered the
others in as fast as possible. The captain of the "galvanized troops" did not wait until the cavalry came up,
but ordered his men back instanter. Some of the Company I boys had gone out on foot nearly to the point
where the "galvanized troops" had been stationed. As
soon as they heard the howitzer, they ran to where the
relief had been stationed, and as soon as they passed
the returning "galvanized troops" they cursed their
captain for being a coward for leaving his post before
the cavalry had overtaken him. The captain, however, paid no attention to their jeers, but pushed on to
the station, although some of his men turned back to
help the others. The cavalry advanced until they
overtook the boys on foot, and then most of them turned
to assist the four men on outpost from Walker's command, although Lieutenant Walker's horse got under
such headway that it did not stop until it had carried
him safely into the station, without his having fired a
shot. About fifteen Indians had appeared out of a
ravine and charged for the four men from the north
side of the river. The men discharged their carbines,

and then commenced to unload their revolvers. They were not noticing anything on the south. Several Indians came out of a ravine on the south close by, and before they were even observed, one of them had driven a spear into Porter's heart and he fell dead from his horse. Another Indian gave Hilty a stab with a spear which penetrated his lung. The savage withdrew his weapon as Hilty fell forward on his horse's neck. This Indian attempted to strike McDougal as he went by, but he was so close to the sergeant that there was not room to use his weapon effectively. McDougal turned his head, and seeing that it was an Indian who was attempting to bore him with a spear, pressed his revolver against the Indian's body and pulled the trigger. The Indian fell from his horse, shot through the heart. It was the last cartridge McDougal had in his revolver, but it saved his life. By this time the boys on foot began to reach the Indians with their carbines, and as the Indians who had gotten into this skirmish were comparatively few in numbers, they did not press any closer. Hilty clung to his horse until it carried him into the station, where he was cared for. I will state here that he eventually recovered.

About the time Lieutenant Walker's party had started from the station, we observed that the firing had ceased at the train. Soon after, a large smoke arose, and we saw that the wagons were burning fiercely. We then knew that the fighting there was all over, and that the brave men who had so well defended themselves were all dead. They had made a gallant fight for four hours, but had been overpowered at last. The Indians hung about the place, watching the wagons burn, until nearly nightfall, and then a great many of them moved back to the bluffs north of the river. We expected that during the night they would make some demonstration against the station, and the guards were doubled and extra vigilance enjoined on them, so that we would not be taken unawares. Just after midnight a few of the savages came prowling about, but the guards were on the alert and fired at them. They responded with a few arrows, but made no further demonstration. About ten o'clock that night, Major Anderson arranged with the half-breed Snake Indian to go to Deer Creek and report the situation to the commanding officer there, and have him telegraph down the road, and also to carry orders for the garrison at Deer Creek to march to our assistance and bring us a supply of ammunition.

During the fight of the day before, we had captured a number of Indian ponies whose riders had been shot off their mounts, and which had followed along with Collins' party into our lines. The half-breed selected one of these which he said had belonged to an Indian chief, and had been noted for speed and endurance. He started out a little after ten o'clock, going directly south toward the mountains, and after striking them he took a trail which he knew and worked to the east until he reached the Deer Creek station in safety. Here about fifty men of Company K, Eleventh Kansas Volunteers, with about five thousand rounds of ammunition, were dispatched for Platte Bridge.

The next morning everything appeared about as it had been the previous night. The Indians were in sight on the bluff, but we noticed parties of them going off in a northwesterly direction all the morning. About noon the last of them disappeared. Toward three o'clock in the afternoon we noticed a body of men coming from the direction of the Deer Creek station. They proved to be Company K with the ammunition. We gave them a hearty reception, and as soon as they had rested a few minutes they, in company with a detachment of Company I, started on the trail of the Indians. It was soon ascertained that the savages were in full retreat, and then the command was ordered to the spot where the wagon train had made such a gallant fight.

On arriving there a horrible sight met our gaze. Twenty-one of our dead soldiers were lying on the ground, stripped naked and mangled in every conceivable way. I noticed one poor fellow with a wagon tire across his bowels, and from appearances, it had been heated redhot and then laid upon him while still alive, so that the red devils might gloat over the torture they were inflicting before the breath of life had entirely left his body. From the appearance of the other bodies I believe he was the only one tortured, and therefore I believe he was the only one left alive at the time they captured the train. Every one of them were scalped, but the Indians had left the scalps lying around on the ground, which was a sure sign that their loss had been so heavy they did not think they had cause to exult over their victory. We counted about forty lodge-pole trails on which they had fixed stretchers to carry off their wounded. We heard, some time after, that their loss was over sixty killed and about one hundred and thirty badly wounded. The loss on our side was Lieutenant Collins and twenty-seven men killed, eleven or twelve wounded and one missing. We presumed the missing man was killed but we could not find his body. It may have been possible that the Indians captured him and carried him away to torture at one of their villages.

The command returned to the station, and next morning we went out and buried our fellow heroes in the ground upon which they had so nobly, yet unavailingly, fought. The most of those who had been killed with the train had belonged to Company H of the Eleventh Kansas, and it was always considered the best company in the regiment when there was any real fighting to be done, and yet, up to this time, the company had escaped with fewer fatalities than any other company in the regiment. It seemed so much harder to bear to think that after three years fighting against the rebels they were ordered out on the plains to fight Indians, and now, when the orders were out for their return home, where they were to be mustered out, they were so ruthlessly slaughtered. We have the consolation of knowing that they died with their faces to the foe, and that in death, as in their three years' service, they sustained the proud reputation gained by this regiment of always doing its duty, no matter what odds were pitted against them.

About two days later the Sixth Michigan Cavalry came to relieve us at the bridge, and we marched for home without further molestation.

The Bozeman Trail

Not only was gold discovered in California during the days before the event of the railroads into the West, but other localities yielded enormous fortunes of the precious metal. Colorado, during the summer of 1859, had one hundred and fifty thousand gold seekers within its present boundaries. True, this was largely a restless, floating population, one-third of which in time returned to the states, disgusted with the West and the mining districts within sight of Pike's Peak. Nevada, Idaho, and Montana proved rich fields for those who had become discontented with other districts, and the trails to new mining camps were now filled with an eager throng seeking new localities wherever there was a rumor of a great "strike." There is no doubt that in time the fields the prospector had left, proved to be quite as rich in returns as the new locality, but the desire to acquire in a night a vast fortune was too much of a temptation to be overlooked. Although Wyoming did not experience the intense and prolonged gold excitement as was felt in the territory outside of her boundaries, South Pass City, a few miles north of the famous South Pass, contributed materially to the sum total of gold mined in the sixties. Gold in paying quantities was first discovered in this camp as early as 1842 by a member of the American Fur Company, though no developing was done until 1857 when forty men prospected the entire length of the Sweetwater. Gold was found everywhere in the stream and its numerous trib-

utaries. In the fall of 1861, when gold was being
found in abundance in Colorado, Idaho, and Montana,
three-score of men located claims along Willow Creek
on which stream South Pass City was located. By 1863
mining was carried on in Carissa Gulch and from that
time to the present day there has intermittently been
gold developments in this gulch. James Stuart, when
at Fort Bridger in August, 1863, found many teams
there congregated to go to Bannack camp, having deserted the gold-fields of Pike's Peak.[49] Among the
number of those disgruntled were many who tried their
luck at South Pass City, as did hundreds of other miners
from Montana, Colorado, Utah, Idaho, Nevada, and
California. By 1868, this little hustling mining camp
boasted of more than four thousand people, which number was greatly increased in the following year. All of
the roads in 1869, leading to South Pass City, were full
of eager jostling prospectors. But the camp soon experienced a decline after the rich "pickings" had been
mined. Today South Pass City camp is a picturesque
ghost city containing less than a score of people and a
few relics in the way of log cabins, of what was for a
number of years the most prosperous mining camp in
Wyoming.[50]

[49] Montana Historical Society *Collections*, Vol. i, p. 222: "Nearly all
of the mountaineers are going to Beaver Head or Deer Lodge. There are
plenty of Pike's Peak emigrants passing all of the time. They don't like the
Peak and are hunting a better country."

[50] South Pass City won world wide notoriety in 1869 when William H.
Bright, a citizen of the camp, became a member of Wyoming's first territorial
legislature, introducing and successfully championing his bill for suffrage for
women. The enactment of the suffrage measure on December 10th, which
was approved by Wyoming's first Governor, John A. Campbell, gave the
few women then living in the recently created territory the distinction of
being the first women in the world to have full and unrestricted franchise.
Again, in 1870, this frontier town became known internationally by having
the first woman Justice of the Peace, Mrs. Esther Hobart Morris, being ap-

SOUTH PASS CITY, WYOMING, IN THE SIXTIES

Situated about twelve miles northeast of Pacific Springs the first stopping place of the emigrants on the Oregon Trail where the waters flowed toward the Pacific Ocean. South Pass City formed with Atlantic City and Miners Delight (also called Hamilton) a nest of gold mining camps yielding during the sixties millions of dollars in gold.

The discovery of gold in southwestern Montana during the last days of 1862 gave rise to the city of Bannack (at that time in Idaho) the camp by January, 1863, having a population of from two thousand to three thousand people. Bannack, for a short time, was the capital of the territory after it was organized in 1864, being moved to Virginia City when the scramble for gold was discovered in the new mining camp in Beaverhead Valley. Virginia City was first named "Varina" in honor of Mrs. Jefferson Davis, but the people of the camps soon changed the name to one that did not so constantly remind them of the South and the civil strife then being carried on in the States. With the discovery of this new camp, the population of Bannack pretty generally moved en masse to Virginia City, which, by 1864, had a population of ten thousand typical mining people. Virginia City remained the capital until 1866, when it was moved to Helena, another camp of unusual promise. Telegraph lines in 1866 were running to both of these camps by the way of Salt Lake, John Creighton operating this line as a branch of his main line along the Oregon Trail. The amount of letters sent from one of these western mining camps was evidence of the number of people in the camps. From Virginia City in one day in 1863, six thousand letters were dispatched to the east by the way of Salt Lake, being an accumulation of ten days when the stage was not in operation.

Helena, first called "Last Chance Gulch," became a roaring camp in 1864, and soon grew to be a shipping point for mining supplies, as it was on a direct road from Fort Benton to Virginia City and Bannack being

pointed to the judicial position by Acting Governor Edward M. Lee, February 14, 1870.

one hundred and forty miles from the Fort and one hundred and twenty-five from Virginia City. The road between Helena and Fort Benton was on the west side of the Missouri and easy to travel, though there was a trail through the mountains on the east side of the river. The class of people who came to Montana were respectable and law abiding, the usual rough and tumble population incident to the finding of gold was not conspicuous. As early as 1868 Helena established a public library to meet the demands of the reading public. Alder Gulch, also rich in precious metal, yielded from 1863 to 1869 ten million dollars worth of gold and contained in 1864 fourteen thousand people. Summit, Virginia City, and Nevada mined thirty million dollars in the first three years of their existence. But these camps, as Junction, Montana City, and Central City which had come into existence in a day, soon worked themselves out, the population drifting to the larger camps; the population of Bannack in 1870 was three hundred and eighty-one; Virginia City, eight hundred and sixty-seven; Helena, three thousand one hundred and six; Gallatin, one hundred and fifty-two; Nevada City, one hundred; Bozeman, five hundred and seventy-four.

The Idaho and Montana mines were easily reached from Fort Hall by the way of the Oregon and California Trails, which connected with a newly established road running northeastward from the old fort. In 1862 gold was discovered in Boise Basin (Idaho) the richness of this camp creating a stampede from other camps. By the spring of that year the trails and roads leading to Boise Basin were crowded with eager miners coming from the camps of California and Nevada; the agriculturalists from Oregon and Washington and all sorts and conditions of emigrants from the country east of the Rocky Mountains. In the year following the finding of the gold, at least thirty thousand people, in their frenzied desire for the yellow metal, arrived at the diggings in Idaho. The gold excitement in Montana and Idaho were concurrent making the living conditions in that northwestern part of our country one of intense activity, great richness and lawlessness.

Supplies poured into these camps from Walla Walla during the month of November, 1863, twenty thousand dollars worth of dry goods being shipped over the trails into camp, while Utah rushed over the Salt Lake and Virginia City road a pack train loaded with provisions. Gallatin Valley (Montana) was a favored spot for homeseekers with an agricultural inclination, from where were grown quantities of grain and vegetables which were used to feed those who toiled, not in the soil, but in the sands. The Gallatin Valley was an extensive meadow in which, in 1867, were grown wonderful crops of wheat, oats, barley, buckwheat, and vegetables, crops more than sufficient to supply the growers who sent provisions to places in Montana where crops were not grown.

The changing, feverish population in the camps was first composed of earnest and respectable people who had come to work for their gainings; following these came those who did not toil nor spin, but who lived illicitly off of the earnings of others; the gamblers, the road agent, the murderer. The time soon came when decency asserted itself, and another class arose which believed that some semblance of law and order should be established, and having the courage of their convictions, organized themselves into Vigilance Committees. The people who had moved from regions where there was an established government did not long tolerate the law of the gun and organizations of desperadoes and road agents. Public opinion gradually began to crystallize for law and order. These vicious bands were perfectly organized, raiding into all camps and operating along the roads between the camps. In Montana the insignia of this red handed band was a peculiar knot tied in their neckties, so that outlaws' identity might be easily established. Often hundreds of thousands of dollars were taken at one haul from the miners and merchants by these "desperate, crackshot bands of robbers and cut-throats." In order to protect life and property the Vigilantes were forced to organize, arrest members of the outlaw band and act as judge, jury, and executioner. The hanging of a few of these robbers would always check, at least temporarily, the lawlessness of the outlaw bands.

The people of Montana did not resort to a vigilance code until forced to take drastic measures in order to disorganize and drive from the country the band of rapidly increasing desperadoes, which had created a reign of terror that was spreading over the camps. It was hardship enough to wash the sands of the stream, working under the hostile eyes of Indians, but to have the fruits of toil taken by bandits could not long be tolerated. No one individual dared to punish the guilty who openly and publicly boasted of their crimes. True, high handedness continued until regularly established courts were created and laws made by the legislature, but a wholesome fear of the Vigilantes made living conditions more peaceful and bearable.

Into Montana had come many deserters from the South and many who were not in sympathy with the cause for which the Civil War was being fought. Some measures were taken to test their loyalty to the Union, the first being made when the emigrants and miners arrived at Fort Bridger, where each member of a party that was going over the Salt Lake-Virginia City Road had to take the "iron-clad" oath of allegiance to the United States. Anyone refusing to take the oath was not permitted to advance.

In order to facilitate transportation through the country situated between the Yellowstone and the Columbia, Congress, early in 1857, made an appropriation for a proposed wagon road which was to run from Fort Benton, the western end of navigation up the Missouri, to The Dalles, the head of navigation on the Columbia. It was believed that the mining camps would be helped in the district covered by the proposed roads if supplies coming from Missouri and California, as well as from Oregon to Montana, could be more easily and quickly transported over a constructed road than one that was not much more than a trail. The construction of this military wagon road from Fort Walla Walla to Fort Benton, was supervised by Lieutenant John Mullen, hence the name, who did his preliminary work in 1858, the hostilities of the Indians preventing the early completion of the road. The first work on the road was from Fort Benton to the Snake River; in 1860 the road was put into operation, though not entirely completed until 1862.[51] Thus was established a connecting line

[51] In 1859 the American Fur Company came up from Missouri in their steamboat Chippewa to a point in the vicinity of Fort Benton. Thus establishing a new route to the West and relieving the over crowded condition on the Oregon Trail. For twenty years Fort Benton was the center for transporting freight, amounting to millions of dollars annually, to the camps and other places, the returning steamers carrying ore to the East. In 1859 there was one steamboat with supplies at Fort Benton; 1862, 4; 1866, 31; 1867, 29; 1869, 24, the intervening years having corresponding numbers of arriving boats.

for transportation of supplies to forts, camps and homes from the Missouri to the Columbia, which might be called a rival transcontinental road of the Oregon Trail. As a matter of fact, the operation of the road relieved to a degree the congestion of freight on that central trail. Three reasons existed for the Mullen Road: it shortened the distance to be traveled by wagons, lessened the hardships of the emigrants and avoided the Indian raids along the Sweetwater and North Platte Route. "There was a large migration in 1862. Some stopped on the eastern flank of the Rocky range in what is now Montana. . . Four steamers from St. Louis ascended to Fort Benton, whence three hundred and fifty emigrants traveled by the Mullen Road to the mines of the Salmon River." [52]

For many miles the Mullen Road followed the old trail made by the Indians on their annual hunts from the Pacific on the way to the east of the mountains for buffalo. Some places in the old trail were twelve inches deep, made so by the centuries of travel back and forth to and from these annual hunts.

Bozeman City, just west of Bozeman Pass, was established in 1864. Fort Ellis was built in 1867 to guard the Pass, which was within sixteen miles of the ground of thousands of hostile Indians to the east. [53] Before the fort was used in April, 1867, the governor of Montana, when Fort C. F. Smith was infested by Indians, called for six hundred mounted volunteers for service for ninety days to go to the pass and hold back the red men. Many members of these militia or Mounted Volunteers, when started on an offensive campaign,

---

[52] Portland *Oregonian*, August 28, 1862.

[53] Completed in the fall of 1867, about three miles east of Bozeman City, when Captain La Motte with a command of three companies of United States troops appeared at the fort. Abandoned 1889-1890.

FORT ELLIS, MONTANA

On the Bozeman Trail, near the present city of Bozeman. The arrival of a military escort at the Fort. Reproduced from a contemporary drawing.

had a pan and other implements of the best quality for digging gold while clearing the road of Indians. These men were finally equipped for fighting by the government until the regular soldiers took their places. In 1867 a messenger brought word to the soldiers guarding the pass of the desperate condition of the garrison at Fort C. F. Smith. The alarming information started Bozeman and his companion over the trail to the besieged fort, on the way to which Bozeman was killed by Blackfoot Indians.

By 1865 Montana had a population of one hundred and twenty thousand, which had to be fed and furnished with supplies that were not produced within that territory. Gold seekers had come over the mountains from the Pacific into the gold-fields of Montana, a population producing nothing but gold; a population totally dependent on the outside for things to eat, clothing to wear and supplies for their mining outfits. Products could be brought by way of the South Pass and Fort Hall, but the continental divide had to be twice crossed before reaching Montana. By boat on the Missouri to the head of navigation at Fort Benton was another way of transportation, but this road, after leaving the river to the camps, was through three hundred miles of Indian territory, and about five hundred miles longer than a proposed road to go east of the Big Horn Mountains. The mines of Idaho and Montana were the point of greatest traffic, and, to make them more accessible, steps were taken in 1865 to establish a new road running north from the North Platte west of old Fort Laramie. This road, which has been called the Montana Road, the Jacobs-Bozeman Cut-off, the Bozeman Road, the Powder River Road to Montana, the Big Horn Road, the Virginia City Road, the Bonanza

Trail, the Yellowstone Road, the Reno Road, the Carrington Road, ultimately became known as the Bozeman Trail.

In the fall of 1860 and the spring of 1861, the Stuart brothers, James and Granville, found gold while prospecting in the Rocky Mountains of Montana. Writing to their brother Thomas, who was then mining in Colorado, they told glowing tales of the rich finds in that land to the northwest, urging him to come to the new gold-fields. Thomas showed this letter to other young men who were there with him digging for gold. A party of twelve young men was easily induced to leave Colorado in the spring of 1862, arriving in Montana in June of that year. Among these young men was the sturdy and adventurous John M. Bozeman, for whom the Bozeman Trail was named, as were also the city of that name and the Bozeman Pass, between the Gallatin and Yellowstone Rivers.

The desire for adventure and seeing the West brought Bozeman from his home in Coweta County, Georgia, where he had left his wife and two children. After settling in Montana, Bozeman became interested in finding and locating a possible cross country road to the States, a road that would materially shorten the distance that then had to be traveled by old trails, to reach the mining camps in Montana, particularly Bannack and Virginia City.

Bozeman and John M. Jacobs, in the winter of 1862-1863, left Bannack, then one of the most promising of young mining camps, for the Missouri River, with a determination to find this shorter route for the emigrants and freighters on their way to the Montana gold-fields. The customary longer routes then being used were the water route up the Missouri, the established trails, the Oregon and Overland, to Fort Hall, and the Fort Hall-Virginia City route.

Skirting along the south side of the Yellowstone in search of a possible road to the North Platte, the two young men found that they were being followed by the Sioux, who finally overtook Bozeman and his companion on the Powder River. The Indians stole their horses, ammunition and guns and set the men afoot, doubtless believing that no white man could long survive in the dangerous red man's country without gun, horse, or food.

Bozeman and his companion experienced all the hardships possible. Wandering for days, starving, shoeless and footsore, existing on a diet of grasshoppers, the exhausted but undaunted couple finally reached the Missouri. In the spring of 1863, at the Missouri, Bozeman took command of a wagon train of freighters and emigrants, with a determination to retrace his route on the east side of the Big Horn Mountains. When about one hundred miles into this unknown country northwest of Fort Laramie, the Indians contested the right of the white men to use this part of their hunting grounds for a wagon road, and drove the train back to the Sweetwater, from where the men sought the western slopes of the Big Horn Mountains, ultimately making safe passage into Montana. Bozeman did not accompany the train, but made another attempt to go over his road.

From the North Platte, Bozeman and nine of his men decided to defy fate by pushing up north into a country filled with hostile Indians, a roadless distance of seven hundred miles. Making the journey by night to escape the vigilant eyes of the red men, and enduring untold hardships, Bozeman finally reached the top of the Belt Mountains between the Gallatin and the Yellowstone. It was at this time that the pass was given the name of Bozeman by George W. Irvin, a member of Bozeman's train.

From the journal of Captain James Stuart for May 11, 1863,[54] is to be found an additional page of the life of Bozeman. "Looking across the river, about a mile above us, I saw three white men with six horses, three packed, three riding. They were coming down the river and I waited until they got opposite of us and then hailed them. They would neither answer nor stop, but kept the same course and at a little faster pace. I then sent Underwood and Stone across ahead of our pack train to overtake them and hear the news. . . We started to meet the strangers, not doubting but our men had overtaken them. . . We met our men returning without having seen anything of the travelers. . . We followed them for ten miles and then gave up the chase. It seems that as soon as they got out of our sight, they had started on a run, and kept in ravines and brush along the creek for about three miles till they got into the hills. . . We found that we could not overtake them. We found a fry pan and a pack of cards on their trail. None of us have the least idea who they are, where they come from or where they were going."

It was afterward learned that this party of three lone travelers consisted of John Bozeman and his partner, with his little eight year old daughter, being on their way from the Three Forks of the Missouri to Red Buttes on the North Platte. They were looking, it was ascertained, for a new wagon road which they found and which was afterward known as the "Jacobs and Boze-

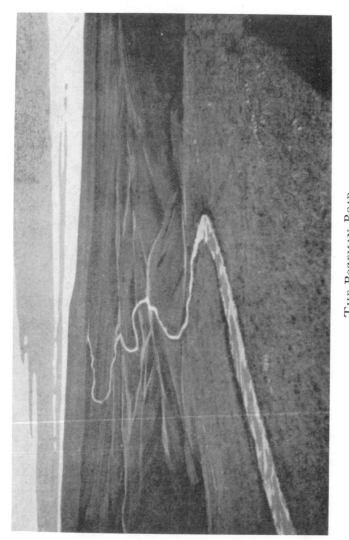

THE BOZEMAN ROAD

Showing the endless plains toward Back-bone Ridge, Wyoming.

man Cut-off," the name used at times for the Bozeman Trail. A few days previous to the adventure with Stuart and his men, Bozeman had had a brush with the Indians, and seeing Stuart's men made Bozeman believe that there was to be an encounter with another band of Indians, and he did his utmost to make a safe escape.

In 1864 Bozeman brought back with him a large train from the Missouri, his line of travel being between the Black Hills and the Big Horn Mountains, his cherished road. Jim Bridger also was taking a train through by a new way he had found possible on the west side of the Big Horn Mountains and down Clark's Fork. Bridger had declared that Bozeman's proposed road east of the mountains was an impracticable route. Over the rival road on the west side of the Big Horn Mountains, Bridger, with several weeks' start, finally reached the Yellowstone ahead of Bozeman.[55] But his road took him into the Gallatin Valley, up the Shields River and Brackett Creek, and down Bridger Creek, a very roundabout route. Bozeman's more direct route landed him in the Gallatin Valley ahead of Bridger. From this point the two trains raced from the West Gallatin into Virginia City, arriving but a few hours apart.[56]

[55] This road was at times along the course of the Big Horn River which was crossed in the vicinity of the present city of Basin, Wyoming. From here for many miles through northern Wyoming and southern Montana the old wagon route followed the present day route of the Burlington Railroad.

[56] In the Bridger-Bozeman race to reach Virginia City, the following statement is made by Olin D. Wheeler in *The Trail of Lewis and Clark,* Vol. ii, page 327: "Bozeman traversed what has since been known as the Bozeman Pass, into the Gallatin Valley, and Bridger entered the valley via Bridger Creek. The route and pass which Bozeman followed were those used by Capt. Wm. Clark in 1806 (pointed out as the right path by Sacajawea, the Shoshone Indian woman guide) and it became a well-known thoroughfare, following particularly the old Indian and buffalo road, and

Again in 1864, trailmaker Bozeman successfully conducted another emigrant train over his chosen route to the Yellowstone River into the Gallatin Valley. The ease of travel, the shortening of the miles, the abundance of water, timber, grass, and game, and the saving of time by using this road, at once made this the most desired trail to Montana, largely to the exclusion of the more-frequented lines of travel. For a time this way to the mines was known as "the Virginia City Road" and "the Bighorn Road," but the original title for the man who dared to defy the Indians, became the accepted appellation, hence, the Bozeman Trail. During the month of July, 1864, one emigrant train consisting of one hundred and fifty wagons, three hundred and sixty-nine men, thirty-six women, fifty-six children, six hundred and thirty-six oxen, one hundred and ninety-four cows, seventy-nine horses and a dozen mules, of a valuation of one hundred and thirty thousand dollars, reached the gold-fields over this forbidden path.[57] Invasion of even one caravan of this magnitude enraged the Indians to hostile activity, for the penetration of this, their land, meant the destruction of the wild game

it was in constant use until the construction of the Northern Pacific railroad supplanted it. The entrances to the valley used by these frontiersmen are within a few miles of each other, the one used by Bridger being to the north of the other. The names of both of these men are perpetuated by Bridger creek, Bridger mountains, Bridger pass and Bridger peak; and by Bozeman pass, Bozeman creek and the city of Bozeman, all in and about Gallatin valley. Bozeman pass, which should have been called Sacajawea pass, is supposed to be the one by which John Colter made his way across the mountains to Lisa's fort on the Big Horn river after he escaped from the Blackfeet at the time Potts was killed.

"In 1902 I drove across this pass from Bozeman. The trail and road are things of the past. The former can be seen here and there where deeply fissured by constant travel, later by running water after heavy rains; the latter is more plainly marked but its washed-out condition at many places and a decayed bridge or two show that time is rapidly obliterating it."

[57] *Journal of George Brundage.*

and the influx and control by the whites. If fight it must be, the country of the Powder River and its minor streams was an inviting battlefield.

In April, 1867, Bozeman and Tom Coover, on their way down the Yellowstone, en route to Fort C. F. Smith, made a camp where they encountered Indians, who stole many of their horses. The following day (April 18th) after this attack, while cooking the noon meal, five Indians entered the camp leading the stolen horses of the day before. Bozeman, believing the Indians to be friendly Crows, invited them to the meal, when without warning, two Indians shot Bozeman through the body. Coover escaped into the bushes. The Indians stole the horses and blankets, but did not scalp Bozeman. It was afterward learned that these Indians were the Blackfeet, fugitives from their own tribe on account of having killed one of their chiefs, and that at this time were living with the Crows.

Two days after the killing of Bozeman, his partner, Coover, wrote for the public the following account of the murder:[58]

GENERAL T. F. MEAGHER, VIRGINIA CITY.

Sir: – On the 16th inst., accompanied by the late J. M. Bozeman, I started for Forts C. F. Smith and Phil Kearney. After a day or so of arduous travel, we reached the Yellowstone River and journeyed on it in safety until the 20th inst., when in our noon camp on the Yellowstone, about seven miles this side of Bozeman Ferry, we perceived five Indians approaching us on foot and leading a pony. When within say two hundred and fifty yards I suggested to Mr. Bozeman that we should open fire, to which he made no reply. We stood with our rifles ready until the enemy approached to within one hundred yards, at which Bozeman remarked: "Those are Crows; I know one

---

[58] Taken from the Montana *Post*, May 4, 1867, printed at Virginia City, Montana Territory. Copy furnished by W. Y. Pemberton, librarian of the State Historical and Miscellaneous Library, Helena, Montana.

of them. We will let them come to us and learn where the Sioux and Blackfeet camps are, provided they know." The Indians meanwhile walked toward us with their hands up, calling, "Ap-sar-ake" (Crow). They shook hands with Mr. B. and proffered the same politeness to me, which I declined by presenting my Henry rifle at them, and at the same moment B. remarked, "I am fooled; they are Blackfeet. We may, however, get off without trouble." I then went to our horses (leaving my gun with B.) and had saddled mine, when I saw the chief quickly draw the cover from his fusee, and as I called to B. to shoot, the Indians fired, the ball taking effect in B's right breast, passing completely through him. B. charged on the Indians but did not fire, when another shot took effect in the left breast, and brought poor B. to the ground, a dead man. At that instant I received a bullet through the upper edge of my left shoulder. I ran to B. picked up my gun and spoke to him, asking if he was badly hurt. Poor fellow! his last words had been spoken some minutes before I reached the spot: he was 'stone dead.' Finding the Indians pressing me, and my gun not working, I stepped back slowly, trying to fix it, in which I succeeded after retreating say fifty yards. I then opened fire and the first shot brought one of the gentlemen to the sod. I then charged and the other two took to their heels, joining the two that had been saddling B's animal and our pack horse, immediately after B's fall. Having an idea that when collected they might make a rush, I returned to a piece of willow brush, say four hundred yards from the scene of action, giving the Indians a shot or two as I fell back. I remained in the willows about an hour, when I saw the enemy across the river, carrying their dead comrade with them. On returning to the camp to examine B, I found but too surely that the poor fellow was out of all earthly trouble. The red men, however, had been in too much of a hurry to scalp him or even take his watch — the latter I brought in. After cutting a pound or so of meat, I started on foot on the back track, swam the Yellowstone, walked thirty miles, and came upon McKenzie and Reshaw's camp, very well satisfied to be so far on the road home and in tolerable safe quarters. The next day I arrived home with a tolerable sore shoulder and pretty well fagged out. A party started out yesterday to bring in B's remains.

From what I can glean in the way of information I am satisfied that there is a large party of Blackfeet on the Yellowstone, whose sole object is plunder and scalps.

Yours etc.   (Signed) T. W. COOVER.

GALLATINE MILLS, BOZEMAN, April 22, 1867.

The Indian side of the killing of Bozeman is given in the following dictation (dictated by George Reed Davis, Crow interpreter, otherwise "Crow" Davis, of Laurel) :

In the year 1867 about the last of May or the first of June I was at Fort Laramie in the service of the government, and here the tribe of the Crows were at that time gathered for the purpose of signing a treaty with the government. At this time a war party of young bucks (Crows) set out from the vicinity of Fort C. F. Smith for the purpose of stealing horses from the settlers in the Gallatin Valley. With this party of Crows were five (four) Piegan Indians, renegades from their tribe at that time, among them being Mountain Chief and three sons, one of whom was named Bull. Being successful in their raid for horses the band started on their return with about two hundred head of horses and had reached a point six miles below Mission Creek and about sixteen miles east from the present town of Livingston, when they met two white men traveling up the river. One of these was J. M. Bozeman and his companion, I have learned, was T. W. Coover, one of the discovers of gold in Alder Gulch.

Not wishing to harm the whites or to be harmed by them the Crows passed on but the Piegans shortly disappeared from among them which fact was not discovered for some time. The latter not putting in an appearance for some time, the Crows started back to hunt them up and found that they had killed Bozeman while away. The Piegans returned to camp with the Crows, but in November returned to the Piegan tribe in northern Montana. Afterwards, during the following years, the three sons of Mountain Chief, together with two other Piegans, set out as a war party for the purpose of stealing horses from their former friends, the Crows. [They] were discovered by a band of Crow warriors under the leading warriors of the

Crow tribe, Pretty Eagle and Ball Rock, in the Judith Gap in Judith Basin. [They] intercepted them and killed five of them. They were recognized by the Crows as the sons of Mountain Chief who had just left their camp and who killed Bozeman.

April 1st 1896   (Signed) George Reed ("Crow") Davis.

Nelson Story, a pioneer of Bozeman, who has caused a monument to be erected in the Bozeman cemetery over the grave of John M. Bozeman, a grave that stands at the brow of the bluff which the cemetery crowns, and overlooking the beautiful city which has grown up since Bozeman ushered in its first settlers, presents new materials as to Bozeman's death which information was given to him by W. S. McKenzie.[59]

The two (referring to Bozeman and Coover) had just finished dinner when the five Indians who had stolen our horses came up. . . They asked for food and Bozeman good naturedly consented to cook something for them. The only weapon the Indians had with them was an old gun which we call a Mississippi yager. Bozeman had a Spencer gun, which he laid aside while cooking, and Coover, who stood near by, had a first class Henry gun. I had advised Bozeman not to let any Indian get close to him. The thing to have done when those Indians appeared with their demand for something to eat, was to have killed them, for their presence meant no good, but Bozeman was a reckless man and never could see danger anywhere. While Bozeman cooked he talked to one of the Indians. Suddenly an Indian from behind the shelter of the one to whom Bozeman was talking, fired at Bozeman. The ball struck him in the abdomen, killing him instantly. . . They found Bozeman's body and buried it where it lay, but could not get the Indians. Three or four days later the body was disinterred and brought to Bozeman and buried in the cemetery. . . Mountain Chief, one of the renegade Blackfeet, I saw at Fort C. F. Smith the year after. I tried to get the commanding officer to put him under arrest, but the officer

---

[59] W. S. McKenzie was a Gallatin pioneer, an old Indian fighter, and knew Bozeman well, both having come from the same county in Georgia.

feared the Indian would be hanged and trouble would ensue, so he would not accede to my request.[60]

The monument on the overlooking hill bears the following inscription:

> In memory of John M. Bozeman, aged 32 years, killed by Blackfoot Indians on the Yellowstone, April 18, 1867. He was a native of Georgia, and was one of the first settlers of Bozeman, from whom the town takes its name.

A newspaper correspondent[61] writing from Union City, Montana Territory, October 21, 1867, a few months after Bozeman's murder, makes this comment:

> The three murderers of Colonel Bozeman came in and received their annuities recently at Fort Benton, and bore their gifts straightway to the hostile camps. Two of them were sons of a chief who professes to be at peace with the whites. He does the part of diplomacy, while his sons and followers rob and butcher. A large portion of the annuities received by this tribe go to those who are on the warpath; he shields the fraud and aids the merciless enemy.

David B. Weaver crossed the plains on the Oregon Trail to Fort Laramie and to Montana via the Bozeman Trail in the summer of 1864, leaving the Missouri River at Omaha on the 21st of May, arriving at Emigrant Gulch, Montana, the 27th of August. The data preserved of this journey and the incidents occurring on the way, are not only interesting but informing of the daily travel and the dangers avoided and encountered. The trip by wagon train from the starting point to Fort Kearney (Nebraska) took until June 2d. Traveling along the north side of the North Platte, commonly called the Mormon Trail, Fort Laramie was a resting place on the 25th of June. The warpath of

---

[60] From Boulder *Monitor*, Montana, October 25, 1919.
[61] McClure, *Three Thousand Miles Through the Rocky Mountains.*

the Indians north of the fort being full of red men the small train of twenty wagons was advised not to proceed until recruit wagons might be added to the train. Crossing the Platte on a toll bridge kept by a Frenchman named Richard (pronounced, however, "Reshaw") to the south side, the few wagons waited until July 12th, when reinforcements were added to the train until it numbered sixty-eight wagons. A few days previous to the departure of this newly organized train, Captain Townsend had gone north on the Bozeman Trail with a wagon train, meeting, as was soon learned, serious disaster from Indian depredations.

Cyrus C. Coffenbury, having many wagons at the crossing, added Weaver's wagon train to his own, made up a train for Montana, being elected commander of the train, with the title of Major, divided into four divisions, with a captain for each section. Leaving the Platte on the 12th, no difficulties were experienced until the train reached the Powder River on the 22d of July. Here the men learned of the tragedy that had met Captain Townsend. Ten days before the train's arrival Townsend had been attacked by the Sioux, having four of his men killed, the naked and mutilated bodies of the soldiers bearing witness to the ravages of the Indians. Four empty graves near the bodies gave testimony to the savagery of the foe, who had not only dug up the bodies, but had robbed them of clothing and the blankets in which they had been wrapped for burial.[62]

Reburying the bodies, the train marched on, reaching Tongue River on the 29th of the month, being at that time one hundred and seventy-two miles from the North Platte. By the 4th of August the train was

---

[62] Montana Historical Society *Collections*, Vol. viii, p. 288, for complete account of Townsend's disaster.

sixty-two miles beyond the Tongue, at which place a camp was made on the Big Horn River. Here was found the "object of our quest," color in the sand and gravel. Stretching toward the Yellowstone which was finally reached on the 14th, the train followed the stream for nine days before they found a fordable place. The trail ultimately took them west to a canyon which was one hundred and fifty miles from the place where the train had first obtained sight of the Yellowstone. In the valley many men were prospecting for gold, which attracted some of the men from the train who decided to go no further, but try their luck with washing for gold.

It was at this point on the Bozeman Trail that the party separated, as the members of the train had different and varied destinations. Some expressed a wish to continue on the trail to Virginia City; others were allured to prospect along the valley of the Yellowstone. On the 27th of August, Emigrant Gulch was reached by Mr. Weaver with a few of his men who wished to try their fortunes in the Yellowstone Valley. In this gulch excited gold washers were feverishly working over the gravel. Thus, the "quest" being found in the hills surrounding the Bozeman Trail the train disbanded, leaving each man to seek his fortune and destination as luck and wisdom might dictate. A recital of the experiences of this train, protected by its members and organization, justified the government in its contention that the real dangers on the Bozeman Trail from the red men were inadequate mobilization of the trains and incompetent commanders or leaders of the trains.

In the summer of 1866, Hugh Kirkendall and others were on the Bozeman Trail on their way with a long train of household goods and merchandise for Montana. When the train reached Brown's Springs, a branch of the Dry Fork of the Cheyenne, the train was attacked by Indians, and a running fight was kept up the entire day. As the hours of fighting increased, the Indians grew in numbers, until it seemed as if all the Indians in the Powder River country had assembled for a final blow. Being able finally to push the train forward, after the Indians were repulsed with heavy loss, the merchants came to within forty miles of Fort Phil Kearney, from where a scout was sent to the fort for soldiers to protect the train and conduct it beyond the fort. Word came in the morning that there were not enough soldiers to even protect the fort with a small degree of safety. The wonder to the members of the train was that the three forts on the "Powder River Road" should have been built if enough soldiers were not in them to not only protect the fortifications, but to assist and protect emigrant trains. "The fact is, the soldiers in the forts are practically bottled up, with the Indians galloping around on the hills nearby, and like Goliath of old, defying them in an insulting manner." [68]

The difficulties of one wagon train over the Bozeman Trail in the summer of 1866, when the Sioux were so intensively irritated, are but the repetition of many caravans to the Montana gold-fields.

"The trail followed the Union Pacific construction up the Platte. It was monotonously dull, plodding along beside the train. And there were no variations in the monotony when the train left the railway line and swung up to Fort Laramie. But at Fort Laramie the pilgrims left the beaten path. They were planning to take the Bozeman Trail from there into Montana,

---

[68] Kuykendall (W. L.) *Frontier Days*, p. 106.

and the condition of the country ahead of them made it necessary that they travel with a big outfit." [64]

At Fort Laramie other freighting outfits were waiting for reinforcements, the government authorities having again issued a warning to small groups of emigrants of the immediate and certain danger from the Indians unless strongly guarded and moving in large numbers. At the fort this small group of freighters found a stockman [65] with three thousand head of cattle from Texas to be taken into the Gallatin Valley for feeding, and also with a wagon train of groceries to be sold in the mining camps of Montana. The forces all united, starting for the Powder River country, the Big Horn, Bozeman and Virginia City. Had this combination of trains been always used, the depredations on the trail would have decreased, and human lives, cattle, supplies and ammunition and guns been saved. "Along the trail the government was erecting a chain of military posts. General Carrington, who afterward negotiated the removal of Charlot on the Bitter Root, was in command of the troops engaged in the construction. One post, Fort Reno, had been completed. The building of Fort Kearney was in process. The posts further north had been located but not built. Some of them never were built."

"The train moved on without serious incident. The country was alive with Indians. There were signs of fighting—burned wagons and dead stock in places, and at times the Story outfit would spy Indians at a distance. But it was not until within about ten miles of Fort Reno that there was any open hostility toward the train. That was probably due to the keen outlook which Story kept

[64] Stone (A. L.) *Following Old Trails.*
[65] Nelson Story, of Bozeman, Montana.

and to his intimate knowledge of the country. There were thousands of Indians within striking distance of the train, but the train was not molested until it reached a point so close to the new post as to seem safe. In the edge of the Bad Lands the train was attacked. There was a brisk engagement, but it didn't last long; probably the Indians who had been spying on the train were merely trying it out, or perhaps they could not resist the stealing of the stock cattle that were being driven with the train. However as it was, the reds swooped down on the travelers with a flight of arrows, but nobody was killed. The cattle were finally recaptured and messengers sent to Fort Reno for an ambulance."

An hour before the train had its brush with the Indians, it met a Frenchman and his boy with a trapper's outfit, the two making camp for the night. Though the large train invited the Frenchman to unite with the larger band, the old man refused the offer, saying his fear for the white men was greater than that of the Indians. The next day proved the fallacy of the lone emigrant and hunter, for the scalps of both were taken; their bodies, badly mutilated, their wagons were burned, food scattered over the prairie, and their horses stolen.

Leaving Fort Reno the train pushed north and west toward Fort Phil Kearney, where General Carrington was surveying and actively assisting in the construction of the main fortification that was to be built on the Bozeman Trail. The soldiers from the fort came down three miles to meet the train, forbidding further advance to the fort, as the meadows around the site of the fort were reserved for government stock. Further instructions were given not to attempt to go further north, as there were danger signals about Indians north of the fort.

"We were camped about three miles from the post, so far that the soldiers could not have rendered us any assistance if we were attacked; we were forbidden to proceed, as the soldiers couldn't leave their building operations to escort us; we just had to sit still and twirl our thumbs. While waiting, the freighters built two corrals, one for the work cattle, one for the Texas stock. One night after two weeks of impatient waiting for permission to advance, the entire train oxen, wagons, cattle and men disappeared moving on beyond the fort in the silence and darkness of night. The Indians were more afraid of the twenty-seven men of the train than they were of the three hundred soldiers at the partially built fort on the Piney. The troops had the old style Springfield rifles, while the freighters had Remington breech loaders, a style of gun not introduced on the plains for the forts until the following year. Twenty-seven of these Remingtons were enough to stand off three thousand reds with bows and arrows after we got them scared."

The success of traveling by night convinced the train that this was a safer method of travel than going by day, hence, they rested during the day and traveled after sundown. The train was attacked only three times, this being during the day, and the Indians were easily stood off, the men being on their guard. As the train moved further north, the Indians became less numerous, an estimation placing the number of red men around Fort Phil Kearney on October 22nd, when the train was near the fort, as three thousand. Two months from this date occurred the Fetterman fight, the initial big fight with Indians in the Powder River country.

These night marches brought the train finally to the

site of Fort C. F. Smith, around which the Crows had their villages. From this point the party journeyed to the northwest, forded the Yellowstone at the place where there was to have been built another Bozeman Trail fort, to be called Fort Fisher. For lack of adequate soldiers, General Carrington was not able to construct the needed and promised fortification. Down Emigrant Gulch the train slowly made its way to Bozeman, no Indian troubles being encountered, when at last the end of the trail was reached at Virginia City.[66]

The principal freighting to the Bozeman Trail forts was done by oxen, for the reason that the red men did not care for cattle, the country through which the trail passed being full of wild game of many kinds. What the Indians coveted were the white man's horses and mules for which he was willing to make tremendous sacrifices. There were no regular stage lines on the Bozeman Trail; all of the mail was carried by the military forces from the Platte to Fort C. F. Smith. Mail for Fort Ellis, Bozeman, and beyond to Virginia City was received by the river route from Fort Benton or by the Virginia City Stage Road from Salt Lake City. During those months when the Missouri was open

[66] Montana Historical Society *Collections*, Vol. ii, p. 135; Peter Koch: "During 1864-6 the principal immigration into Montana was by the Bozeman road and across the Bozeman Pass, and many of our leading citizens came over the road in those years and could doubtless tell many a moving tale of accident by flood and field during their long overland journey. Forts Reno, Phil Kearney and C. F. Smith were built by the government to protect the trains on the road; but on December 21, 1866, the Fetterman massacre took place, and with characteristic pusillanity, the government ordered all the forts abandoned and the road *closed to travel*!

Last year the Reno and Phil Kearney route was pronounced open for emigration, and hundreds of graves along its entire length with the Phil Kearney massacre as the central figure, attest how the promise was kept with the emigrants. This year it is accepted as hostile and impossible."—McClure, *Three Thousand Miles Through the Rocky Mountains*, p. 109. (Written May 20, 1867).

Virginia City, Territory of Montana, 1868

The objective point of the Bozeman Trail. From a contemporary drawing by A. E. Mathews.

to navigation there was not heavy freighting over the Bozeman Trail west of Fort C. F. Smith, the supplies being shipped to Fort Benton or to Benson's Landing at the head of navigation on the Yellowstone, about thirty miles southeast of Fort Ellis, from these two points being redistributed to the various camps and cities in Montana. In the fall of 1866 at Bozeman, Nelson Story took his oxen and wagon team filled with flour and vegetables to Fort C. F. Smith where he sold the supplies to the government for the soldiers at the fort. From that date until the old trail was abandoned in 1868, Story continued to regularly supply this fort with food though not any traffic was carried on east of the fort, where the hostilities were constant from the Sioux. The hostile Indians, the Sioux, Cheyennes and Arapahoes were seldom troublesome west of Pryor's Creek. The hostilities in that part of the country crossed by the Bozeman Trail were carried on by the Blackfoot Indians.[67]

If the Santa Fé Trail was a road of commerce, the Oregon Trail, the path of the homeseeker, the Overland Trail, the route of the mail and express, the Bozeman Trail was the battleground of the fighting Sioux.

[67] F. G. Burnett who furnished the above data about the oxen and freighting west of Fort C. F. Smith, contributes the following about the Blackfoot Indians against whom he had to defend himself many times: "The Blackfoot Indians were a treacherous set of sneaks; they never fought openly as other Indians, but would come into camp representing themselves to be Crows who were at peace with the whites. The Blackfeet would then take advantage of any carelessness on the part of the white man and in cold blood murder an entire outfit. They murdered many miners during the winter time who had gone down along the Yellowstone, where game and timber were plentiful, there to live until the mining season opened in the spring."

The Powder River Indian Expedition

As General Dodge had predicted, the Indians, in the summer of 1865, not only became restless, but grew keenly suspicious of the white man and his repeated invasions, by the use of the Bozeman Trail, into the heart of their hunting grounds in the region of the Powder and Tongue Rivers and their numerous tributaries, represented by the Cheyenne, Belle Fourche, Little Big Horn River and the Goose and Crazy Woman's Creeks, all north of the Platte River, having their origin in the hills and mountains situated in what is now Wyoming, emptying into one another, or, in the greater number of cases, into the Yellowstone River in Montana.

The successful policy of General Dodge had been to strike and to strike hard; to concentrate all of the available military forces possible along the Platte, and then prove to the red men that trained and disciplined soldiers could control the country claimed by the Indians. To further carry out the effectiveness of such a campaign as had been inaugurated by him in the fall of 1864, General Dodge ordered an expedition to go into the Powder River country.

Three divisions were sent into this campaign of 1865, all under the command of General Patrick Edward Connor, who at this time was at the head of the District of the Plains, a division of western warfare created for him in March of this year. In command of the right, or eastern division, was Colonel Nelson Cole, who was to march from Omaha to Columbus, Nebraska, and from there to the northwest, going around the north end of the Black Hills, and then west to the Powder River country, where he and his men were to meet General Connor and his men, as well as the soldiers of the middle division of the expedition.

Over the middle division was placed Colonel Samuel Walker, who was to start from Fort Laramie, from there going north to the Black Hills, where his troops were expected to unite with those of Colonel Cole's command, the united command going to the waters of the Little Missouri River. The left or western division under General Connor, also starting from Fort Laramie, had in its command ninety-five Pawnee Indians, acting as scouts, under the command of Major Frank North, an experienced and successful Indian scout, for many years doing active campaigning against the Indians on the plains and in the mountains. This command was to follow the recently established Bozeman Trail which ran along the eastern side of the Big Horn Mountains.

The eastern division consisted of eight companies of the Second Missouri Light Artillery, and eight companies of the Twelfth Missouri Cavalry, numbering about one thousand four hundred soldiers, besides a train of one hundred and forty six-mule wagons. Colonel Walker had about six hundred men of the Sixteenth Kansas Cavalry and a pack train. General Connor's men were from the Seventh Iowa Cavalry, the Second California Cavalry, a signal corps from the United States army and other scouts than the Pawnee, amounting to about one hundred, from the Winnebago and Omaha tribes.

Not only did the commanders have a hazy and indefinite idea of the exact part of the Powder River country where were to be assembled the forces of the three divisions, but they were confronted from the very first with mutiny and a refusal to fight Indians. At Columbus, Colonel Cole's men stood in open rebellion, declaring that they had enlisted for the war and not to fight Indians; that as the war was over they should, in reason and justice, be discharged. When questioned as to where the command was to go and how long the expedition was to last, the commander could give no definite answer, for he was without knowledge, as his orders from General Connor and the maps given him for the route, only took the command to the Niobrara River, when new instructions were to come from the general commanding the expedition, which would explain the route and final destination. After anxious hours of indecision, the troops were persuaded to continue with the command.

When Colonel Walker with his men reached Fort Laramie, his soldiers also mutinied, refusing to go north to fight Indians. By bringing the artillery to bear on the mutineers, General Connor, who was at the fort with Colonel Walker, convinced the men that the possibility of escaping alive from the Indians was to be preferred to immediate death from firearms. By July 5th the middle command left the fort to meet and join forces with Colonel Cole somewhere, destination not known, in the region of the Black Hills.

From an interview with one[68] who was with Colonel Cole's division from Omaha to the return, serving all through the expedition, many new and instructive facts

[68] William Devine, Sheridan, Wyoming. Mr. Devine was a member of Company F, Seventy-first Penn. Vol. Inf. He was a civilian with the Powder River Indian Expedition.

have been collected, which are embodied in the following:

When the command, early in July, 1865, camped near the mouth of the Loup River, one of the cavalrymen brought dispatches from General Connor containing full instruction as to the general route to be followed, and the destination in the Powder River country where all three divisions were to assemble, and where additional food and supplies were to be distributed. From the Loup to the Niobrara was an unknown country; the road chosen was sandy; the wagons sank to the hubs in sand, the troops having to pull them out with drag-ropes. From here the path was filled with difficulty—marshes, then dry streams, gulches, over which corduroy bridges had to be constructed, then bluffs. On August 8th a fork of the Cheyenne River was reached, where the wagons had to be let down the banks with ropes. Still swinging in a northwestern direction, with stock falling by the wayside, suffering from lack of water and hard traveling, the sun hot, the streams dry, fresh trails of Indians became more numerous, all leading in the exact direction that the command was to march.

About the middle of August, Colonel Walker came into the camp from the West, having followed the command under Colonel Cole for several days without being able to overtake it. From here the route was as direct as possible to the Little Missouri, where was found an extensive burial ground of the Indians. Up and down the valley were scaffolds for the dead Indians, the branches of all the large trees being filled with dead papooses. No Indians had been encountered, though the trails clearly indicated that they were only one day's distance ahead. By this time scurvy was claiming a large toll; men were dying from lack of properly balanced food; no wood, grass or water was to be found. "The sun was like a ball of fire." Horses and mules died from exhaustion, until the trail was marked with their dead bodies.

The instructions from General Connor had been to proceed to Panther Mountains (Wolf Mountains)[69] at the base of which, on the Tongue River, would be found a depot of supplies. But a deplorable lack of accurate knowledge of the country in this region had allowed General Connor to be misleading in his instructions and his map, which sacrificed many a life and caused a heavy loss of livestock, for when arriving at the spot very clearly indicated on the map, there were no supplies. Future developments showed that the directions were wrong—which, of course, made serious complications, particularly in regard to obtaining food supplies. In place of the needed food there was found a country barren of grass, covered with prickly-pear, sagebrush and greasewood. The only thing to be done seemed to be to turn toward the south and move in the direction of rations, the nearest place being Fort Laramie, to be reached by the route of the Powder River, the Big Horn Mountains and the North Platte River. Just at this point of desperation scouts came into camp reporting Indians who, giving battle, killed four of the soldiers, with others mortally wounded. Out of the five hundred attacking red men, twenty-five were killed.

The command never before had been in the West. It had hence never had previous experience with Indians, with the exceptions of the scouts. The soldiers'

---

[69] Near where the Tongue crosses the present boundary between Montana and Wyoming.

idea of the Indians was that they would be dressed as people now see them in the "movies"—war bonnet and beaded clothing, or, as the red man is described by James Fenimore Cooper. What the soldiers did see was what they thought to be a part of Colonel Walker's command, for the Indians could not be distinguished from the white men until so close that the color of their eyes could be seen. Their skins were as dark as that of the white man who had long been exposed to the sun and scorching winds. Many of the Indians were in United States army uniforms. "That was all that was needed by them to make a success. The blanket Indians would make a dash out of some of the gulches, and charging up to within one hundred yards or so would move rapidly away so as to get small parties of our men to follow them. When a small party got far enough away from the main command, the blanket Indians would make a stand. About that time the uniformed Indians would emerge from a ravine in the rear of our men, and get right in among them before our men knew they were Indians. They made their bows and arrows just as effective as our Spencer carbines. An Indian could drive an arrow through a man at one hundred yards' distance. So the uniform was a great handicap to us. There were times when they got almost into camp before we knew them."

By the 2d of September all of Colonel Walker's command had joined forces with those of the right wing, when it was decided that in place of skirting to the south, it would be wise to drive to the north, in hopes of finding the Yellowstone River. During the march down the Powder River two hundred and twenty-five horses and mules died from excessive heat, exhaustion, starvation or extreme cold (a mountain storm of hail and snow having caught the troop the day before). In order not to leave wagons, harness, saddles and other supplies now rendered useless by the loss of stock, to be used by the Indians, instructions were given to have everything, not to be immediately utilized, burned, including a large amount of quartermasters' stores. Two days after this the cry of "Indians!" was given, while just behind the man who gave the alarm, were six men dressed in the full uniform of United States soldiers. From everywhere—ravines, rocks and hillsides, the red man sprang up, until a thousand hostile savages were in sight, the bluffs being literally covered with the enemy, who were yelling and signaling with a red flag and flashing mirrors in the sun. Two pieces of artillery, opening with shells on the Indians, soon dispersed them. On the 8th reports came into camp that the advance guard, which was building roads, had been attacked by four thousand Indians. Again, after a hard skirmish, the artillery saved the men. That night a terrific storm swept the camp, rain, hail and wind lasting for thirty-six hours, during which four hundred and fourteen animals perished at the picket-ropes or along the trail between camps. Again destruction was necessary of wagons, cavalry equipment, harness, tools and implements not absolutely necessary to continue the march. The Indians were very gleeful at the distress of the troops, shouting in good English to the men, calling them all the vile names they could invent, and finally telling them that the white men had come to that country to kill the Indians, declaring that not a single white man would be able to return and tell the story. The soldiers were positive that white men were leading the Indians. Then those things which could not be burned and would only hinder progress if taken with the command, such as horse-shoes, blacksmith forges, tools and mowing machines, were buried.

On September 10th the commands again turned around, going up the Powder River headed toward Fort Laramie. That day they passed over a large Indian village site of two thousand lodges, which had recently been moved. The doleful record of the command now was, that they had been on the road for eighty-two days, existing on sixty days' rations, twenty per cent of which had been lost or destroyed in loading and unloading wagons at crossings of streams and gulches. Again the soldiers were surrounded by a superior force of Indians. "If we had been armed with the old muzzle-loading gun instead of the Spencer repeating carbine, they would have annihilated us." Finally General Connor's scouts, with the Pawnee Indians, after traveling up and down the Powder River, struck the trail of Colonel Cole's command and eventually reached the troops and gave directions how to reach Fort Connor,[70] which place of safety was gained September 10th by shoeless, almost clothesless, starving and weary soldiers of the east and middle command. But there were no shoes or clothing at the fort, for the west command had taken nothing in the way of extra supplies for wear.

From the time the eastern wing had left Omaha to its arrival at Fort Connor, the troops had traveled twelve hundred miles over a territory all but unknown to white men, through a barren and desert country. It had taken eighty-two days to make the journey; days of struggle and fighting; days of road building

---

[70] Near the mouth of Dry Creek of the Powder River; not far from Sussex, Johnson county, Wyoming.

through the valleys and over the mountains; days of combat with the Indians; days of starvation; days of despair; days of burning heat; days of perishing cold; days of no water, of deluging rain and blinding snows.

Fort Connor was a disappointment, for only food could be obtained where supplies of all kinds were expected to be given the threadbare soldiers. The dissatisfaction was expressed in no uncertain terms; the blame was placed upon General Connor and his indefinite instructions as to the place of meeting in the land of the Sioux in the neighborhood of the Tongue River, just northwest of the Powder. Someone had blundered through a lack of exact information as to the geography of the country north of the Platte. When on September 24th, General Connor came into the camp at Fort Connor, his reception was not one calculated to warm the heart of an officer who himself had met disaster, experienced hardships innumerable and unsuccessfully fought the hostile Indians.

After resting two days the command started for Fort Laramie, with only forty wagons to carry the wounded and sick, including the five hundred barefoot soldiers, many of whose feet were swollen to twice their natural size on account of cactus spines which they had encountered. Added to these misfortunes, were a large number of men who were in a pitiful plight, suffering from scurvy. Arriving at Fort Laramie on the 5th of October, there were additional grievances to make up the toll of misfortunes of the expedition. Quoting from William Devine: "The quartermaster at Fort Laramie wanted to hire ten citizens, but all he could get were four – three and myself. When we went to our quartermaster for three and a half month's pleasure trip, we got a sheet of legal cap paper, which stated that the said 'voucher would be received by the United States treasurer at its face value,' and any United States paymaster who had more money than he knew what to do with, would swap his greenbacks for it and it would be received by the treasurer as money. We went to the sutler's store to see how much money we could get for it, and all that was offered was fifty cents on the dollar in trade. We then asked the quartermaster at the fort if that was the kind of money he was going to pay us in; if so we were not going to stay. He told us he would pay us in greenbacks. During that fall and winter we built the stockade at the Platte Bridge, which was afterward made into a fort and called Fort Caspar."

The sudden recall by the War Department of General Connor, when he was surrounded by Indians in the country of the Powder River and north of the fort bearing this officer's name, greatly incensed him, and while smarting under the injustice of the act, he made no official report to headquarters, but boxed up all his records, maps and notes and shipped them to his headquarters at Salt Lake City, where all of the papers in the case were destroyed by fire, the building in which they were stored being entirely consumed. Fortunately, one of General Connor's men had kept a diary of the expedition. It is from this detailed account that information has been obtained that would otherwise have left no report of the left or west command of the Powder River Indian Expedition. Captain Henry E. Palmer of the Eleventh Kansas Cavalry served in the capacity of quartermaster for General Connor, his special duties being to provide transportation, forage, extra clothing and other essential supplies for the expedition—an outfit of such proportions that it filled to overflowing one hundred and eighty-five large wagons.

Five days after the tragedy at Platte Bridge, July 26, 1865, when Lieutenant Caspar Collins was killed, General Connor, with his command of soldiers, Indian scouts, teamsters and wagonmen, making in all about nine hundred men, left Fort Laramie to go into the Sioux country on a mission of annihilation. In the official record are found the instructions which General Connor gave his men before they started on the Powder River Indian Expedition: "You will not receive overtures of peace or submission from Indians, but will attack and kill every male Indian over twelve years of age." To this order came, in due time, a severe reprimand from General Pope, countermanding these instructions in no uncertain terms: "These instructions are atrocious, and are in direct violation of my repeated orders. If any such orders as General Connor's are carried out, it will be disgraceful to the government and will cost him his position, if not worse."

That at least three thousand Indians, on the day after the killing of Lieutenant Collins, had left their ravaging on the North Platte, traveling north to the Powder River, was a well known fact to both officers and the command. It was also as well known that the retreating Indians were going into a country that was inhabited by thousands of other Indians who had not gone on the raids along the Oregon Trail—Indians who were perfectly familiar with every step of the ground of the Powder River country, and knew every waterhole, stream, ravine and path leading to safety. With only as many hundreds of men as there were thousands of Indians, General Connor was sent into a territory unknown to him, except by maps, additionally hampered by the fact that his necessary supplies did not reach him until he arrived at Fort Laramie on his return from the Sioux country.

To follow the march of the west command under General Connor, the diary of Captain Palmer must be frequently consulted and variously quoted. From Fort Laramie, on the thirtieth of July (1865) the command started toward the country north of the Platte River, the official title of the command being "The Powder River Indian Expedition." In this command were also many soldiers who had served as volunteers in the Civil War, who believed that their enlistment ended with the war for which they had enlisted. Protests were many over the forced fighting of Indians, and particularly the going into an unknown country where were known to be thousands of hostiles.

In this west command were soldiers from Iowa, Ohio, California, Missouri, and Michigan, a detachment from the United States army signal corps, seventy-five Pawnee Indians under the direct command of Major Frank North, also seventy Winnebago and Omaha Indians. The two companies, one hundred and sixty men, of the Michigan cavalry were to garrison the first military post to be established on the Powder River.[71] Not including these, there were in the command four hundred and four soldiers, one hundred and forty-five Indians to act as scouts, one hundred and ninety-five teamsters and wagon makers, and with other scouts was the chief of all western guides, Jim Bridger, who by this time in his life of varied experiences had won the title of "Major James Bridger." Marching along the south side of the North Platte from Fort Laramie, a crossing was made at the old La Bonte Ford, from where a march

---

[71] These men were left at Fort Connor until relieved by Colonel Carrington the next year.

was made along the north side of the Platte to a point where Fort Fetterman was afterward located. The journey from here was northwest to the sources of the Powder River, the command moving with the scouts some miles ahead, always alert for the unseen foe, which the command learned was more dangerous than when in sight; the Pawnee Indians acting as flanking parties on each side of the command. The other Indian scouts, with Captain Brown and his troops, had been sent to the Platte Bridge, to push north from there to the south slope of the Big Horn Mountains and the Wind River Valley, so as to thoroughly reconnoiter that country, and then rejoin the main command within twenty to twenty-five days near Crazy Woman's Creek, a fork of Powder River. Pushing toward the Powder River, General Connor's command only made camps at springs, owing to the scarcity of water, for the region was barren and the streams at this time of the year were dry; roads were rough, grass poor; any water that was found was either stagnant or alkali, and the miserable roads threatened to be a serious menace. At this point Captain Palmer makes an error in his diary, August 4th, when he writes: "Almost impossible to get the train through, having traveled, as before stated, in a country where no wagons ever before passed." Father De Smet records in his diary under date of August 22, 1851, when he was in the Powder River country on his way from the Yellowstone to Fort Laramie: "For several days we had had to camp by ponds filled with disgusting water. How agreeable the contrast to find ourselves on the borders of this beautiful river (Tongue) the waters of which are as pure as crystal. How eagerly did we allay our burning thirst. On the 23rd we left the Tongue River. For ten hours we marched over mountain and valley, following the course of one of its tributaries, making, however, only about twenty-five miles. On the following day we crossed a chain of lofty mountains to attain the Lower Piney Fork, nearly twenty-five miles distant. We arrived quite unexpectedly on the borders of a lovely little lake about six miles long, and my traveling companions gave it my name. On the 27th of August we reached Powder River, one of the principal tributaries of the Yellowstone. Our wagonmen will not soon forget the difficulty of conducting their teams through this vast route, for it was a very miserable, elevated, sterile plain, covered with wormwood, and intersected with countless ravines, and they vowed they would never be caught driving a wagon there again. The valley of the Powder River, in the neighborhood of the Gourd (Pumpkin) Buttes, which are in sight, is three or four miles wide. Although the soil was light, the verdure was fine and the grazing abundant."[72]

General conditions of the road became better as the command went farther north, though the miles covered each day did not indicate special speed – "ten miles," "eight and one-half miles," "twelve miles," being the record for three successive days. August 5th – "General very diligent and careful about being surprised; he superintends every movement himself, and is very sanguine that our expedition will be successful. Some careless soldiers fired the grass near our camp last night. The fire getting beyond our control served as a beacon

[72] General W. F. Raynolds, commander of the government "Yellowstone Expedition" of 1859-1860, stated, "I traveled through this region with heavily loaded wagons in the fall of 1859 without embarrassment." (United States Senate *Executive Document* 77, 40th Congress, 1st Session).

Bozeman, also with wagons, went through the Powder River country in 1864, as did others in the years following.

light to the hostiles and gives great uneasiness to our
guides, who fear that the Indians will be signaled thereby, and may congregate in large numbers – too large for
our little command. At the start of the fire the flames
ran across the camp towards two powder wagons."
The seemingly inevitable explosion and destruction of
ammunition was avoided by the prompt aid of volunteers, who took the wagons to a place of safety. Next,
the Dry Fork of the Cheyenne River was reached,
where not only water and grass were found in abundance, but wood, with which the meat of the fine buffalo
could be cooked; not only buffalo, but a large number
of antelope were seen both to the east, toward the Black
Hills and the west, toward the Big Horn Mountains.

By the 9th of the month the command caught its
first glimpse of the glorious Big Horn Mountains,
which loomed up to the northwest at a distance of
about eighty-five miles, the view of which was described as follows: "The sun so shone as to fall with
full blast on the southern and southeastern sides, as
they rose toward Cloud Peak, which is about ten thous-
and feet above sea level, and the whole snow-covered
range so clearly blended with the sky as to leave it
in doubt whether all was not a mass of bright cloud.
Although the day was extremely warm, so soon as we
struck this ridge we felt the cooling breezes from the
snow-clad mountains, which were most gratefully ap-
preciated by both man and beast. In front, and a
little to the northeast, could be seen four columns of
the Pumpkin Buttes, and fifty miles further east, Bear
Buttes, and beyond, a faint outline of the Black Hills.
The atmosphere was so wonderfully clear and bright
that one could imagine he could see the eagles on the
crags of the Pumpkin Buttes, full forty miles away."

The first view of the Powder River was obtained on the 11th of the month, a river rapid but narrow, which, in the springtime, overflowed its banks, inundating the country on both sides. The clay through which the river ran was, and is, generally of black, brittle, gunpowdery material, hence, the particular name given to the stream. The next day part of the command was on the Bozeman Road, where Indians were discovered, and every mile were found places where had been Indian villages, some of them indicating that there had been inhabitants in the locality within the past few days.

On the 14th came the selection of a site of the first fort to be established in the Powder River country, the land which, according to the treaty signed with the Indians, was only to have a road traverse it, but on which there were to be no fortifications and no soldiers to garrison the forts. The fort was named Connor, retaining this name until next year, when it was enlarged and renamed Fort Reno. The ground selected for the building was on the left side of the Powder River about four miles below the mouth of Dry Fork. Here was cut timber for the construction of a stockade, situated on a large mesa about one hundred feet above the bed of the river, the ground being as level as a floor, and in extent about five miles, running to the bluffs. Generally speaking, the site was a fine one, the only great drawback being the lack of hay land. The timbers used in the construction were twelve feet long and eight to ten inches in thickness, the posts being placed in a trench four feet deep, leaving the posts above ground some five to seven feet. All of the men assisted in the erection of the stockade, which was constructed in a surprisingly short time.

August 16th – "Command still in camp waiting for a train of supplies from Fort Laramie before we proceed. Indian scouts discovered a war party today, and the soldiers gave them a running fight, Captain North's Pawnees in the advance, with only a few staff officers, who were smart enough to get to the front with the Pawnees. Captain North followed the Indians about twelve miles without their being aware of our pursuit; then the fun began in earnest. Our war party outnumbered the enemy, and the Pawnees, thirsty for blood, and desirous of getting even with their old enemy, the Sioux, rode like mad devils, dropping their blankets behind them, and all useless paraphernalia, and rushed into the fight, half-naked, whooping and yelling, shooting, howling – such a sight I never saw before. Some twenty-four scalps were taken, twenty-four horses captured, and quite an amount of other plunder, such as saddles, fancy horse-trappings and Indian fixtures generally. The Pawnees were on horseback twenty-four hours, and did not leave the trail until they overtook the enemy. On their return to camp they exhibited the same savage signs of delight, and if they felt fatigued they did not show it; they rode with the bloody scalps tied to the ends of sticks, whooping and yelling like so many devils."

Captain Palmer has well described the spirit into which many of the officers and men went into this expedition, as of enjoyment and pleasure, when he says: "Then the fun began in earnest." Utterly oblivious to the seen and unseen dangers, the officers seemed to take for granted that the expedition was quite as much for adventure, to be of pleasing remembrance, as for Indian hunting; many days were spent in buffalo and antelope hunts, unfitting the horses for active service.

Often while game was hunted, other officers would report the appearance of thousands of Indians in the immediate neighborhood. Among these scouting officers was Captain Nicholas J. O'Brien, mentioned particularly at this point, due to the fact that after numerous Indian wars, in which he took a fearless and active part, he remained in what was to become Wyoming, identifying himself not only with Indian warfare, but the growth of the territory and the development of the state of Wyoming. At Fort Connor, the two companies of the Sixth Michigan Cavalry were left in command, while the balance of the left wing pushed on to Crazy Woman's Fork, a branch of the Powder, where fresh Indian trails were discovered; also poor grass, abundance of sagebrush and alkali water. Going north from Crazy Woman again, the command was on the Bozeman Road, where hunting was tempting to the point of yielding, water plentiful and "cold as ice," the first experience of most of the command with direct mountain water. In these streams we found plenty of fish, where trout were caught with hooks made of willows. Not only this diversion engaged the acute attention of the men, but grizzly bears were shot, one weighing eighteen hundred pounds, which had taken twenty-three well aimed balls to end its existence.

"From this point on to Montana, in fact along the whole base of the Rocky mountains to the British possessions, the country is perfectly charming; the hills all covered with a fine growth of grass, and in every valley there is either a rushing stream or some quiet, babbling brook of clear, pure snow-water, filled with trout, the banks lined with trees, wild cherries, quaking asp, some birch, willow and cottonwood. No country in America is more picturesque than the eastern slope of the Big Horn Mountains." By the 25th Lake De Smet came into view. Here coal was found in abundance, which enabled the forges to be put in operation, and the blacksmith to do some sadly needed repairs on the wagons. General Palmer states that Lake De Smet was about two miles long and three-quarters of a mile wide, the waters being "strongly impregnated with alkali." In this neighborhood was discovered "a flowing oil well." Camp was made this night on the Piney Fork of the Powder River, at a place two miles below the present site of Fort McKinney and Buffalo in Johnson County, Wyoming. From this point the course taken by the command was north to the divide between the Powder and Tongue Rivers, Jim Bridger blazing the way. Bridger's ears had become well trained by this time, for he could drop a pebble down a deep canyon, and by counting, could determine how many feet it had fallen when it struck the water. Not only were his ears thus accurately trained, but his eyes not only estimated distances to a wonderful degree of accuracy, but they were trained for elevations to an amazing degree. The following instance is recorded:

"Which of those passes is the lower?" an engineer once asked Bridger.

"Yon," said the scout pointing to the South Pass.

"I should say they were about the same height."

"Put your clocks on 'em," said Jim, "an' if yon gap ain't a thousand or two feet lower, you kin hev 'em both."

A test was made, and the South Pass proved to be fifteen hundred feet lower than the other.

For the next two days, traveling down Peno Creek

and Tongue River, Major North and his Pawnee scouts brought back information that an Indian village had been discovered, the Indians being found the next day, the 29th. The village numbered many hundreds of Arapahoes under Black Bear and Old David. The Indians, with three thousand ponies, a thousand dogs, squaws and children, were just breaking camp, when General Connor and his mounted men charged down on the village without halting their horses, firing volley after volley, finally entering into a hand to hand encounter with warriors and squaws, "for many of the females of this band did as brave fighting as their savage lords." Driving the Indians from their village, General Connor finally made a fearless dash after the retreating red men, when he himself was attacked, but with the reinforcements coming to his relief, his life was saved. In this fight one piece of artillery became useless. "The axletree of the guncarriage, a mountain howitzer, was broken. We left the wheels and the broken axle near the river and saved the cannon. The command rendezvoused in the village, and the men were set to work destroying Indian property. Scores of buffalo robes and furs were heaped up on lodge poles, with teepee covers and dried buffalo meat piled on top, and burned. On one of these piles we placed our dead, burning their bodies to keep the Indians from mutilating them. During our halt the Indians pressed up close to camp, making several desperate attempts to recover their stock, when the mountain howitzer, under the skillful management of Nick O'Brien prevented them from completing their aims. . . . We destroyed an immense amount of property—fully two hundred and fifty Indian lodges and contents. . . The Indians pressed us on every side, sometimes charging up within fifty feet of our rear guard. They seemed to have plenty of ammunition, but did most of their fighting with arrows, although there were some of them armed with muskets, with which they could send lead in dangerous proximity to our men. Before dark we were reduced to forty men who had any ammunition, and those only a few rounds apiece. The Indians showed no signs of stopping the fight, but kept on pressing us, charging upon us, dashing away at the stock, keeping us constantly on the move until twelve o'clock (midnight)."

In this fight two hundred and fifty lodges and all of the winter's supply of food belonging to the Arapahoe Indians were burned, sixty-three of the warriors and a son of Chief Black Bear were killed, and eleven hundred ponies captured.

On September 1st, while marching down Tongue River, a cannon shot was heard, presumed to be from the command of Colonel Cole, who was supposed to be in the rendezvous of General Connor at the mouth of Rosebud River,[73] about eighty miles to the north. In response to the shot, Major North, with a portion of the Pawnee scouts, started to the relief of the men of the right wing of the command. On the 4th of September, scouts from Colonel Walker's middle command came into the camp, telling of the attack on their command by Indians, supposed to be the band that had the day before fought the west command. Doleful news was also given that Colonel Cole was killed, which was not true, and that "about twenty-five wagons and one hundred men were en route from Sioux City to Bozeman, by way of the Big Horn, or Bozeman route; that they had passed over the country by the way of

[73] Near the present site of Rosebud, Montana.

the Niobrara, North Fork of the Cheyenne, between Pumpkin and Bear Buttes, intersecting with our (Connor's) trail near Fort Connor; that Colonel Kidd, whom we had left in command at Fort Connor, had sent Captain Cole with twenty men as additional escort for the train, to help them through the Arapahoe country." Next day the scouting party to relieve Colonel Cole, supposed to be at the Rosebud, returned, with no news of the missing command, which it is now known, was never in the place where relief had gone.

On the 6th, the west command was about-faced, commencing its retreat up the Tongue River "to find better grass for the stock," but in reality to get back to Fort Connor as soon as possible, for thus far nothing had been accomplished, as far as subduing the Indians was concerned. But on the 11th, Major North came back to camp from the Powder River with the report that he had found five or six hundred cavalry horses, all dead, and which had undoubtedly belonged to Colonel Cole's command, together with the remains of burned saddles and other supplies. "His trail was well marked and showed that he had pushed up the river in an opposite direction from the course which he had been ordered to take." The reason for this seeming disobedience of orders has been explained in the account of the troubles of the east command. "The startling news gave evidence that we were nearing the end of our expedition, which we feared must end disastrously."

Now realizing the dangerous condition in which Colonel Cole and his command must be for lack of food, General Connor sent a force of men to the relief of the east command. "The general is risking our entire force for the salvation of Cole's men. If our force should be attacked now, it would be short work for the

Indians to massacre the entire party." Finally on the 7th, word was received that the scouts had located the missing commands, and that they were on their way to Fort Connor. Gradually, General Connor worked back toward the fort, and when camping on Crazy Woman's Fork, a message was brought to him stating that he had been removed from the command of the District of the Plains. Why, he did not know, and just how word at this time could have been received by the War Department that the expedition had not been a success, has never been explained. With this crushing message came also the word that Colonel Cole and his men had arrived at Fort Connor in a very destitute condition, "half of his men barefooted, and that for fifteen days they had had no rations at all, and had subsisted entirely upon what little game they could get close to camp, and on mule meat." At noon, the 24th of September, after an absence of forty days, General Connor reached his fort, where he found Colonel Cole's command, looking starved, torn, ragged and dirty, more like tramps than soldiers. With the ending of this day, the Powder River Indian Expedition came to an inglorious end. General Frank Wheaton had been made commander of the Plains District, while Colonel Cole was placed in command of the expedition, which was to make its way back to the States by slow marches. The first section of the march terminated at Fort Laramie, which was reached on the 4th of October.

While the justification for the final statement made by Captain Palmer may raise a question in one's mind, after carefully following the expedition step by step and day by day, it is made to say: "As a summary of general results I can only say that, even with the disastrous ending of Cole's expedition, the Powder River Indian Expedition of 1865 was not a failure. The general's plan to 'carry the war into Egypt' succeeded admirably; the warrior element, by the movement of these columns, were compelled to fall back upon their villages to protect their families, and during the process of the campaign the overland line of travel became as safe as before the Indian outbreak."

General Connor has been characterized as one who had few equals who were braver, nobler or more enterprising, and whose ability, sagacity and courage as an Indian fighter remains unchallenged. Colonel Walker was an able, fearless and untiring officer, whose march to the Black Hills and into the Powder River country was an achievement of no ordinary kind. Colonel Cole won renown as an Indian fighter, and bore the general reputation of a brave and skillful commander.

What the Indians thought of the expedition may best be expressed in what they did upon the retirement of General Connor and his three commands from the Powder River country. "The Indians, thinking that the commander had voluntarily retired from their front, again hastened to the road, passing General Connor's retiring column to the east of his line of march, and again commenced their devilish work of pillage, plunder and massacre." In one account General Connor is reported to have said in substance of the expedition: "You have doubtless noticed the singular termination of the late campaign against the Indians. The truth is, rather harm than good was done, and our troops were, in one sense, driven out of their country by the Indians. I am more solicitous for the honor of the service than I am for my own. I do not feel sore over the treatment accorded me, but think the policy of the government toward the Indians mistaken and very unjust to the Western people."[74]

Quotations have been made from the diaries of the men who were under General Connor's command; there are those who knew him well and saw the extreme difficulties under which he had to operate. F. G. Burnett,[75] in a personal letter, bearing date of March 6, 1919, gives the following testimony as to General Connor's work among the Indians: "General Connor was a brave commander of men, fearless and discreet, never asking a man to go where he would not lead. His men loved him; he despised disobedience and cowardice. There were three regiments under his command in 1865; he loved these men – the Second Colorado, the Second California and the Eleventh Ohio. I have heard him say that with these three regiments and ninety Pawnee scouts under Major Frank North, he could whip all of the Indians on the plains, and I believe that he could have done it."

[74] Salt Lake *Tribune*, December 21, 1891.

There is every evidence that Connor went into the Powder River poorly equipped, through no fault of his, for the contracts for furnishing supplies to the troops on the plains was loosely made by our government, the War Department, and the officers in command had no control of the prompt delivery of the commodities. As a result of this failure to make food and men arrive at the same destination at the same time, Connor did not receive his promised supplies until he returned to Fort Laramie after his expedition to the north. Not only were the soldiers short of food but they were poorly equipped, one regiment having only sabers and revolvers to kill Indians at long range.

[75] Mr. Burnett, in 1920, residing at Fort Washakie, Wyoming, crossed the plains in 1865 in the interests of A. C. Leighton, an army sutler who had stores at Forts Reno, Phil Kearney and C. F. Smith. Mr. Burnett was at one of these forts on the Bozeman Trail from the time of the establishment of Reno to 1868 when the forts and Bozeman Road were abandoned.

The Hated Fort on the Little Piney

The Powder River country has been called "the Land of the Sioux," when, in reality, it had been known for years as the Land of the Crows (or "Absaraka") embracing the fertile lands along the south side of the Yellowstone River, and the country drained by the Tongue, Rosebud, and Powder Rivers. Not only were the lands rich in food for the Indians, and likewise for their animals, but the streams had, in years past, been the storehouses for the wealth to be obtained from the beaver which had been hunted by the fur men. The Crow Indians had gone through years, first of bitter strife, in order to hold the rich lands, and then, years of bloody combat to regain their ancestral hunting grounds. Always anxious to ally themselves with the white men, against whom they claimed they had never raised their hands except in self-defense, in order to conquer the Sioux and Northern Cheyennes with whom they had combined to hold the Powder River country, the Crows realized that they had not only the red man to fight, but the white man as well. The coming of the soldiers to build forts in their lost territory, made the Crows realize that the last hope was slipping from them to regain the cherished lands between the Big Horn Mountains, the Black Hills, the Yellowstone and North Platte Rivers.

In an interview with Black Horse, a Cheyenne chief, the question was once asked him, when in council with Colonel Carrington:

"Why do the Sioux and Cheyennes claim the land which belonged to the Crows?"

"The Sioux helped us. We stole the hunting grounds of the Crows because they were the best. The white man is along the great waters, and we wanted more room. We fight the Crows because they will not take half and give us peace with the other half."

Those who intended to use the Bozeman Road not only proposed to traverse the land through which it ran, the land in controversy, but were determined to construct forts along its route and distribute soldiers in the fortifications in such proportions that protection would be given to the emigrants on their way from the States to Montana and the gold-fields. To carry out this plan of our government, Colonel Henry B. Carrington was sent into the Powder River country in the early summer of 1866, the year after General Connor's expedition had penetrated into the land of the Sioux as far as Tongue River.

The Indians, after General Connor's unceremonious removal from his command, celebrated their victory by a renewal of the raids on the overland roads and the Bozeman Trail. Red Cloud had gained great ascendency by this time among his warriors for his successful raids, and in his encounters with the emigrants and the soldiers. Peace terms were scorned by this Sioux chief, for he knew the only terms on which peace would be accepted by the red men, and he was confident that the government would not accept these terms, viz: the removal of the troops from north of the Platte River, and prohibiting the white man from going into the Powder River country. Of the great Sioux chiefs, Spotted Tail advocated peace in accordance with the white man's terms, believing that eventually the government with its soldiers would force the red man back from the transcontinental road and the trails going into Montana. Because this warrior preached the doctrine of peace, he lost prestige with his band of warriors and won disfavor with Red Cloud, who was rapidly acquiring fame as a great medicine man.

The people in the East, ever glorifying the red man, and criticising the efforts made by the white man fighting in the Indian country, rejoiced that peace was to be an established fact, for a council had been called of the government officials and the warring chiefs, to be held at Fort Laramie in the early summer of the year in which Colonel Carrington was to go into the country controlled by the Sioux. General Pope and General Dodge, knowing Red Cloud's ability in organization, remained firm in their contention that the red men were not easily to be subdued, and that their hunting grounds were to be effectively guarded. In order to carry the war into this land north of the Platte, General Pope, at the head of the Mountain Division, organized an expedition to go into the contested country and there establish forts—three of them—to be beyond Fort Connor on the Dry Fork of the Powder. The fort which was to take the place of Fort Connor (which was to be dismantled and abandoned) was to be forty miles westward toward the Yellowstone, along the Bozeman Road, the new fort to be called Reno,[76] North of this was to be Fort Ransom on the Big Horn River,[77] and the third fort was to be at the junction of the Big Horn and Yellowstone Rivers. This new route, operated by the government and protected by the soldiers, extended from Bridger's Ferry (near the present Orin Junction, Con-

---

[76] Named for General Jesse L. Reno, a hero of the Civil War, killed at the battle of South Mountain, Md., Sept. 14, 1862.

[77] Subsequently changed to Fort C. F. Smith.

verse County, Wyoming) on the North Platte, to Virginia City, Montana, though no fortifications were built west of the Big Horn River.

From Fort Kearney, Nebraska, on May 19, 1866, Colonel Henry B. Carrington of the U.S. Eighteenth Infantry, took command of this expedition to go into the newly organized district, having with him officers and soldiers from the infantry and cavalry, two surgeons, one physician, and among other guides, that greatest of frontiersmen, Major James Bridger, who was assisted by guide H. Williams, also of wide Indian warfare experience, the route being along the North Platte to Fort McPherson, to Fort Sedgwick west of Julesburg, across the South Platte to where Pumpkin Creek empties into the North Platte; from here over the Oregon Trail to Fort Laramie. In the command were about two thousand troops, but from this number were to be taken thirteen hundred men to relieve the volunteers who were then guarding and protecting the mail roads and the telegraph lines on both sides of the Overland Route and the Oregon Trail, leaving soldiers for the Powder River country amounting to only seven hundred, not all trained for the service that they were about to enter. Most of the men belonged to the infantry, but were to be mounted at Fort Laramie, which was reached by the command on the 13th of June, at which place the Indians had assembled for a great council, which it was hoped would result in an abiding peace between the Indians and the United States government. Several thousand of the red men were at and near the fort, where their chiefs had assembled, to make the final negotiations for the peace treaty. What the government expected, and hoped to obtain by this council, and a treaty, was the right to use the Bozeman Road unmolested, and to establish the military posts along the route which went through the hunting grounds, not only of the Ogallala and Minneconjou Sioux, but the lands of the Northern Cheyennes and Arapahoes and the mountain Crows. Red Cloud and Man-Afraid-of-His-Horses would not join the conference, which was in session for several weeks, though both of these warriors were at Fort Laramie. With disdain and loftiness they kept separate and apart from the proceedings. Before the conclusion of the treaty, these two chiefs, with their followers, withdrew from the locality, refusing to accept the presents from the government commission, which was to give all signing tribes numerous gifts as a partial compensation for the right to invade their country. Red Cloud and Man-Afraid-of-His-Horses took their departure, with the firm determination to resist any steps that might lead to the occupying of their treasured territory, muttering as they went that "in two moons the command would not have a hoof left."

When Red Cloud first saw Colonel Carrington, he drew his blanket closely about him, disdainfully refusing an introduction. Standing Elk, chief of the Brules, asked Colonel Carrington where he was going. Upon being told to the Powder River country, he made this answer: "There is a treaty being made at Laramie with the Sioux that are in the country where you are going. The fighting men of that country have not come to Laramie, and you will have to fight them. They will not give you the road unless you whip them." To all of the chiefs, Colonel Carrington was introduced as "The White Chief who is going to occupy Powder River, the Big Horn country and the Yellowstone," a challenge in itself. In each instance the White Chief was treated with cold disdain and was looked upon with distrust and scorn.

Leaving Fort Laramie on the 16th of June, the commander found that there could be furnished him only a supply of hard bread in poor condition, enough to last four days; no utensils to bake bread in were given him, and only one thousand rounds of ammunition could be obtained, which, added to what he might find at Fort Connor, made a total of sixty thousand rounds, "obviously very inadequate;" this lack of a proper amount of ammunition rendering the troops from Fort Laramie to Connor almost powerless.

To the Powder River country Colonel Carrington took mules and horses, tools for the erection of buildings, machinery for agriculture, a brass band of forty pieces, potatoes and onions for seed, surveyors' instruments, rocking chairs, churns, washing machines, canned fruit, turkeys, chickens, pigs, and cows. About five hundred and sixty of the raw recruits were armed with old-fashioned muzzle-loading Springfield muskets, though the band had Spencer breech-loading carbines. All of the materials for the construction and operation of two sawmills were also carried, as well as axes and saws for the woodcutters and choppers, mowing machines, shingle and brick machines, wagons and carts – blacksmiths, wheelrights, painters, harness makers, carpenters – in fact, the expedition was well outfitted for construction work, though seriously lacking in officers, troops, ammunition, and firearms. Added to all these conditions, the troops now knew for the first time that they were to occupy a region that would be surrounded by Indians. Many absurd rumors were started as to the extreme dangers soon to be encountered, though Colonel Carrington was ready to meet any danger and difficulty, true soldier that he was. "Patience, forbearance and common-sense in dealing with the Sioux and Cheyennes will do much with all who really desire peace, but it is indispensable that ample supplies of ammunition come promptly." Again, on the day of the departure of the command for the north, another plea was made for those supplies which would protect the men of the command: "I find myself greatly in need of officers, but must wait the arrival of new appointments." This condition was typical of all of Colonel Carrington's half year in the Indian country; handicapped at the start for lack of sufficient ammunition and men and proper food; handicapped from day to day; handicapped at the crucial moment when the lives of his entire garrison hung in the balance. The wonder is that he was able to save any of his men, not that he lost a large percent of them in raids, skirmishes and open fights.

No Indians were encountered on the road from Fort Laramie to Fort Connor, except near Horseshoe Station along the Platte, and at Bridger's Ferry, though when arriving at old Fort Connor on June 28th, report came into camp that the sutler's (A. C. Leighton's) stock had been run off by the Indians. After scouting for ninety miles, no trace of the stock could be found, although one pony of a squaw was captured which had strapped to its back bags of sugar, coffee, tobacco, one army stable frock and unfolded goods which had either been given away at the Peace Conference or had been purchased at Fort Laramie. Thus was Colonel Carrington introduced to the hostilities which were to greet him in the Powder River country. Several trains of emigrants were waiting at the fort (Connor) for protection on their further journey to the gold-fields, their understanding being that troops were to be furnished all along the Bozeman Road.

At Fort Connor, which was soon to be called Fort Reno, were found two companies of Michigan volunteers,[78] left there by General Connor to protect the fort built in the fall of 1865, the orders being to now return these soldiers to their command, and from Colonel Carrington's scant seven hundred soldiers there should be left two companies of eighty men each to protect the new fort which was to replace Fort Connor. In place of abandoning this fort, Colonel Carrington concluded it was wise, not only to maintain a fort at this site, but to enlarge its capacity and establish it as one of the three forts on the Bozeman Trail. The original instructions had been to abandon Fort Connor, move down the Powder River and over to the Piney or the Tongue and build a fort there. With the enlargement of Fort Connor the new fort became known as Fort Reno.

The invasion of this country into which the troops were now going was looked upon by Red Cloud with great distrust. The occupying of the Indians' sacred burial grounds and their traditional hunting territory was not viewed with any friendliness, but with intense hostility and distrust toward our government for the violation of previous treaties made with the red men, and the one being consummated at Fort Laramie at this very time. To allow the emigrant to traverse their grounds was an invasion, but to establish forts along the road was a deep insult. The Indians felt that they were being gradually crowded out of their ancestral lands, and nothing, to their minds, made this a greater possibility than the building of the hated forts along the

---

[78] A number had deserted, departing for the more attractive gold-fields of Montana.

trail and the garrisoning of the buildings with soldiers. Red Cloud was now through with all treaties – those of the past, those being made and those that in the future might be made – treaties as quickly broken by the white man as they were made. The only way to retain the lands of their fathers was to annihilate, by overwhelming forces, all of the white men, officers and soldiers who dared trespass on the Sioux territory. The chief declared war againts any and all intruders – they were all invaders and thieves. Forts were a symbol of subjection, of force, of power, hence, war must be centered on them; they must not be erected, but if built, they must speedily be destroyed. The concentrated campaign from this time on must be for the preservation of the Indian lands, by the abolition of the hated military forts. Red Cloud further stated that the treaty being consummated at Fort Laramie was but another evidence of the desire of the white men to rob the Indians of their lands, and thus starve their women and children. So far as he was concerned he preferred to die fighting, rather than by starvation. He believed that he would be successful in the war, which would be a long and bloody one. He and his chiefs would sign no more treaties; that was left to Spotted Tail, Big Mouth, Swift Bear, and Two Strikes.

From the date of the arrival of the command at Fort Connor, June 28, 1866, until the abandonment of the forts, in August, 1868, there was never a day, never an hour, but that the Indians attacked, or would have attacked if not properly watched, or would have raided if they had found an opportune moment, any or all of the three forts. Eternal vigilance was not only the watchword, but the living necessity. Horses were stampeded, emigrant outfits raided – more often for the guns and ammunition than the killing of the people. The soldiers were killed at every opportunity, for they represented the hated forts.

Almost immediately upon leaving Fort Reno, Jim Bridger acting as guide and doing the reconnaissance for the site of the main fort to be built, Colonel Carrington received a message from Chief Black Horse saying: "We wish to know – does the White Chief want peace or war?" As a result of this message Carrington consented to hold a conference with the Indians, which was to be held on the site that was to be selected for the new fort in the region of the Piney River. At this proposed site Bridger had reported there was to be found an abundance of grass, water, and timber, and which, upon the personal examination of Colonel Carrington, was pronounced as a "good post site." On the thirteenth of July the definite location was made; the name of the new fort was to be Fort Philip Kearney,[79] though for some time it was called and known as Fort Carrington. The day before arriving at the newly-selected site, the command came in view of Lake De Smet, having previously crossed Crazy Woman's Fork of the Powder River.

The location of Fort Phil Kearney, as it came to be known (the name of Philip being abbreviated to

---

[79] General acceptance of the spelling of "Kearney," though the general for whom the fort was named spelled his name "Kearny," warrants the nomenclature as used. Authors of recognized authority spell the name with and without the "e." United States documents are as inconsistent. The spelling of the fort with an additional "e" does not seem to be a recent fact, for as early as January, 1867, the government had acquired the habit. In United States Senate *Executive Document 16*, 39th Congress, 2d Session, O. H. Browning, Secretary of the Interior, uses the spelling "Fort Phil Kearney," as did Lewis V. Bogey, Commissioner of Indian Affairs; Special Agent E. B. Chandler, at Fort Laramie, uses "Fort Philip Kearney" as did General U. S. Grant. General Carrington used both ways of spelling. The United States Superintendent of Documents also uses both spellings.

FORT PHIL KEARNEY — "THE HATED FORT ON THE LITTLE PINEY"

Planned and erected by Colonel Henry B. Carrington, in 1866, in what was then Dakota Territory (now Wyoming). Evacuated and abandoned by the United States in 1868, and immediately burned to the ground by the Sioux. In the immediate vicinity of this post more battles and skirmishes with Indians took place than around any other fort on the Western frontier. Sioux Indians skulking on skyline. Sentries stationed at intervals (east of top of flag). Soldiers drilling (in center). Trees are along the banks of Big Piney.

From a sketch drawn by Bugler Antonio Nicoli, Second U. S. Cavalry, at Fort Phil Kearney, in 1867.

"Phil") was on the Little Piney, a fork of Clear Fork of the Powder River. Letters sent from this fort to the U.S. War Department were always headed "Fort Phil Kearney (or Kearny) Dakota, Piney Forks." Hurried preparations were made to have everything as imposing as possible for the coming conference to be held on the 16th of July with the Indians who had sent the message to Colonel Carrington upon his departure from Fort Reno. The grounds were surveyed for the garrison, the parade ground staked out, the tents put into position, the wagon train and artillery parked – everything possible being done to make the camp have the appearance of a strong military fortification. Woodchoppers were sent to the mountains toward the west, to cut timber for the erection of the buildings; one of the saw mills was also immediately set up and put into operation to prepare the material for the buildings. About six miles above the fort, the two Piney streams left the Big Horn Mountains, the headings being about five miles apart. It was between these streams, just before they united, that the new fort had its foundations constructed, though the fort was nearer the Little Piney than the other fork. Placed on a plateau which was gradually sloping from its fourside, six hundred by eight hundred feet, the fort had a commanding view of most of the surrounding country though the view to the northeast was rather restricted; an abundance of grass was to be found around the post. The Little Piney was so near the fort on its southeast side that its waters were easily diverted and carried within the stockade. The timber in the mountains was near enough so that two loads by the same teams might be brought daily to the fort; the hills and slopes all about the fort being commanded by artillery, which had been brought from Fort Reno, not only for this fort on the Piney, but also for the fort on the Big Horn, which was to be called Fort C. F. Smith.

A signal hill was selected on which was kept a day picket, which commanded a view of the Bozeman Trail for eleven miles to the northeast. A coal mine was at once opened two miles south from the post, furnishing an unlimited amount of fuel for the forges. The selected site was in the very heart of the hunting grounds of the Indians—bear, buffalo, elk, deer, antelope, rabbits, and sagehens abounded in great numbers. In the Big Horn Mountains, with glorious Cloud Peak to the west, were pine, hemlock, ash, balsam, boxelder, fir, willows, spruce, and cottonwood trees, while wild plums, cherries, currants, strawberries, gooseberries, raspberries, and grapes grew in profusion; the grapes being "very grateful to the taste and an excellent antiscorbutic." Bright colored flowers cheered the women's hearts, for there were to be found wild tulips, larkspur, sweet peas, convoloulus; added to which were Indian potatoes and wild onions.

Colonel Carrington's report, sent to the government, stated that the country was susceptible of the highest development; that there was no land on the Platte that would rival the bottom-lands of the streams which were fed by the snows of the Big Horn Mountains. "The angle of the Pineys will make a fine government farm, and is readily irrigated." The little valley was the semi-neutral ground of the Snakes, Crows, Cheyennes, Sioux, and Arapahoes. Not that all had an equal right to this paradise, but to all it was a favorite field. It was to this place that the Indians were to come and ask the White Chief what were his intentions in regard to their chosen hunting land.

With the coming of the 16th came the Indians flying a white flag. Much had been done to impress the red men with the importance and gravity of this meeting. The national flag was displayed, epaulettes and dress hats were taken from trunks, polished and carefully brushed; the band played, and everything possible was done to make the occasion one of state and great dignity. But the Indians were not to be outdone. The very tall Cheyenne warriors wore their richly embroidered and beaded moccasins and fancy breech-cloths – one even appearing with a large bright colored umbrella over his head, which, as his pony briskly galloped along, offered "a grotesque and ludicrous appearance," rather than one that should have been warlike and fearful to the white men. Some wore large silver medals, with medallion heads of Jefferson, Madison, and Jackson – medals that had been given to their fathers when they had visited Washington, or were obtained as trophies of battle or of trade. Among the chiefs at the conference were Black Horse, Pretty Bear, Dull Knife, Red Arm, Little Moon, Man-that-Stands-on-the-Ground, Wolf-That-Lies-Down, Rabbit-That-Jumps, Bob Tail, Dead White Leg, and The Brave Soldier, representing in all, one hundred and sixty-seven lodges of the Cheyennes.

The chief result of the conference was that if Colonel Carrington would go back to Fort Reno and make no further attempt to enter and possess the Powder River country, he and his men might stay there unmolested, provided that even in that territory he would build no more despised forts. Without promise from the commander, the Indians took their departure. Black Horse, upon his return to his tribe from this council, was asked by a party of Sioux what the white man had said to him, and if the "White Chief" was going back toward the North Platte River. He told the Sioux, "he was not, but was going on." Black Horse further said that the White Chief gave them all they could eat, and that the Sioux and Arapahoes and all of the Indians in Tongue River valley might obtain from the Great Father at Fort Laramie all the presents they wanted; and that they could get them when they went down there and signed the treaty, which was all ready for them to sign. "The Sioux then unslung their bows and whipped Black Horse and the other Cheyenne chiefs over their backs and faces, saying 'Coo!' (coward), which, by the Indians, is deemed a matter of prowess, and a feat that gives them credit, counting their 'coos' in a fight almost as proudly as they do scalps." Black Horse's response was: "Let us take the white man's hand and what he gives us, rather than fight him longer and lose all." But Red Cloud, realizing that this would be to barter all of the Indians' rights away, answered: "White man lies and steals. My lodges were many, but now they are few. The white man wants all. The white man must fight, and the Indian will die where his fathers died." [80]

On July 30th Colonel Carrington telegraphed to the War Department (the message going by couriers to

---

[80] Carrington (H. B.) *Some Phases of the Indian Question*, p. 13: "I watched the departing Cheyennes led by old White Horse, with hair as white as snow, Black Bear, Bull Knife, Big Wolf, and the Man-that Strikes-Hard. They started for the Wind River Mountains. Their lodge poles, laden with all of their effects, dragged behind the ponies in slow procession. The squaws bent under the weight of dried game, skins, arrow-wood, and the supplies furnished them from the post. Children were packed with all they could carry. The old men rode, or slowly trudged along the middle of the train, compelled to keep up or to be abandoned. They were going to seek new hunting grounds; leaving an Indian paradise, before the shadow of the advancing white man had fallen upon their trail. They were *passing away*."

Fort Laramie and from there sent by wire): "The Sioux on Tongue River, a few miles distant, threatened (by Cheyenne messenger) to drive out the troops, but will not dare make the venture. Eight Cheyenne chiefs, with six hundred of their tribe, met me in council and promised peace. It is yet a question I can only solve by a visit in force to their village, whether they have public stock and have kept faith. They are, however, at war with the Sioux. I submit that I should have either Indian auxiliaries or additional companies from my own regiment. It is a critical period with the road, and many outrages will injure it. Still, if emigrants are properly armed and kept together, having due warning, I have confidence in the route." [81]

The travel was heavy over the Bozeman Road. The emigrants, being assured at Fort Laramie of the perfect safety over the road, often failed to supply themselves with guns and ammunition, although all other information pointed toward a general raid over the entire road. The emigrants were being scalped and mutilated, and what few arms they possessed were taken from them to assist in the raids. These supplies for fighting, which were stolen from the emigrants, were added to by purchases from the agencies, all to be accumulated for the day when there would be a concerted attack from the North Platte to the Yellowstone Rivers.

During the early days of August, Colonel N. C. Kinney of the Eighteenth Infantry, with two companies of soldiers, Jim Bridger acting as guide, was sent to the Big Horn River to establish Fort C. F. Smith.[82] It was necessary to garrison Fort Smith with two com-

---

[81] United States Senate *Executive Document*, 1887, vol. i, ex doc. No. 33.

[82] Named for General Charles Ferguson Smith, who received three brevets for distinguished services during the Mexican war. General Smith died April 25, 1862.

panies, because a large force of miners from Virginia City (Montana), who had established themselves in the mountains near the fort, were ready to ally themselves with the hostile Indians. Further, the fort was near the western limits of the best hunting grounds. The fort thus assured the Indians that the garrisoning of the Big Horn Valley was no temporary expedition, but a substantial, permanent occupation.

It is also true that this fort suffered less from Indian depredations than Reno and Phil Kearney because many of the Indians in its vicinity were the friendly Crows, and the fort was west of the main hunting grounds of the Arapahoes, Cheyenne, and Sioux. It was the last building on the trail until Bozeman City was reached. The building of the fort was timely, as the Indians had robbed an emigrant train of one hundred mules just before the soldiers came to the selected site. Even after the fort was erected, reports were frequently made of Indians stealing stock. That Colonel Carrington fully realized his dangers, and that more men were needed to adequately protect the forts now constructed, as well as the Bozeman Road, may be seen from the following messages:

"FORT PHILIP KEARNEY, D.T., PINEY FORKS,
July 30, 1866

"My eight companies of 80 effective men each, with quarters to build, and 560 of them new recruits from general depot (although largely from old volunteers) do not give me a fixed adequate command for the present emergency. My own supply trains are to be guarded, trains are to be escorted, a courier line is to be maintained. Whatever my own force, I cannot settle down and say I have not the men, but I must do all of this, however arduous. The work is my mission here and I must meet it. But when with this dispatch I send two officers from the ten on recruiting service (four being already on the same service); when two officers for ten days alternate as officer of the day, and in turn command detachments; when I am my own engineer, draughtsman, and visit my pickets and guards nightly, with scarcely a day or a night without attempts to steal stock or surprise pickets, you will see that much is being done, while I ought to have all my officers and some cavalry or Indian auxiliaries at each post. . . I need not say I want men, as the general commanding has had experience in the same warfare."

Then came the word to headquarters that if the supply of soldiers was insufficient to protect the entire route, the abandonment of Fort C. F. Smith might be a wise movement. To which proposition Colonel Carrington made reply:

"The protection of emigrants simply to Fort Phil Kearney, which indeed took the heart of the Indian hunting grounds, could furnish no protection to travel through the valley of the Tongue River and westward to Virginia City. To refuse to advance to Big Horn River was the surrender of the purpose of my entire movement. It subjected me to compliance with the very demands the Sioux had made, and its importance is fully seen by my official reports." August 29th – "I think Yellowstone post should be established this fall. The Big Horn post is successfully established. I need cavalry, but they will be here very soon. (They never came). If I had five more companies of infantry it would be well to establish a subpost at Reno at South Fork of the Cheyenne, half-way to the ferry, with one company; next, to divide a company between Crazy Woman's Fork and Dry Fork of the Cheyenne, and to place one company on the mouth of Goose Creek on Tongue River and two at Yellowstone." Again, on November 15th, additional information was sent East: "There is no doubt of this bitter hatred of our every movement, but they (the Indians) do not understand the nature of our resources. For example: Red Cloud informed the Crows that by cutting off communications when bad weather set in, he would starve us out this winter. He does not comprehend the idea of a year's supplies, nor that we are now prepared to not only pass the winter, but next spring and summer, even if he takes the offensive. On the whole, the condition of affairs is more favorable than I expected would be the case when I left Laramie. I have not the slightest confidence in the result of the proposed treaty, and so wrote you. And in fact, during the whole result of the negotiations, there was a mere temporary suspension of hostile acts, if it even amounted to that. I look for this month to determine their purpose, and hope yet to be able to strike a blow which they will feel more than the last, and not risk a single post on the line in the attempt. In no case will any rash venture be made, or any that will not meet the favor of the general commanding. What was intended and understood; his views and those of General Sherman, and the purpose I held on the march, will be realized, and the increase of troops, which will undoubtedly be furnished, will ensure a sane spring emigration and open a fine country, as well as a short route to the far West."

After the latter part of August the depredations and raids became more frequent and by larger parties. On the 13th of September a band of Sioux attacked a herd of mules and horses belonging to Fort Phil Kearney. One of the men serving as a picket was shot in the hip with an arrow, and another received a ball in the side. Captain Ten Eyck and Lieutenants Brown and Bisbee tried to overtake the Indians, but after riding for fifteen miles and coming within half a mile of the fleeing savages, gave up the chase, the Indians retreating into buttes where horses could not travel, and where the stock could not be recovered. On the following day, one of the haying force, riding ahead of the train at a distance of about three hundred yards, was cut off and killed by a band of twenty Indians. On the 17th, Ridgeway Glover, artist and correspondent for Frank Leslie's Illustrated Weekly, was killed while taking a walk a few minutes' distance from the fort. He was found naked, scalped and with his back cleft by a tomahawk. That same day a band of Sioux attacked the pickets stationed between the Pineys, but were driven off by the firing from the twelve-pound field howitzer. Of this gun the Indians had great fear, calling it "the gun that shoots twice." The same day a mining party of forty men, belonging to Bailey's mining camp, came to the fort on their way from Virginia City, reporting the loss of two of their men who were scalped near Tongue River. The indications were that there had been a hard fight and that many of the Indians had been killed in the skirmish while the two miners fought from behind their dead horses. To add to these and other disasters, word came from Fort C. F. Smith on the 23rd that one of the contractors (Grull) had been attacked, he and two of his men being killed. All of the depredations were not confined to Fort Phil Kearney, for at Fort Reno horses and cattle were driven off every few days. One of the soldiers was killed on Dry Fork of the Cheyenne, and two citizens were wounded.

Colonel Carrington, faithfully reporting conditions in the East, sent these as his conclusions: "While more troops are needed, I can say (and I am in the hostile district) that most of the newspaper reports are gross exaggerations. I gather and furnish you, as requested, all the bad news, neither coloring nor disguising facts." The Indians were well armed with rifles and revolvers; Red Cloud was commanding the attacking parties; there were in the bands those who dressed and appeared like white men, talking and swearing in English; the Indians were determined to burn the country, cutting off all the supplies, and would hamper every movement of travel, even to the trains going for timber. Jim Bridger and Jim Beckwourth were sent frequently to Fort C. F. Smith on scouting parties and to visit the Crows in their villages. Beckwourth was a mulatto who had married a Crow woman, and was on friendly relations with that tribe, living more or less with the Crows. While on one of these expeditions to the Crows, Beckwourth was taken sick and died, Colonel Carrington being thus unable to obtain the result of Beckwourth's council with the Indians. In September the soldiers at Fort C. F. Smith had only ten rounds of ammunition to the man. The Springfield rifles used by the entire force under Colonel Carrington's command, were useless to men on horseback. The arms for which he requisitioned in the early summer of 1866, reached Fort Phil Kearney in January, 1867, just in time to be turned over to his successor! Is there any wonder that the following was the tale of injustice? "During this time, by order from department headquarters, I was directed to keep up a weekly mail, traveling at a rate of not less than fifty miles per day. As has already appeared, more than half of the horses properly attached to the four companies at Fort Phil Kearney (thirty-three in one day) have been stolen by the Indians. Snow fell, even in September, and nineteen days were occupied in one trip to Fort Laramie and back, the party stopping but one day at that post. My recommendation to authorize the establishment of sub-posts as relay stations was never responded to. I, however, sent three mails in October, and on the return of the last, had but twenty-eight horses reported serviceable, and these hardly fit for duty. The commanding general called my attention to the fact that I was disregarding the order to keep up the weekly mail."

The requirements to keep up a mail service was a serious matter, owing to lack of men, horses and ammunition, all of which had to be used at the three forts, where there were scarcely enough horses to keep up the picket duty. Facts showed that the mail had been sent regularly every week to Fort Laramie, even though under the most adverse circumstances. Added to these difficulties, there had to be kept open communication with the most distant fort to the north, Fort C. F. Smith. General Hazen had come to the Powder River country on a tour of inspection, and men and horses had to be furnished him – twenty-six men and that many mounts. Escorts were constantly being demanded for the emigrants. During this period one contract train, with supplies for Fort C. F. Smith, also asked for men, the train consisting of thirty-one wagons and having but five firearms in the entire party! The last escort sent to Fort Laramie to carry the mail required sixty members of the cavalry, taking twelve days, due to the four feet of snow, bad roads and severe weather; for though the wind blew the snow from the level ground, the ravines, valleys and gulches over which the men had to travel were packed with snow. Then word came that Major Bridger and the other guides, who all knew so well the country in which the soldiers were operating, must be dismissed, "in order to reduce expenses," but an earnest remonstrance from Colonel Carrington, permitted him to retain these valuable men. Not only, now that winter had come, were the Springfield rifles needed to replace broken and worn-out arms, but mittens were needed for the men, and another plea was made for more officers, the cavalry having none, and there being but six officers for six companies, including staff.

It has been estimated that during the first six months of the occupation of the command at the three forts along the Bozeman Road, one hundred and fifty-four citizens and soldiers were killed by the Indians, two score were wounded, and about seven hundred head of horses, cattle and mules were captured; that every train going over the road was attacked, or hostile demonstrations were made, with a record of the Indians appearing before Fort Phil Kearney fifty-one times in hostile array. Woodchoppers were attacked on their way to and from the mountains for timber for the completion of the fort, though a heavy guard was always detailed for their protection. All of the men worked faithfully and diligently to complete the fort and stockade before winter should come, which, with its heavy snows, would prevent the wood trains from going to the mountains for timber. Every day heard the hum of the sawmill, the pounding of hammers, and the rip of the saws, until, when the 28th day of October came, the fort was completed and ready for the raising of the flag-staff.

When General W. B. Hazen visited Fort Phil Kearney in the fall of 1866, he pronounced the structure to be "the best he had ever seen, excepting one in British America, built by the Hudson Bay Company." The following is a detailed description of the stockade, given by those who were at the fort at the time: The fort proper was six hundred by eight hundred feet, located on a natural plateau, giving a gradual slope on both front and back, falling off nearly sixty feet in a few rods, thus affording a natural glacis, and giving to the position a positive strength, independent of other defenses. A rectangle, two hundred by six hundred feet was occupied by warehouses, cavalry stables, laundress quarters and non-commissioned staff. Around the parade ground were the officers' and men's quarters,

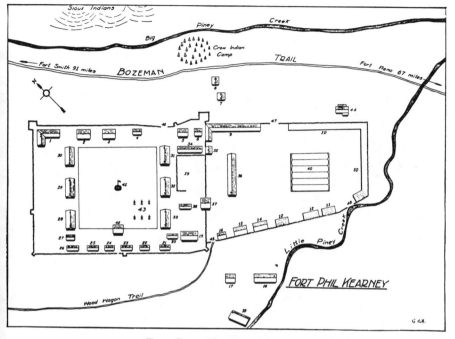

FORT PHIL KEARNEY, IN 1867

Redrawn from an original drawing by Samuel Gibson

(1) Hospital; (2) Sutler's store; (3) Adjutant's office; (4) Guard house; (5, 6) Quartermaster's department; (7) John Phillips' house; (8) Jim Wheatley's house; (9) Teamsters' quarters; (10) Stables; (11-16) Cavalry and quartermaster's stables; (17) Engineer's house (presumably sawmill engineer); (18) Sawmills; (19) Theater; (20) Major Powell's quarters; (21-26) Officers' quarters; (27) Dr. Horton's quarters; (28) Company A; (29) Company H; (30) Company B; (31) Company C, Twenty-seventh Infantry; (32) Company K, Twenty-seventh Infantry; (33) Company C, Second Cavalry; (34) Laundry; (35) Wagon master's house; (36) Civilian employes; (37) Quartermaster's quarters; (38) Commissary; (39) Cavalry yard; (40) Haystacks; (41) Flagstaff and magazine; (42) Colonel Carrington's quarters; (43) Battery; (44) Mr. and Mrs. Washington's cabin; (45) Mill gate (through this gate Captain Fetterman and his men went to their death, Dec. 21, 1866); (46) Main gate and sentinel's box at right; (47) Gate; (48) Water gate; through which John Phillips, unobserved, rode into the night to notify civilization of the Fetterman disaster.

Near Building 24 was a small gate; just east was a sentry box; there was another small gate on the west wall opposite Company A's quarters with a sentry box just north. At 46 on the north side were the double gates south of the Bozeman Road, to the east of which was another sentry box. On the northeast corner of the main stockade, and the northwest corner, were substantial blockhouses, while on the southwest and southeast there were sentry boxes. Blockhouses and sentry boxes were occupied night and day.

offices, guard house, sutler's and band buildings. The stockade was made of heavy pine logs, eleven feet long, hewn to a touching surface of four inches, so as to join closely, being pointed and loop-holed and firmly imbedded in the ground three feet. Block-houses were at two diagonal corners, and massive gates of plank, with small wickers, all with substantial locks, were on the three fronts, and on the fourth, or south front, back of the officer's quarters, was a small gate for use when suddenly beseiged. The three warehouses, the hospital and the quarters for the four companies were eighty-four feet long and twenty-four feet wide, with ceilings ten feet high. All of the windows. in the soldiers' buildings were made with three sashes. In the center of the parade ground was an octagonal band platform, in the center of which was erected a flagpole. Diverging from the band-stand were walks dividing the parade ground into four squares; in one of these squares was located the powder magazine. East of the fort, and adjoining it, was the corral or quartermaster's quarters, with an area equal to the fort. This was surrounded by a rough cottonwood stockade, containing buildings for mules, hay and wood yards, hay scales, quarters for the teamsters and mechanics, the blacksmith, wagonmakers, carpenters, saddlers and gun repair shop. From this corral the woodchoppers left by a gate towards the mountains. Another gate was toward the Powder River and the third gate was toward the Piney, which "made a convenient bend perfectly protected by the re-entering angle of the stockade just at this point." Two sawmills were just above the mill gate and only a few rods distant. In all, the entire stockade or enclosure, embraced a circuit of two thousand eight hundred feet. The altitude of the post was five thousand seven hundred and ninety feet, which insured excellent health for the garrison.

The last day of October was a holiday, when all of the garrison took part in the celebration of the completion of the fort and the raising of the flagpole, which had been fashioned by William Daley[83] and Principal Musician Barnes, upon which floated that day our national flag, the emblem being twenty-four by thirty-six feet in size. It was the first garrison flag raised in the Powder River country, and also in the country between the Platte and Yellowstone Rivers. Colonel Carrington made an address, speaking with pardonable pride of the work accomplished and the heroic efforts of all of the men. Part of his address is as follows:

Three and one-half months ago stakes were driven to define the now completed outline of Fort Philip Kearney. Aggressive Indians threatened to exterminate the command. Our advent cost us blood! Private Livenberger of Company F was the first victim, July 7th, 1866. Lieutenant Daniels, Private Callery of G Company, Gilchrist and Johnson of E Company, Fitzpatrick and Hacket of D Company, Patrick Smith of H Company, and Oberly and Hauser have also, in the order named, given their lives to vindicate our pledge to never yield one foot of advance, but to guarantee a safe passage for all who seek a home in the lands beyond.

Fifteen weeks have passed, varied by many skirmishes and both night and day alarm, but that pledge holds good. In every work done, your arms have been at hand. In the pine tracts or in the hay fields, on picket or general guard duty, no one has failed to find a constant exposure to some hostile shaft and to feel that a cunning adversary was watching every chance to harrass and kill.

And yet that pledge holds good. Stockade and blockhouse, embrasure and loop-hole, shell and bullet, have warned off danger, so that women and children now notice the savage

---

[83] Now (1920) residing at Rawlins, Wyoming.

when he appears, only to look to you for fresh occasion for you
to punish him, and with righteous anger to avenge the dead.

. . . The steam whistle and the rattle of the mower
have followed steps in this western march of empire. You have
built a central post that will stand comparison with any for
security, completeness and adaptation to the ends in view, wherever the other may be located or however long in erection.

. . . Coincident with your march to this point was the
occupation of Fort Reno; first by Company B, afterwards reinforced by Company F of this batallion, and the advance of
Companies D and G to Fort C. F. Smith, nearly one hundred
miles further west. All of these, like yourselves, having a share
in the labor, the exposure and the conflicts that throughout the
whole length of the line attended its occupation, have sustained
the past good record of the Eighteenth Infantry, and thus have
vindicated your pledge.

When one realizes the dangers and the constant
lurking of the Indians in every direction, and in every
place large enough to hide, it is beyond understanding
how women were ever permitted to make the journey
to the Powder River country and to go into exile in
the land of these hostile Indians. Yet, when the command was at Fort Kearney (Nebraska) General Sherman "personally advised the ladies to accompany the
expedition, as very attractive in its objects and wholly
peaceful!" Alas, there was no romance on the expedition! Tragedy was written on every mile of the
road and in every day of Fort Phil Kearney's existence.
Hiding in ravines, secreted in depressions, concealed
behind trees in the heavy timber in the mountains to
the west of the fort, prowling around partially-con-
structed buildings, killing both the guarded and un-
guarded soldier, scalping the more venturesome civilian and slaughtering the careless emigrant, were the
red man's daily programs, making difficult and dangerous the protection of the men in occupations necessary

for the construction of fortifications, not to mention the
lives of the women and children, who were hard to
teach of the dangers for those who dared to go beyond
the stockade. So regular were these onslaughts that
it seemed important enough on one day for Colonel
Carrington to report to headquarters: "For two days
no Indians have appeared."

On the part of the Indians there was a general concentration of the allied tribes; more firearms were collected, replacing to a degree the bow and arrow; with
a strategic chief who was learning to follow up a victory, an art unknown to the red men. The year of
1866 solved many problems as to the strength and
weakness in both of the contending forces, for the emigrants were, on their part, required to be better armed
and to protect themselves behind corrals made of their
horses and wagons, while those who were in the forts
were given strict orders as to their conduct, and greater
protection given to the wood trains and the choppers
in the mountains. The timber men always had their
armed teamsters, their armed choppers and their armed
guards, the choppers in the woods having from sixteen to thirty soldiers or armed men, the special guard
containing about that number also. These, with the
drivers of the timber wagons, gave a resisting force of
seventy to one hundred armed men. Up to this time the
Indians had never made an attack on the fort, or the
trains, or teams into the mountains in large forces, their
tactics being to pick off a few more daring people who
left the shelter of the fort without adequate protection,
believing that in this way the number of the whites
would be gradually reduced for the day when there
would be a concentrated attack on all three forts and
every mile along the Bozeman Road. As the horses

and mules grew less in numbers by theft and by death, the mounted escorts could not always accompany the wood wagons to the pinery for timber. The wood trains were then sent out to the mountains on two roads, running parallel to each other, with an intervening space of fifty or one hundred yards, so arranged that when an alarm of "Indians!" came, the front wagons turned in to meet the other wagons; those on the flanks were hurried up, with the mules covered by the next wagon in advance; then the last wagon of each train obliqued in to fill the fourth or rear side of the square. "It was a singular commentary on the recklessness of travelers, their ignorance of the feelings of the Indians, their want of correct advice at Laramie and the wisdom of the Indians themselves, that, of all the outrages committed on trains in 1866, there was not a single consistent attack upon a good corral; neither was there loss of life when proper rules were regulated."

At the fort the gates gradually became more securely fastened, the keys being handled only by specially designated officers; the waste of ammunition for needless hunting was forbidden; the number of pickets was increased; no one was allowed to leave the fort after dusk, and at no time might soldiers or civilians leave the fort without orders, and, as a consequence sacrifice their lives. With all these precautions, however, there were many violations of the orders. Women would leave the fort unescorted, for a gallop, to relieve the monotony of life within the stockade, but after two narrow escapes, one on the Big Piney and another beyond Pilot Hill, they realized the risk they were incurring and abandoned this form of unescorted amusement. To relieve the tension incident to the close quarters of a stockade, the women amused themselves with cooking, dancing and the outdoor game of croquet, for the mowing machines had made a short turf suitable for this recreation. There were but few women servants in the command, although Mrs. Carrington had brought a colored maid with her. The lack of servants necessitated the general work of the fort to be performed by the wives of the officers, the work all being done with good cheer, as was the work of the men, in whatever the duties seemed to demand.

There were five wives of officers at the fort, viz: Mrs. Carrington, Mrs. Grummond, Mrs. Bisbee, Mrs. Horton and Mrs. Wands, the latter being always ready for adventure, and had twice been nearly captured by the Indians. There were also a number of children at Fort Phil Kearney. It is not known that there were women at the other two forts, although the fact that there was at each post a "laundress building" might, though not necessarily, indicate that some of the privates had taken their wives into the wilderness. Of the children at Fort Phil Kearney, one of them was James B. ("Jimmie") Carrington,[84] his brother Harry and Bobbie Wands. Captain Ten Eyck had a colored butler who made company for Mrs. Carrington's maid. F. M. Fessenden, whose experiences are detailed in a separate chapter, and who was a member of the Eighteenth Infantry Band, being promoted the last six months of his service to Principal Musician, with the rank of sergeant, was also accompanied by his wife and baby daughter, who remained at Fort Phil Kearney with Mr. Fessenden until April 9, 1867. Just outside the stockade there was a cabin occupied by a civilian named Washington and his wife, who, strange as it may seem, were never seriously molested by the

[84] Now (1920) on the editorial staff of Scribner's Magazine, N. Y.

Indians. True the red men would surround the cabin, but the couple were such good shots that after a few of the Indians were killed, the cabin was not further molested.

Two cows had been brought from Nebraska, but they were driven off by the Indians; wolves stole the turkeys and the climate claimed the chickens, thus depriving the women of three sources of civilized supplies. The provisions were mostly canned goods, though a few potatoes were obtained from Bozeman and sent down by Captain Kinney from Fort C. F. Smith, who also at one time sent down "half a cabbage and eleven onions," which must have been an unusual treat, to receive special mention in Mrs. Carrington's diary.

To each at the forts Jim Bridger was a "sterling friend," having a headful of maps, trails and ideas, "all of great value to an expedition which now was in a country where, with the single exception of Fort Reno, there was not a resident white man or woman between Bridger's ferry, Dakota Territory, and Bozeman, Montana."

On December 3, 1866, President Johnson addressed Congress, in his message, saying: "Treaties have been concluded with the Indians, who have unconditionally submitted to our authority and manifested an earnest desire for a renewal of friendly relations." The incorrectness of this statement and the false conclusions thus derived were made manifest in the "Fetterman Disaster," for this harrowing drama of the plains was now ready for enactment. The players in a life and death struggle had unconsciously been assigned their parts. December 21, 1866, was the eventful date when the curtain rose. The Indians scored the first victory. The soldiers, dazed, outnumbered and outgeneraled, counted the cost, one division being completely annihilated; with the red men defiantly jeering and tauntingly challenging for renewed combat.

The Fetterman Disaster

The days of December 1866 were tragic ones for the forts on the Bozeman Road, particularly the one on the Little Piney. Some of the younger officers at Fort Phil Kearney became restless, even to the point of secretly disobeying orders in regard to the conservative and cautious methods of Colonel Carrington in dealing with the Indians. Fretting and chafing over the impediments thrown in their way for sudden glory, they determined to play with danger to achieve their ambitions. The commander of the forts well knew that his small army at any one of the forts, or, as a matter of fact, the combined forces of the three forts, was absolutely inadequate, even at its full quota, to meet the Indians in hostile array. The tactics of guarding with the utmost precaution each man, or small body of men, leaving the fort, had proved to be reasonably successful. A realization of the precarious condition of the fort and men, especially the women and children, if some tragedy of surprise or successful storming of the garrison should take place, forced Colonel Carrington to move with the utmost prudence, avoiding any rash or spectacular operations. This method of warfare was distasteful to some of the younger officers, who, having had no special training or experience with Indians or in Indian warfare, with nerves raw from restraint, became determined to show the military world exactly how, in one decisive battle, the Indians, no matter how large their number, could be annihilated.

It must, in justice to all concerned, be admitted that the officers and men, and strange to state, even the women of the fort, were anxious to have something done that would be brilliant and explosive in the way of punishing the Indians for some of the outrages perpetrated during the six months of isolation in the Powder River country. Colonel Carrington did not see his way clear to immediately put into operation the aggressive policy advocated by General Phillip St. George Cooke, the department commander at Omaha, who believed, and so expressed himself, that Indian warfare in the Powder River country could be successfully ended once and for all by engaging in open battle with the Indians during the winter. Some of the officers at Fort Phil Kearney being thoroughly in accord with Cooke's scheme of Indian combat, questioned, and quite openly criticised the methods then being used to subdue the warriors, who were fighting for their treasured hunting grounds.

General Cooke had advised a short winter campaign, because he believed that three hundred infantry in winter, even though experiencing great hardships, could do more in severely cold weather than three thousand cavalry in summer. Though fully realizing the dangers this campaign would incur to his small detachment, Colonel Carrington was determined to put into operation this method of surprise and extermination as soon as his reinforcements arrived, long since asked for and promised, but not yet having reached their destination, knowing that the test would involve a risk to the safety of the post, for he well knew and so reported, that to destroy the villages of

Red Cloud, involved great danger from this successful fighting chief and his warriors, "his knifing squaws and shooting papooses."

In contrast with Cooke's methods of Indian warfare were those of Carrington, "that in Indian warfare there must be perfect coolness, steadiness and judgment. . . . They cannot be whipped or punished by some little dashes after a handful, nor by mere resistance of offensive movements. They must be subjected and made to respect the whites."

The contention for a conservative campaign, and also for an excessively agressive one made conditions at the fort intense. Civilization, meaning the East where the actual hectic conditions surrounding the fort were not known, insisted that any method that did not instantly subdue the Indians was all wrong; while Carrington knew he had an insufficient command to attempt anything spectacular. When an officer was detailed to Phil Kearney he usually insisted upon going out single-handed to chase the Indian, regardless of the repeated orders against this dangerous procedure. After the skirmish of December 6, 1866, Captain William J. Fetterman confessed that he had learned a lesson and "that Indian warfare had become a hand to hand fight requiring the utmost caution."

On the morning of December 6th, danger signals had been sent from Pilot Hill that the wood train had been surrounded and relief was needed. When this signal for immediate help was sent down from the hill, the Indians appeared in great numbers upon the Lodge Trail Ridge to watch the movements of the garrison, some of the Indians having field glasses while others were signaling with mirrors. Captain Fetterman, with mounted infantry, was sent to the scene of conflict, accompanied by Lieutenant H. S. Bingham with cavalry to assist. The instructions being to drive the Indians back over the Lodge Trail Ridge while General Carrington and Lieutenant George W. Grummond with thirty mounted men were to cross the Big Piney to intercept the Indians driven by Fetterman, thus preventing any chance of retreat by the red men. While in the midst of a fight with three hundred Indians Fetterman suddenly found himself without the help of Bingham who had mysteriously disappeared taking fifteen of his cavalry with him. Why he had departed at this period no one has ever known. Colonel Carrington pushing forward to reinforce Fetterman came upon the small detachment of cavalry, dismounted, waiting for a commander and instructions. All information that could be obtained was that Bingham with Sergeant C. R. Bowers and a few men had struck out toward the mountain, followed by Lieutenant George W. Grummond, and they all had suddenly disappeared from view. For what purpose the unannounced departure had been made there was no opinion. Doubtless the dashing spirit of the young officer (Bingham) seized him and he rode to his death, fearlessly, believing that his great adventure was now to be realized.

A young bugler also gave the information that Lieutenant Bingham had disappeared around a hill and nothing more had been seen of him. To General Carrington this all seemed impossible as Bingham's place was with Fetterman, but a recall failed to bring any response. Following the indicated direction, which the missing man had taken, Carrington finally heard some one calling "for God's sake come down quick!" With a dash forward, it was not long before Grummond and three soldiers were found as they were about to be killed with spears by seven Indians. Rescuing this small band, an immediate search was made for Captain Bingham and any escort he might have had. After an hour's exploring, the body of the lieutenant was found, as well as the mortally wounded sergeant whose skull had been cleft by a tomahawk. In close range to Sergeant Bowers were the bodies of three Indians who had been shot by him with his revolver. Private Donovan also had been killed in the skirmish. An ambulance was hurried from the fort to the place of disaster, but too late for Bowers died before its arrival.

In making his report, Colonel Carrington wrote:

Reference is had to Captain Fetterman's report also. He knew but little of the country, but carried out his instructions promptly. Captain Brown, who accidentally accompanied him, knew the ground, and the result would have been a good fight if he had retained Lieutenant Bingham's command. By hard riding I reached the point I hoped to attain, the Indians fleeing before me; but by the decease of Lieutenant Bingham, all clue is lost to his leaving his commanding officer, or his object. If he left to join my party he neglected to report to me. His sergeant says his horse ran away with him, and that the lieutenant told him he could not hold him. My regimental quartermaster, Lieutenant A. H. Wands, by mistake, joined the wrong party, supposing I took the road to the woods, but did good service. Captain Brown, always quick after an Indian skirmish, and whose operations September 25, 1866, deserve public mention, went as volunteer, and greatly contributed to the success of Captain Fetterman's movements. Much was done. The loss of Lieutenant Bingham makes all seem loss, but the winter campaign is fairly open and will be met. I do, however, most earnestly ask for more men. . . If Captain Burrows goes before the retiring board and Captain Kinney's resignation is accepted, the upper post will suffer also. This is all wrong. There is much at stake. I will take my full share, but two officers to a company is small allowance enough, with mercury at zero and active operations at hand.

"And thus, at last, but not the last, after all the random skirmishes and frequent pursuits of stock stealing parties, there had been a pitched battle to increase and intensify the Commandant's assurance, backed up by guide Bridger, that the enemy was increasing in force and watchful of every exposure or recklessness of parties leaving the fort, for whatever purpose, to destroy ultimately. Out-of-door life in that climate was conducive to health, and sickness, other than scurvy, was rare, so a cemetery became necessary only for graves caused by violence." [85]

From this time on, until the great disaster of the 21st of December, Indians appeared daily about the wood party or within sight of the fort. The picket on Pilot Hill reported on December 19th that a wood train had been corraled and was threatened by a large party of dancing Indians. Relief was at once sent from the fort under the command of Brevet Major James W. Powell, who drove the warriors over toward Lodge Trail Ridge. Explicit instructions were given not to cross the ridge, but to return with the relieved wood train. Major Powell afterward reported having seen Indians in great numbers and that "if he had crossed the ridge he never would have come back to his command." The next day Colonel Carrington went to the woods to the west to ascertain the force of the operating Indians and to "test their animus." At the same time he wished to personally supervise the construction of a bridge across Piney Creek to facilitate the hauling of timber and lumber on the wagon road. No Indians were seen on this trip, and no fresh trails were seen in the snow which had fallen the night before. On the following day, the 21st, Colonel Carrington, anticipat-

---

[85] Carrington (F. C.) *Army Life on the Plains*, p. 135.

ing that the Indians might have seen him at his construction work, gave the wood train an additional guard, which, with the soldier-axmen and armed teamsters made a formidable party of eighty men.

Captain and Brevet Lieutenant Colonel William J. Fetterman arrived at Fort Phil Kearney in November, 1866. It did not take him long to win his way into the hearts of the people of the garrison, for he possessed unusual social and professional characteristics, and soon became a general favorite. He became restive and impatient because the Indians were not summarily punished for the depredations they had committed, having a profound contempt for the warriors of Red Cloud, underestimating their strength in battle, and never having had any previous experience in fighting the red men. Captain Frederick H. Brown joined his company at Phil Kearney late in 1866, becoming at once attached to the country around the Powder River, and at the same time displaying an intense desire to obtain Red Cloud's scalp. He felt that to win a coveted promotion, which had repeatedly passed over his head, and to gain honors which were being given to others (and he always being overlooked) something spectacular must be done by him, and soon, for he was in a short time to return to civilization. He, hence, became not only restless, but impatient, eager and reckless. The tension had become heightened by the results of the November fighting, until a time had now arrived when the officers must give leash to their passion to destroy. Of this feeling, Colonel Carrington had received full information. These officers had conceived a plan, in which they were seconded by Lieutenant Grummond, to hobble some mules along Piney Creek after dark, between the fort and a cottonwood thicket, where, with a strong detachment, they desired to await until Indians appeared to capture the mules, when the savages were to be annihilated. The scheme was submitted to Colonel Carrington, who, while having no expectations of decisive results, allowed the officers to carry out their plan. The mules were staked out on a bright moonlight night, so that it was plain to be seen that the animals appeared to be unprotected, but the officers were doomed to disappointment, as no savages appeared on the scene, "although within three hours after Fetterman's party returned to the fort, the Indians ran off a herd not a mile distant."

Just the night before the Fetterman disaster, when Captain Brown saw no opportunity offering itself for the special service he craved, and realizing that he was soon to leave his command, he again expressed regret that he had to leave without the chief's scalp-lock. He wished that reinforcements might be hurried up, as he was going to have one more fight, no matter what the odds. In addition to this, he was sorry that Colonel Carrington did not permit him and Captain Fetterman to go to Tongue River valley on a trip with the cavalry, although he himself realized the request was an impossible one with the forces at hand; only he felt that he could kill a dozen Indians single-handed.

That Captain Brown's impulsiveness influenced Captain Fetterman to disobey orders at the sacrifice of himself and his entire detachment, those who knew both officers, firmly assert. It was a well known fact that each of the captains had said he would always reserve a last shot in his revolver to be used upon himself as a last resort, in case either were overwhelmed by the savages. Lieutenant George W. Grummond, serving as had both Fetterman and Brown, in the Civil

War, miraculously escaped death on December 6th, to meet a worse fate on the 21st of that month. His ambition prompted him to join the Fetterman party. The fact that his remains were found, with those of Sergeant Augustus Lang and a handful of faithful men, more than a quarter of a mile ahead of those of the rest of the command, showed that he was endeavoring to cover the retreat, or was wounded and killed in defense of his own and others' lives.

Captain Fetterman, having had no experience on the frontier, once said: "A single company of regulars could whip a thousand Indians," and that "a full regiment (officially announced from headquarters to be on the way to reinforce the troops) could whip the entire array of hostile tribes." He had further stated that "with eighty men he could ride through the Sioux nation." It was this spirit of reckless bravado possessed by Fetterman, Brown and Grummond which brought them and seventy-eight brave soldiers to their death.

The morning of December 21st was bright and clear. The hillsides were covered with heavy snow, though the ground between the timber and the fort was bare and devoid of snow. On this morning the unusually long wood train moved out from the fort with its extra enforcement of armed guards, and had gone but a mile and a half distant when the picket on Pilot Hill signaled that there were many Indians threatening on Sullivant Hill. The report also came that the wood-choppers, though entrenched in their wagon corral, were engaged in active defense. At once (this being at eleven a.m.) a relief train was organized, consisting of fifty infantry and two officers, twenty-six cavalry and one officer, and two civilians, James Wheatley and Isaac Fisher, who had volunteered their services for this fight. These two men were thought to be a very valuable asset to the fighting party, because of their long experience on the frontier, and their equipment, which consisted of the new model sixteen-shot Henry repeating rifle, just invented that year, and which both Wheatley and Fisher were very desirous of experimenting with on the Indians. Both were employed at the fort in the quartermaster's department. Major J. W. Powell was placed in command, but upon the insistent request of Captain and Brevet Lieutenant Colonel Fetterman (claiming his right by seniority) Colonel Carrington placed him at the head of the party. Lieutenant Grummond then asked to have charge of the cavalry, a request which was also granted. Captain Brown joined the troops, though assigned to no command, nor was this act approved by, nor known at the time, to Colonel Carrington. The fighting force was eighty-one men – just the number Captain Fetterman had declared necessary to wipe out all the Sioux in the Powder River country. Knowing the impulsive nature of the two officers, Colonel Carrington warned Fetterman that he was fighting brave and desperate enemies, who, by their cunning and deceit, were trying to outdo all of the advantages which the white man possessed by intelligence and better arms. Well knowing the ambition to win distinction, which would mean promotion, these instructions given by Colonel Carrington were both peremptory and explicit. To Lieutenant Wands, regimental quartermaster and acting adjutant, he gave this command, to be delivered to Captain Fetterman: "Support the wood train; relieve it and report to me. Do not engage or pursue the Indians at its expense. Under no circumstances pursue over the ridge (viz: Lodge Trail Ridge) as per map in your possession." Still fearing that the spirit to win might override prudence (for Captain Fetterman still resented the commander's refusal to let him go to Tongue River) Colonel Carrington crossed the parade ground, and from a sentry platform, halted the troops and repeated to Fetterman his orders: *"Under no circumstances must you cross Lodge Trail Ridge."*

That Colonel Carrington was justified in his order is verified by the statement he made in his report to the War Department bearing date of December 21, 1866: "I knew that the Indians had for several days returned, each time with increased numbers, to feel our strength, and to decoy detachments to their sacrifice, and I believed that to foil their purpose was actual victory, until reinforcements should arrive, and my preparations were complete. I was right. Just as the command left, five Indians appeared at the crossing. The glass revealed others in the thicket, having the apparent object of determining the watchfulness of the garrison or cutting off any small party that should move out. A case-shot dismounted one and developed nearly thirty more, who broke for the hills and ravines to the north."

The picket on Pilot Hill, within half an hour after the departure of the command, signaled that the wood train had broken corral and had moved on toward the pinery. From the detachment of eighty-one officers, soldiers and two well-armed civilians, there came no report. The cavalry were armed with new carbines, but the infantry had the old muzzle-loading muskets. In another thirty minutes came the sound of firing toward Peno Creek, beyond Lodge Trail Ridge; then followed a few scattering shots; then was heard the sound of such rapid firing that the shots could not be distinguished; there were also a few volleys, apparently, fired. Immediately upon this unexpected change of warfare, Captain Tenedore Ten Eyck was dispacthed from the fort with infantry and cavalry, two wagons, ambulances and two doctors. Not a moment was lost; the troops were moving on the run within twelve minutes after they were ordered into action, but within one-half hour after the firing of the first shot by Fetterman's command, and just as Captain Ten Eyck reached the hillside overlooking the battlefield, all firing had ceased.

At once a mounted orderly named Sample was sent by Captain Ten Eyck to the fort, with a message stating that nothing could be seen of Captain Fetterman's command; that the Indians, in countless numbers, were on the road below, dancing, yelling and challenging him to come down and fight, and that other large bands of Indians were in all of the valleys for a distance of several miles. Captain Ten Eyck also asked that a howitzer be sent him, but no one in his command could handle the gun, hence, it was not sent. Colonel Carrington's answer to the message brought by Orderly Sample was: "Captain: Forty well-armed men, with three thousand rounds of ammunition, ambulances, etc., left before your courier came in. You must unite with Fetterman; fire slowly and keep men in hand. . . I ordered the wood train in, which will give fifty more men to spare." The howitzer mentioned could not have been used if it had been sent, as subsequent events showed that it could not have reached the battlefield in time, as the Indians had retired and were at a safe range, removing their few dead.

In response to this call for help from the fort, everything possible was done; yet there was not much to do, for the supply of men, horses and ammunition was limited. Extra ammunition for the troops and the wood train was started from the fort; every available man was put into service, even the prisoners in the guardhouse were immediately released and placed on duty. Messengers were hurried to the timber to bring back the guards and the wood train; these to assist in the defense of the fort, and also for the fear that Captain Fetterman, in leaving the designated road, might have involved the destruction of the choppers and their guards. At this most critical moment there were but one hundred and nineteen men left to protect and guard the fort, as well as the women and children! All of the force for fighting at Fort Phil Kearney at this time was represented by three hundred and ninety-eight men, this including soldiers, civilians, employes, teamsters, mail parties and escorts, and prisoners in the guard house. As for ammunition, the long-expected and promised supply having failed to reach the fort, left not a full cartridge box (twenty rounds) to each man!

The wood train finally reached the fort, having seen nothing of Captain Fetterman and his command, and having heard no firing.

In order to save the strength of his men, and thus be of service to Captain Fetterman and his party, Captain Ten Eyck moved cautiously forward with men and wagons—when the scene of carnage came into view. The battlefield was indescribable, not a living soldier, civilian or horse was to be seen, though the Indians, in their retreat, were keeping up their shrill warwhoops and jeers. The bodies of Captains Fetterman and Brown, with forty-seven other bodies, were found and placed in the wagons, when a slow backward movement was made, though the Indians did not follow. After dark the procession reached the fort, where had been long and heartbreaking waiting, without additional accident, but bearing the astounding information that "there were no survivors"—all had paid the price of death to gratify an ambition. Implicit orders had been disobeyed. The remains of the two dashing officers were taken from the wagon, beside which were the bodies of their friends, who had known how they had craved for "just one more brush with the redskins," Fetterman, sure of his ability to whip the Sioux if he were only allowed eighty trained men; and Brown, who went into the fight without the knowledge or consent of Colonel Carrington, to battle with Indians, no matter how adverse the odds might be, determined to at least get one scalp before he was required to rejoin his company.

The next morning the officers held a council, at which was expressed a universal disinclination to attempt to search for the remaining bodies of the command, the safety of any small party being doubtful, and the protection of the fort deemed a necessity. Colonel Carrington, however, was firm in his purpose to not only rescue the fallen comrades, but to impress the Indians with the fact that white men were as courageous in obtaining possession of their dead as were the Indians.. "I will not let the Indians entertain the conviction that the dead cannot and will not be rescued. If we cannot rescue our dead, as the Indians always do, at whatever risk, how can you send out details for any purpose? And that single fact will give them an idea of weakness here, and would only stimulate them to risk an assault." Thus spoke a brave soldier.

On the sad journey that morning were Colonel Carrington, Captain Ten Eyck, Lieutenant Matson, Dr.

Ould and eighty men, every soldier fit for service having begged permission to join the command. Picket guards were stationed on each successive hill, in order to communicate back to the fort, in case the Indians made an attack on the garrison, and to summon reinforcements if they were needed.

Before leaving the fort, Colonel Carrington personally opened the powder magazine and cut the fuses of spherical case-shot, which had been used in the howitzer against the prowling Indians in the brush, and so adjusted all the ammunition in the magazine, by opening all the boxes, that all could be destroyed by the touch of a single match. To the officer of the day was given the following instructions: "Fire the usual sunset gun, running a white lamp to mast-head on the flagstaff. If Indians appear, fire three shots from the twelve-pounder (a large field howitzer) at one-minute intervals, and later, substitute a red lantern for the white. If, in my absence, Indians in overwhelming numbers attack, put the women and children in the magazine, with supplies of water, bread and crackers and other supplies that seem best, and in the event of a last desperate struggle, destroy all together, rather than have any captured alive."

Arriving at the crest of Lodge Trail Ridge, the scene of action too truthfully told its harrowing story. The place where the final stand was made, on the road on the little ridge, was strewn with arrows, scalp-poles and broken shafts of spears. Arrows were found in all directions, which had been spent harmlessly, showing that the suddenness of the attack was an overwhelming one, and that it had been from all sides, which prevented any retreat. Most of the bodies were found in the neighborhood of some large rocks or boulders, located nearest the fort, occupying a space about six feet square. A small number of the bodies were at the north end of the field over which the Bozeman Trail passed, a short distance below Lodge Trail Ridge. Lying with Lieutenant Grummond's body were a few other bodies, about five miles from the fort, and also that distance from the wood train. The wood train could not have protected itself with its guard nor with the detachment's assistance. The odds were too heavy. Within ten feet of Lieutenant Grummond's body were three pools of blood, and within an area of an acre were counted sixty-five such spots, showing where Indians had either fallen to their death or had been badly wounded, though the red men had removed all their dead and wounded before Carrington's soldiers came on the battlefield. A number of horses of Fetterman's command were killed, all with their heads toward the fort, as if in retreat, or, relieved of the burden of a body, had attempted to reach the post and were shot down. The fierceness of the fight with those who madly pursued the Indians to save the wood train and its guards, may be best illustrated by the fact that both Captains Fetterman and Brown had powder marks on their temples, as if a weapon had been held very close to the head when fired.[86] Colonel Carrington said: "As Brown always declared he would reserve a shot for himself as a last resort, I am convinced that he and Fetterman fell by each other's hand rather than undergo the slow torture inflicted upon others." Others have said that, seeing that all hope was lost, they had evi-

---

[86] Controversy has arisen as to the exact conditions under which Fetterman and Brown died. Many years after the battle Chief American Horse (Sioux) positively asserted to a competent authority (Captain James H. Cook) that he, personally, killed Captain Fetterman by knocking him off his horse with a war club and stabbing him to death.

dently stood face to face and each had shot the other dead with his revolver.

Thus fell two brave, impulsive men, one of whom had declared, only the night previous to the tragedy, that no Indian force could overwhelm the trained soldier, and that "with eighty men he could ride through the Sioux nation!" Nothing could have saved them at this time, except a superior force, which did not exist in the Powder River country, even if every soldier, teamster or white man then between the Platte and the Yellowstone were requisitioned.

At the end of the ridge furthest from the fort, between two rocks, were found the bodies of citizens James S. Wheatley and Isaac Fisher, who had volunteered their services, and who possessed sixteen-shot Henry rifles, which were a novelty in that country, and which were supposed to be invincible. That these two men made the Indians pay dearly for their lives was witnessed by the two piles of spent cartridge shells by the dead bodies. In the body of Wheatley were found one hundred and five arrows. The mutilations—some too horrible to pen, consisted of eyes torn out and placed on the rocks, noses and ears cut off, chins severed, teeth torn out, fingers chopped off, brains removed, hands and feet cut off, bodies penetrated with spear-heads, sticks and arrows, muscles slashed from calves, thighs, stomach, back and arms, ribs separated by means of knives and skulls crushed and hacked from trunks of bodies. In other words, most of the men were taken alive and tortured to death; not more than six, according to Colonel Carrington's report, having been killed by bullets. The arrows were doubtless shot into the bodies after the clothing was removed, for all the bodies were stripped naked. The reason

why the Indians used the arrows so freely upon the
bodies of their victims was that it was a part of their
religion and their superstition. Each arrow counted to
the credit of their courage, as did the slashing across
the shoulders with a bow, as happened to the Chief,
after his council with Colonel Carrington in 1866,
when he refused, after returning to camp, to join Red
Cloud's forces against the whites. The "coups," or
"coos," were counted as a victory, and were recorded
by tying knots in the tails and manes of their ponies.
So the arrows used upon the bodies at the Fetterman
disaster, where hundreds were found, showed that a
large force of the Indians was engaged to destroy the
soldiers on that fatal day.

Placing the thirty-two bodies (all who went out to relieve the wood train that morning now having been ac-
counted for) in the wagons, the procession marched
cautiously back to the fort, without having encountered
or seen an Indian. It was after dark before the solemn
train reached the garrison, the rejoicing being intense
when the white light was seen hanging over the fort
from the flagstaff, signifying that all was well within.

The mutilated bodies were placed in the hospital,
tents and cabins. Choice uniforms were contributed to
clothe the fallen comrades. The next day was one of
bitter cold, for the night had brought a terrific blizzard, with the temperature down to twenty degrees
below zero. Then began the sawing of boards and the
hammering of nails in the construction of coffins. Each
box was properly numbered, with data corresponding
to the number given, furnishing information which
might be needed by relatives or the government. The
ground was deeply frozen, making the digging of the
graves extremely difficult, while the cold was so intense

that it permitted the grave diggers to work only in fifteen-minute relays. The graves were not completed until Wednesday, December 26th, five days after the battle. In one grave were placed the remains of Fetterman, Brown, and Grummond, though the remains of Lieutenant Grummond were taken East at the time Carrington's command marched to Fort Caspar in January, 1867. In a pit fifty feet long and seven feet deep, were placed the bodies of the seventy-six soldiers and two civilians, Wheatley and Fisher.[87]

Thus, in the Powder River country, near the hated fort on the Piney, was fought one of the three battles recorded in American history from which came no survivors. On the Little Big Horn River in Montana, June 25, 1876, Lieutenant-Colonel George A. Custer, with two hundred and seven of his immediate command, met their death, leaving no white man to tell the tale. At the Alamo, March 6, 1836, the Texans, under Bowie and Davy Crockett, fell to a man beneath overwhelming forces under Santa Anna. Thermopylae had its messenger of defeat; but from the three foregoing battlefields came no survivors.

A courier was sent out the night of the terrible tragedy with dispatches, his destination being Fort Laramie, two hundred and thirty-six miles to the southeast. The bearer of this first message to reach civilization with an account of the awful disaster, was John Phillips, who volunteered his services. He did not belong to the army, but was a miner and frontiersman in the employ of the quartermaster. Unaccom-

---

[87] The bodies of all the victims of the Fetterman disaster, with the single exception of that of Lieutenant Grummond, were exhumed and buried in the national cemetery on the Custer Battlefield, June 24, 1896. The bodies of thirty-seven other soldiers, buried at Fort Phil Kearney, were likewise removed on this date to the Custer Battlefield burial ground.

panied at the start, and over the most dangerous part of the journey, with no companion but the swiftest horse at the post; braving the Indians, snow, zero weather and hunger (for he carried with him only a few hardtack for himself and a small amount of grain for his horse) this hero forged his way toward Fort Laramie by way of Fort Reno. Exactly the route of the journey over the snowy country has never been known, though it is well authenticated that Phillips traveled by night, hiding from the Indians here and there in bushes and ravines through the day. Guided by the stars at night, his general sense of the road and the intelligence of his horse, greatly assisted in keeping the true direction. When the little fort on the west side of the Powder River was reached, late one night, fresh supplies were obtained from General Proctor, who was still commander of Fort Reno. Information was here given that no Indians had been seen in the immediate neighborhood for the last few days. The remainder of the journey did not present the peril that the first had done, for from this point on, the worst enemy to be encountered was the weather, the thermometer from the start recording from twenty to twenty-five degrees below zero. Pushing on, Horseshoe telegraph station was reached at ten o'clock Christmas day. At this station, John C. Friend,[88] the operator, sent Colonel Carrington's message over the wires to General Palmer

---

[88] On March 1, 1917, Mr. Friend writes: "I sent the telegram from Horseshoe to Omaha on Christmas day, 1866, from Colonel Carrington at Fort Phil Kearney, telling of the killing of Fetterman and his troops by Indians. John Phillips, known as "Portugee" Phillips, was one of the party who brought down the message, Captain Bailey and George Dillon being with Phillips. They reached Horseshoe, the first station between Reno and the North Platte, about ten a.m., and filed two dispatches, one to the department commander at Omaha, and one to the post commander at Fort Laramie. I sent both dispatches. Afterwards Phillips was chief of one of the mail parties that carried mail between Fort Laramie and Phil Kearney."

"BEDLAM," ONE OF THE MOST HISTORIC BUILDINGS YET STANDING AT FORT LARAMIE

Erected in 1852, and used for the bachelor officers' headquarters or club-house. The lumber was hauled by wagon from Fort Leavenworth, costing $60,000 when completed. General Charles King has made "Bedlam" famous through his stories of Western garrison life. The building is 32x48 feet, two stories high, with a double-decked porch on the south side. The Christmas festivities were being held here when John Phillips brought the message carrying the news of the fated 81 men who had gone to their death in the Fetterman disaster. The building is still in wonderful preservation, 70 years since its walls first resounded with the laughter of gaily dressed men and women of the garrison, and the music of the regimental band.

at Fort Laramie, and also a message to the headquarters at Omaha, giving to the world, from the isolated post on the Little Piney, the news of Fetterman's defeat.

Not being satisfied that the long and intensely important message would reach the commander of Fort Laramie in exactly the condition it had been sent by wire, Phillips again mounted his horse and plodded on down the Platte River, completing his two hundred and thirty-six miles when he reached Fort Laramie about midnight of Christmas day, where the message was delivered to the commander in person. A Christmas dance was in full swing at "Bedlam," [89] and it was thought wise not to disturb the merry-makers. But news as terrible as conveyed by the message could not be long kept secret, for gradually the other officers became acquainted with the awfulness of the contents of the letter. Then it was, for the first time, that those who were protected and secure began to realize what those who were protecting the Bozeman Road and the far-distant forts were experiencing, and the dangers through which they had to live.

At once reinforcements, consisting of two companies of cavalry and four companies of the First Battalion of the Eighteenth Infantry, were hurried north, under the command of General H. W. Wessels. The journey was a hard and dangerous one, for the mercury ranged from twenty-five to forty degrees below zero day after day. Soldiers' hands and feet were frost-bitten, and the road was not visible, the men marching in snow knee-deep, and often to the waist.

No additional attacks had been made on the fort or the men during the absence of Phillips. It had been expected that the fort would be besieged as a follow-up

[89] See photograph of this historic old building for explanation.

of the Fetterman victory. The blizzard, the blinding snow and the extreme zero weather were all causes of no renewal of hostilities at this critical time, though had the Indians known the truth and the real situation, an attack on the fort by three thousand of the red men who were in the immediate vicinity at that time, could not have been withstood by the soldiers, whose numbers had been so badly depleted by the last combat.

On January 1, 1867, Colonel Carrington issued General Order Number One, at Fort Phil Kearney, apropos of the Fetterman disaster, a part of which follows:

It is a matter of gratitude that the bodies of all who fell in the 'Fetterman Massacre' [90] were recovered, were suitably cared for and buried by their friends. That they fought bravely, and to the last, need not be said. The officers who fell had served well before, and were ever eager to strike a foe when opportunity offered. Among the non-commissioned officers who fell there were many who were the pride of the garrison. Some were veterans of many fights who were not many weeks from the expiration of their second term of service in the army, and could be daunted by no danger.

As a feeble tribute to their memory, their names are published in this order, so that the records of the post shall bear them in remembrance so long as the post shall remain. [91]

Captain W. J. Fetterman, Second Battalion, Eighteenth U. S. Infantry, Brevet Lieutenant-Colonel, U. S. A.

Captain Frederick H. Brown, First Battalion, Eighteenth U. S. Infantry.

---

[90] Every time a body of troops engages in a fight with Indians and the troops are outnumbered, or caught at a disadvantage, and the battle is continued until the troops are slaughtered, such an affair is popularly called a "massacre;" as "the Fetterman Massacre," "The Custer Massacre." I believe this to be an unwarranted use of the term. Fetterman and Custer attacked the Indians and fought until they and their men were all killed. I call that a "battle," not a "massacre." – Brady (C. T.) *Indian Fights and Fighters.*

[91] List of officers and men taken from United States Senate *Executive Document,* 1886-7, vol. i, *Executive Document* No. 97, 49th Congress, 2d Session.

Lieutenant George W. Grummond, Second Battalion, Eighteenth U. S. Infantry.

Company A, Second Battallion, Eighteenth U. S. Infantry

First Sergeant August Lang.
First Sergeant Hugh Murphy.
Corporal Robert Lennon.
Corporal William Dute.
Private Frederick Ackerman.
Private William Betzler.
Private Thomas Burke.
Private Henry Buchanan.
Private Maximilian Dihring.
Private George E. R. Goodall.
Private Francis S. Gordon.
Private Michael Harten.
Private Martin Kelly.
Private Patrick Shannon.
Private Charles M. Taylor.
Private Joseph D. Thomas.
Private Daniel Thorrey.
Private John Thimpson.
Private Albert H. Walters.
Private John M. Weaver.
Private John Woodruff.

Company C, Second Battalion, Eighteenth U. S. Infantry

Sergeant Francis Raymond.
Sergeant Patrick Rooney.
Corporal Gustave A. Bauer.
Corporal Patrick Gallagher.
Private Henry E. Aarons.
Private Michael O'Garra.
Private Jacob Rosenburg.
Private Frank P. Sullivan.
Private Patrick Smith.

Company E, Second Battalion, Eighteenth U. S. Infantry

Sergeant William Morgan.
Corporal John Quinn.
Private George W. Burrell.

Private John Maher.
Private George H. Waterbury.
Private Timothy Cullinane.

Company H, Second Battalion, Eighteenth U. S. Infantry

First Sergeant Alex. Smith.
First Sergeant Ephriam C. Bissell.
Corporal Michael Sharkey.
Corporal George Phillips.
Corporal Frank Karston.
Private George Davis.
Private Perry F. Dolan.
Private Asa H. Griffin.
Private Herrman Keil.
Private James Kean.
Private Michael Kinney.
Private Delos Reed.
Private Thomas M. Madden, regimental armorer, Eighteenth U. S. Infantry.

Company C, Second U. S. Cavalry

Sergeant James Baker.
Corporal James Kelly.
Corporal Thomas F. Herrigan.
Bugler Adolph Metzger.
Artificer John McCarty.
Private Thomas Amberson.
Private Thomas Broglin.
Private Nathan Foreman.
Private Andrew M. Fitzgerald.
Private Daniel Green.
Private Chas. Gumford.
Private John Gitter.
Private Ferdinand Houser.
Private William L. Bugbee.
Private William L. Cornoy.
Private Chas. Cuddy.
Private Patrick Clancy.
Private Harvey S. Deming.
Private U. B. Doran.
Private Robert Daniel.

Private Frank Jones.
Private James P. McGuire.
Private John McKolly.
Private Franklin Payne.
Private James Ryan.
Private George W. Nugens.
Private Oliver Williams.

With the coming of the additional troops came also the order relieving Colonel Carrington of the command of Fort Phil Kearney, the command being transferred to General Wessels, and Colonel Carrington was ordered to report at once to Fort Caspar, the insignificant fortification on the North Platte. With this message also came a wagon load of accumulated mail, thus giving the people of the garrison a glimpse of the outside world, and a gleaning of how those who did not know, regarded the Indian campaign in the Powder River country. The sympathy was not with the battling whites, but with the "poor Indians," who were "mistreated," the opinion being that the campaign of subduing the Indians was one of extermination. Sentiment, not fact, was the ruling passion. Someone had to be the scape-goat, and the mantle fell upon Colonel Carrington. His enemies, those particularly in the army, sought a sacrificial goat in order to direct public attention from their own mistakes. The unpopularity of the administration of Indian affairs had to rest on some one's shoulders.

"Actual observers," "special correspondents," and "eye witnesses" had filled the eastern papers with their "experiences," while, as a matter of fact, these self-appointed reporters had never been as far west as the Missouri River. No one in the East knew the actual conditions on the Bozeman Trail; there was no one to contradict the false statements, hence, imagination was drawn upon with great freedom and startling success. A tragedy had occurred, some one was to blame, although many of these reports about conditions in the Powder River country were written up before the Fetterman disaster. Those who never saw an Indian outside a circus or sideshow, were the ones who knew most about how to deal with the Indian question. "Reliable Information" had many thrilling tales to relate, one being: "When the last band of survivors was driven to the gates of the fort, knocking and screaming for admission; when the last cartridge from rifle, revolver and carbine was expended; when the sabers and butts of muskets were broken, and when, leaning against the gate, weary and bleeding, and all resistance fruitless, all fell in one heap of mangled humanity, unsupported and uncared-for." It was further stated that "the commanding officer, with two full companies, was looking on, afraid to either fire or open the gates, lest the garrison within should be massacred by the infuriated savages and the post should be sacked. Four howitzers, which could have swept the slope and bottom-land, were silent and innocent of harm to anybody."

It is to be remembered that the Fetterman fight was enacted miles away from the fort, and not within sight of its walls or near the stockade; there were no "eye witnesses" to tell of the battle, for there were no survivors of the tragedy, except the Indians. Therefore, the driveling stories from the excited brains of these addle-headed newspaper and magazine writers, did irreparable harm and damage for years, until the falseness of all these wild-eyed yarns was shown in its true light.

Thus, these brainless reports from carping critics were sent broadcast, and even repeated in Washington and New York papers. Pamphlets, letters, editorials, and pictures gave their opinion of the conditions of the country north of the North Platte, not any of which told an iota of truth, but gave only a garbled, sensational *theory* of what had happened to the Indians at the hands of soldiers. Credence was given to the report that "the commanding officer was giving powder to the Indians," and that "the ladies of the fort threw packages of sugar and coffee over the stockade to the squaws!" The Commissioner of Indian Affairs sent to Congress, on January 4, 1867, the following report:

> Now, I understand this was the fact: These Indians, being absolutely in want of guns and ammunition to make their winter hunt, were on a friendly visit to the fort, desiring to communicate with the commanding officer, to get the order refusing them guns and ammunition, rescinded, so that they might be able to procure their winter supply of buffalo. It has been reported that some three thousand to five thousand Indians were assembled to invest the fort. This is not, and cannot by any possibility, be true. The number of Indians is not there. The whole is an exaggeration, and although I regret the unfortunate death of so many brave soldiers, yet, there can be no doubt that it was owing to the foolish and rash management of the officer in command of the post.

The world now knows that it took a Fetterman Disaster and the Custer Battle, in both of which there were no survivors, to awaken the War Department to the fact that the enemy was not only skillful in the art of war, but formidable beyond comprehension.

The order for Colonel Carrington to report to Fort Caspar was put into execution at the earliest possible date, notwithstanding the Arctic severity of the weather, and the all but impassable roads, covered with a crusted snow all along; added to which was the constant, impending danger of a renewed attack from the

Indians. Colonel Carrington took with him his regimental headquarters staff and officers' families, which included the women and children. From Fort Phil Kearney the train of wagons, on January 23, 1867, left for the North Platte. Canvas tops had been reinforced on the wagons; the fronts had been boarded up, doors placed in the back, and sheet-iron wood-burning stoves installed inside the vehicles. The snow continued; a blizzard raged; for the first day the mercury stood at thirty-eight degrees below zero, finally congealing in the bulb. Half of the escort of sixty men were frosted in the first sixty-five miles. The traveling was so frightful that, although the party left Fort Phil Kearney at 1:30 p.m., and traveled continuously until ten o'clock that night, "by dint of shoveling and picking at proper intervals, nearly six miles had been attained!" Not only by day, but by night, the caravan moved toward the south. All of the men experienced the torture of being frost-bitten before the journey was over, many having to submit to amputation of fingers, and two men, when they reached Fort Reno, had their legs amputated, both dying there from the operation. One of these was the driver of Mrs. Carrington's wagon, in which also rode her two sons, Harry and Jimmie. When the wagon train was crossing Crazy Woman's Fork, this being the point along the journey where the cold was most intense, all preparations to keep warm seeming futile, notwithstanding, that the sheet-iron stoves were kept continually crammed with pine blocks, the younger Carrington lad was crying from the bitterness of the cold, only finding relief when the mother wrapped him in her shawl, taken from her own shivering shoulders. At this point of the journey the thermometer registered forty degrees below zero! Bread had to be cut with a

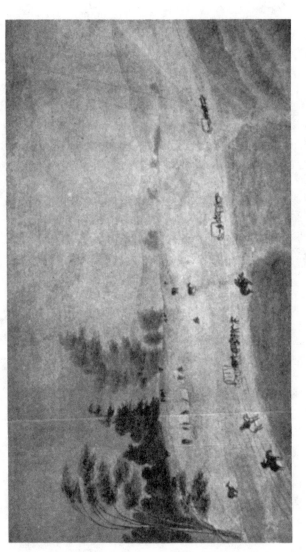

A Blizzard in the Rocky Mountains, June 6, 1853
From an old painting.

hatchet, being frozen solid! Circulation in the men's legs had to be started with the lash of the whip; the men had to be forced into action by stern methods, for their extremities had become insensible from the terrible cold. All begged to "take one more sleep," which, if taken, would have meant death. Mrs. Carrington substantiates the testimony given in regard to the way the starving mules ate anything into which they could sink their teeth. She says:

> Our poor hungry mules did a most unnatural thing. I had heard of goats being indifferent to their fare and very promiscuous in their indulgence of appetite when thoroughly famished, but this was the first instance in which I ever heard or knew of mules chewing wagon covers, gnawing mess chests, spokes of wheels and wagon-tongues, as they attempted, that first night at Reno before their time came to be fed. The best possible was done for them on the journey, but the supply of fodder and food of all kinds was limited. The troops that relieved us did not bring adequate supplies for more than their march, in their hasty departure, so that when our train left Fort Phil Kearney it was augmented by forty empty wagons to return with commissary supplies from Fort Reno.

After "thawing out" and resting for three days at Fort Reno, under the care of General Proctor and Lieutenant Kirtland, "on to Caspar" was the watchword, and the procession again marched slowly toward the south. The journey from Fort Reno was not as difficult as the journey to Reno. No Indians were encountered until the lonely train came within sight of little Fort Caspar, though nothing serious was experienced with the enemy. The command was cordially greeted and tenderly cared for at the fort by Brevet-major Norris, Captain and Mrs. Henry B. Freeman, and Lieutenant Carpenter.

The stay at Caspar was very brief, for upon arrival a

message was handed Colonel Carrington to take his command and report to Fort McPherson (Nebraska) at once. Over the Oregon Trail to Fort Laramie traveled the band of soldiers. In the shadow of this old historic fort the command made a temporary camp, their wants being administered to by Seth Bullock, post sutler. Near Sage Creek, Colonel Carrington had had the misfortune to be wounded in the left leg by the accidental discharge of his revolver, which detained him at Fort Laramie for a time. From here the march, was by way of Fort Mitchell, Scotts Bluffs, Chimney Rock, Fort Sedgwick, Julesburg, and on to Fort McPherson, covering a distance, since leaving Fort Phil Kearney, of five hundred and seven miles.

Colonel Carrington, smarting under the unjust criticism, demanded an investigation of the facts incident to his operation of his campaign in the Powder River country. Twenty unnecessary years passed before complete vindication came to him from the government; not only exonerating him, but commending his tactics in Indian warfare. The blame rested on General P. St. George Cooke, who failed to furnish the long asked for reinforcement of soldiers, for at Fort Laramie (a comparatively safe fortification) there were twelve companies of soldiers, while Colonel Carrington had only eight, and most of the time only seven, poorly equipped companies for *three forts*, situated in the heart of the country of the hostiles, and for the protection of the Bozeman Road, covering a distance between the Platte and Yellowstone Rivers of three hundred and twenty-seven miles!

To follow the statement of Colonel Carrington, made in his defense, as set forth in U.S. Senate Executive Document, Vol. I, No. 97, 49th Congress, 2nd Session,

1887, is helpful, in trying to arrive at a just conclusion of the campaign at and surrounding Fort Phil Kearney.

HEADQUARTERS POST, FORT PHIL KEARNEY, Dak.,
January 3d, 1867

Assistant Adjutant-General, Department of the Platte,
Omaha, Nebraska.

Sir: I respectfully state the facts of fight with Indians on the 21st ultimo. This disaster had the effect to confirm my judgment as to the hostility of the Indians, and solemnly declares by its death roll of dead and the number engaged, that my declaration, from my arrival at Laramie, in June, was not idle conjecture, but truth. It also declared that in Indian warfare there must be perfect coolness, steadiness and judgment. This contest is in their best, and almost last, hunting grounds. They cannot be whipped or punished by some little dash after a handful, nor by mean resistance of offensive movements. They must be subjected and made to respect and fear the whites.

It also declares, with equal plainness, that my letter from Fort Laramie, as to the absolute failure of the treaty, so far as relates to my command, was true. It also vindicates every report from my pen, and every measure I have taken to secure defensive and tenable posts on this line. It vindicates my administration of the Mountain District, Department of the Platte, and asserts that the confidence reposed in me by Lieutenant-General Sherman has been fully met. It vindicates my application so often made for reinforcements, and demonstrates the fact that if I had received those assured me by telegraph and letter, I could have kept up communications and opened a safe route for emigrants next spring. It proves correctly, my report of fifteen hundred lodges of hostile Indians on Tongue River, not many hours' ride from the post. It no less declares that while there has been partial success in impromptu dashes, the Indian, now desperate and bitter, looks upon the rash white man as a sure victim, no less than he does a coward, and that the United States must come to the deliberate resolve to send an army equal to fight with the Indians of the Northwest.

Better to have the expense at once than to have a lingering provoking war of years. It must be met, and the time is just now. I respectfully refer to my official reports and correspond-

ence from department headquarters for verification of the foregoing propositions, and proceed to the details of the Fetterman
massacre.

Again, in a later report, Colonel Carrington, states:

I now return to the published reports of the Secretaries of
War and of the Interior, as to the massacre at Fort Phil Kearney. I first refer to letter of P. St. George Cooke, brevet
major-general commanding, dated December 27, 1866. The
following are extracts:

(1) 'Colonel C.'s statement that, with teamsters, he had
December 21, but one hundred and nineteen men left in the
fort, requires the statement that his December 10 report shows
an aggregate present of four hundred and seventy-five.'

My statement, as already shown officially, was literally
true; and General Cooke could have made no allowance for
wood train and its guard, neither for the dead who fell with
Fetterman, nor for any force sent out to support Fetterman.

(2) 'I hope regular communication can be kept with Fort
C. F. Smith, and that we may be able to chastise the Indians
who may insult the posts, but with great caution. The officers
are not equal to their strategems in the broken ground they
know so well; their numbers, it seems now certain, are very
superior.

'Colonel Carrington is very plausible – an energetic, indus-
trious man in garrison, but it is too evident that he has not
maintained discipline, and that his officers have no confidence
in him. Some of his acts, officially reported, such as shelling
woods, when Indians had appeared on a previous day, may
have by this time settled his appreciation of Indians.'

My statements are these:

(1) Because the country was broken; because most of the
officers had not been with me in reconnaissance and had recently arrived at the post, entirely unused to Indian warfare;
because I knew the Indians to be in large numbers, I would not
authorize them to make hazardous adventures. When Fetterman and Brown asked for fifty mounted men to go with fifty
citizens on a trip to Tongue River to destroy Indian villages, I
showed them by my morning report, for which I sent in the person of Adjutant Bisbee, that I should thereby absolutely break

up my mail parties and my pickets, and then lack eight horses to supply the number desired.

When citizens sent me a similar request I answered that said citizens, with a lieutenant and fifty men, had not been able to protect the same citizens in fulfilling a hay contract for a winter's supply for my stock, and was therefore unequal to the punishment of their enemies and the destruction of Indian villages. I did (as I believe) fail to have the confidence of some officers. Few came from Omaha or Fort Laramie without prejudice, believing that I was not doing enough fighting. Most of those who had no confidence in my judgment as to Indians, have paid the penalty of their lives for their want of confidence. Of the officers who marched from Kearney and went through the whole campaign with me, Captain Ten Eyck alone remains at Fort Phil Kearney. He assisted in surveys, and long commanded the post. Lieutenant Matson came soon after, and he is also at that post. These, with Captain Powell, are the only officers who were there at the time of the massacre, and are still there. Fetterman and Powell did not arrive until November, the former expecting to have command of the post and the Twenty-seventh Infantry, and that I would join the new Eighteenth Infantry.

Lieutenant A. H. Wands (my last adjutant) was able to serve most of the campaign. Lieutenant and Brevet-Captain W. H. Bisbee, who entered my regiment in 1861 as a private soldier, was appointed sergeant-major, and by request, under the laws of 1861, was appointed second lieutenant, marched with me from Fort Kearney as adjutant second battalion, and served the whole summer (until he had orders in December to report at department headquarters) as post adjutant, was also with me. As adjutant he never reported 'irregularities' or 'disorder' that he was not at once empowered to correct. He differed from my views of discipline in physical and verbal abuse of soldiers, requiring my issue of General Order No. 38, already cited. I stand by that order.

(2) I did, with thirty men and howitzer, shell woods where Indians had appeared on a previous day, because the blockhouse of the woodchoppers had been besieged a whole night by Indians, as per written report of post commander, one soldier being shot through a loophole. Because two men

had been killed and another wounded near by, and having been advised by a messenger that Indians were still in the pine woods and thickets, two hundred feet below the ridge, on which the blockhouse stood, where infantry could not operate against Indians unless in numbers, and cautiously, the men also asked to return to post, unwilling to work thus exposed, I did go out and shell the forest below, clear it out and restore confidence to the working party.

(3) The tender of Major Van Voast with five companies to lead a short winter expedition above Reno, not far from my post, where the same number of men would have been invaluable to me, was first approved and finally disapproved, as the 'force was too small' and too uncertain for the risks and suffering. I was expected to surprise Red Cloud in his winter camp, by telegram of September 27th, 1866, and was advised 'that two hundred or three hundred infantry, with much suffering, perhaps might thus accomplish more than two thousand troops in summer;' and again by telegram of November 12, was reminded that 'I had four companies of infantry and some cavalry available for punishing a long arrear of outrages.'

(4) As to the discipline of my command, I refer simply to my previous testimony and to the work done in five months. I had, at first, little drill on parade, except at roll call, but I had willing and obedient soldiers. Drunkenness was rare; the post was orderly and quiet at all times. My men went from guard duty to hard work, and from hard work to guard duty without a murmur. Often they could not have two consecutive nights in bed, and were always subject to instant call. The want of discipline was not in the soldiers and their commander — it was in officers coming fresh to the command who were unequal to the wiles of Indians, and who despised my caution and personal knowledge of the broken ground, which the Indians knew better than all of us, but which I had made my business to study and explore all summer.

(5) A letter from same headquarters, dated January 14, 1867, refers: 1. To 'the impossibility of obtaining from so remote a post reports so soon as desired and expected.' I fully concur, and have experienced this difficulty. It says: (2) 'Colonel Carrington has, before December 21, made no expedition against Indians; all his skirmishes have been with war parties

attacking his supply trains or appearing in sight of the fort.'

I remark that this is true, and it took all of the men I had to do this and prosecute my legitimate work. Again quoting:

'I am informed that on these occasions it was the custom of officers and men to sally forth, mounted or on foot, much at their discretion; and in confirmation of this I enclose (C) a report of Brevet Lieutenant-Colonel Fetterman of the affair of December 6. He says: 'When his command of thirty men reached the wood party, surrounded by Indians, four miles from the post, he was joined by Captain F. H. Brown, with a couple of mounted infantry, who had already started for the relief of the train and was overtaken by Second Lieutenant Wands, Eighteenth U.S. Infantry.' I have already said that the report was a schedule of mine, and mine is not in the pamphlet. Captain Brown went with some quartermasters' employes. He had been relieved as quartermaster, and was closing his papers; but, as was his custom when responsible for the trains, watched them closely. His official report is in my hands for examination. He reached the train before Fetterman and says 'he there volunteered to join him.'

I have before explained Lieutenant Wand's accidental error in joining the wrong party, and refer to order heretofore cited for proof that I suppressed, even by guards at the gate, upon an alarm (more than once directing them in person) the very natural impulse for new men on the frontier to chase the first Indian that appeared. I have no positive knowledge who General Cooke's informant was, and therefore do not give my opinion.

'My reports do not show the facts cited. Again, the size and composition of the party massacred indicates that they were all mounted cavalry and infantry, to just the number of horses in hands of infantry.'

My 13th of October report, 1866, when the district was abolished, and already referred to, shows less than half of that number of serviceable horses then at the post. The infantry had nearly that number in May. Never after were resupplied; but their horses turned over to the cavalry as they required them. Again: 'That the horses were kept saddled.' They were saddled at daylight. I wished to be as quick as the Indians, and therefore always ready for them. I never lost man or animal by being thus ready; but repeatedly foiled the Indians by sending a force out instantly upon their appearance.

Being upon oath to state the truth, the whole truth and nothing but the truth, I do say frankly that I know of nothing in my official correspondence with General Cooke, while he commanded the Department of the Platte, nor in my personal experience during eight months spent in opening the route to Montana, that confirms the conclusions said reports involve. I do, however, remark that a disappointed candidate for a sutlership, a disappointed applicant for a place under my quartermaster, and a disturbed emigrant, furnished the Kearney Herald, the Leavenworth Times, the New York Tribune and the Washington Chronicle, entirely false statements as to myself and command, and gave impressions to the public, which from the first occupation of the line, have been calculated to do mischief, and that only.

Colonel Carrington, in his official report, makes also this statement as to the inadequate force of men at his command at the three forts at the time of the Lodge Trail Ridge Road fight:

At Fort Phil Kearney, including myself, district, regimental, battalion and post staff, seven officers; and for duty, including those on extra or daily duty, as clerks or otherwise, three hundred and eight officers and enlisted men. The nominal aggregate present was three hundred and thirty-nine, and the aggregate proper of the command, including ten commissioned officers (absent) and soldiers absent, the sick, and those in arrest, was three hundred and ninety-eight. Those in arrest I put on duty to avail myself of the relief of the guard and every able-bodied man.

The number of serviceable horses at said post was thirty-seven, and unserviceable, thirteen.

At Fort Reno: Aggregate present for duty, one hundred and thirty-seven; total present, one hundred and fifty-two, including two officers, the total belonging to the command, one hundred and seventy-four, with no horses.

At Fort C. F. Smith: Aggregate, for duty, one hundred and fifty-nine, and three officers; total present, one hundred and sixty-seven; total belonging to the post, one hundred and seventy-nine; total serviceable horses, thirty-eight; unserviceable, eight.

I add in this connection that the aggregate at Fort Phil Kearney included the leader and band of the Eighteenth Infantry (the leader and twenty-four men) the non-commissioned staff and a few unassigned recruits.

With the exception of the recruits of Company K, duly organized, forty-five in number, and Company C, Second Cavalry, about sixty strong, which came in small detachments, armed, as I have heretofore stated, partly with old rifles and partly with Star carbines, no addition was made to the garrison at Fort Phil Kearney until I was relieved from command by the arrival of Lieutenant-Colonel Wessels with two companies of Second Cavalry, and three companies of the Eighteenth Infantry proper. During the same period, although said Company K had been ordered to report to me for garrison duty, I was authorized by General Cooke, if I thought practicable, to send them to Fort Smith. They were perfectly raw recruits from the general depot – should not be sent without other escort. It was impracticable to send them, and they were placed under instructions. Fort Smith, therefore, was never reinforced. (During Colonel Carrington's command). When General Wessels moved from old Kearney to take command of Fort Reno, he brought with him also Company I, forty-three strong, of the same character with Company K, and Fort Reno received no other reinforcements until one company of the Eighteenth Infantry proper, which came with Major Van Voast, was detached to strengthen its garrison.

Each of the posts was deficient in small arms. I had left one mountain howitzer at Reno, sent one to Fort Smith, and at Fort Phil Kearney there was one twelve-pound howitzer (field) and three mountain. The Springfield rifles used by the mounted men on the march, were very much injured by use on horseback, so I deemed it necessary to estimate for one hundred to put the eight companies of the command in possession of perfectly serviceable arms. A few had been carried off by deserters; a few had been lost on the march; both numbers small.

Fort Phil Kearney was established amid hostilities. Fifty-one skirmishes have occurred. No disaster other than the usual incidents to border warfare occurred, until gross disobedience of orders sacrificed nearly eighty (eighty-one) of the choice men of my command. I now know that, dissatisfied with my unwillingness to hazard the post, its stores and the whole line, for an uncertain attempt to strike Indians in their villages (many times my number), at least one of the officers sacrificed, deliberately determined, whenever obtaining a separate command, to pursue the Indians after independent honor. Life was the forfeit. In the grave I bury disobedience. But I will vindicate the living and stand by my acts and record. It will stand, as a simple fact, that in the face of constant night and day attacks, and in the heart of the Indian country, the posts ordered to be established were established during 1866, and that they will control the great highways to the Northwest whenever the aims or the policy of the United States shall fully appreciate and take measures to develop the lines established.

Colonel Carrington obtained information of the Fetterman disaster as to the incidents connected with the Sioux Indians' plans in the campaign which led to this fight, which is quoted as follows:

I take the liberty of sending you Two Moons' account of the Fetterman disaster. Two Moons was visiting his Indian friends at Oklahoma last winter, and I secured this account through his brother-in-law, a half-breed who speaks Cheyenne:

Two Moons says that he and a small party of friendly Cheyenne Indians were sent to the fort to spy about, and see if it could be taken by storm. Here he saw old Bridger, the former scout and guide, and had quite a nice visit. When he returned to the hostile camp he reported the fort too strong to be taken without great loss, so the chief decided to draw the garrison out by detachments, and surprise them, a plan which the recent recklessness of some of the troops in chasing Indians convinced them would succeed.

So they attacked the wood train that day, and when Fetterman's command came out they sent a few Indians, mounted on their best ponies, to decoy them into the hills. Fetterman followed, and then the Indians swarmed out from all sides.

Two Moons adds: 'At this time more troops were coming up behind Fetterman (this was Ten Eyck's relief). Fetterman turned and tried to get away. Then he dismounted his men, and the horses either broke away or were turned loose. After this,' continued Two Moons, 'Fetterman couldn't do anything else but fight, and it was soon all over.

One Arapahoe, two Cheyennes and eleven Sioux were killed.[92] The Cheyenne chiefs in the fight were Strong (or Brave) Wolf, Little Wolf and Dull Knife; Eagle Head and Black Coal led the Arapahoes; Red Cloud, Pawnee Killer and Blue Horse led the Sioux. All the Northern Cheyennes were in the fight, and also the Ogallalas (one thousand Ogallala warriors).

Continuing, Colonel Carrington says:

Two Moons, whom we called Little Moon, from his under size, ought to have mentioned the battery of mountain howitzers, and other things, as well as the interview in my headquarters tent. That was the only place where he saw Bridger; but he saw enough to know that he could never surprise the fort, and that only by decoying men beyond the reach of orders, could give the Indians a chance. He saw the magazine, the blockhouses and the sentry platforms, and I took no little pains to have the officers show them the power I had to help them, if attacked by the Sioux. Their tender of alliance may have been a nice decoy plot itself, but they had enough of their visit.[93]

The following letter, while written for publication, has not before been published. It teems with the spirit of injustice, even after the lapse of thirty-six years:[94]

HYDE PARK, MASS., June 6, 1902

Dear Sir: You are correct as to 'Absaraka.' It was first published before permission was given to publish my official report of the 'Phil Kearney massacre.' That report was sup-

---

[92] This tallies with the number Red Cloud gave as his loss to James H. Cook — see chapter on Red Cloud — *Authors.*

[93] Extracts from a letter dated Omaha, Aug. 11, 1905, from Colonel Carrington.

[94] Letter to George Coutant for vol. ii, *History of Wyoming.* (Vol. one only was published).

pressed for a long time, it being supposed that a living 'scape-goat' would be found as the cause of that disaster. At the suggestion of Governor Dennison of Ohio, approved by General Sherman, Mrs. Carrington wrote her 'Experiences' forming the first edition. An autographic letter of General Sherman fully endorses that volume as accurate. By his permission the second edition contained the report. The then Secretary of War declined to furnish the U.S. Senate with a copy called for by that body. The original, forwarded to Lieutenant General Sherman, than at St. Louis, was accompanied by an endorsement of General P. St. George Cooke, which was so erroneous on its face that General Sherman relieved him from command of the Department of the Platte. It was not published officially until twenty-one years later, as Sen. Doc. 97, 49th Cons. 3d Session . . .

I deem it important as historical matter, to notice the document sent to Congress February 5th, 1867, entitled 'Massacre at Fort Phil Kearney,' being 'Report of the Secretaries of War and Interior,' inasmuch as they were largely made up from surmises of Bogy and others, wholly gossip, or guess-work, or crude contemporary letters aiming to shift responsibility *from the dead to the living.* One (a private letter from a sergeant, name not given) dated Jan. 28, 1867, credits Captain Powell, then the junior captain of the command, 'with having taken the relieving party to the field, and with his having, on the following day, rescued the remainder of the dead from the field.'

He did not leave the fort on either day. Captain Tenedore Ten Eyck was the officer, and accompanied by myself, on the second day.

The surmises of General Cooke were fully exposed by documents, in the subsequent investigations of the Special Commission, vide, Senate Document 33, already noticed. During January, 1890, General Cooke, at Detroit, thus explained his unintentional error: *'The country was greatly excited, and the government very urgent so I endorsed the papers for transmission by one of my staff. I do not remember which. I can do nothing more now than to express my deep pain at what transpired. My memory recalls nothing of the details, except that it was hurried off to General Sherman, and you must take my regrets as sincere, and my congratulations, that in the end you were fully vindicated.'*

On Page 50 are named six persons, who were perfectly cognizant of the occurrence of the massacre, including the orderly (Sample) who accompanied Ten Eyck to the field, and who were at Fort McPherson when the commission met; but the commission declined to take additional testimony after thirty days, nearly, of careful examination of the *original books, letters, documents, and orders* published in Senate Document 33.

A subsequent military commission was dissolved by General Sherman as unnecessary, after examination of the books, documents, etc., which were turned over to them, upon demand, after certified copies had been taken, for personal protection, thereafter.

It is not to be omitted (with reflection upon none) that the former sutler of Fort Phil Kearney, J. F. Kinney (a member of the commission) after the completion of the work at Fort McPherson, Nebraska, visited Fort Phil Kearney, and during that visit an *ex-parte* affidavit was made by Captain James Powell which is not referred to in Judge Kinney's official report of his visit, but was furnished by myself to Mr. Browning, the Secretary of the Interior, with request that my review of it be placed on file for permanent record. He did not recognize the document as of value, knowing the facts to be different since it averred that he, Powell, not Colonel Carrington (at Colonel Carrington's request) was placed in entire command of the post, and that he, Powell, conducted all details, etc., etc. Upon conference with General Sherman it was deemed wise to consider the whole as a matter of *mental aberration*, and not deal with it by military processes. The same course was adopted respecting letters found after Captain Fetterman's decease, which compromised others, in ways, afterwards to be condoned, by their apparent appreciation of the true history, and by good service rendered as late as the Spanish War.

I thank you for your appreciation of the facts which you have gathered, but this analytical summary of documents, long buried in library alcoves, gives some specific elucidation not otherwise patent to strangers. It is my duty, while living, thus to minister to the truth of history, before all shall have passed away, who opened Wyoming to settlement and statehood.

It is almost childish to say that newspaper stories, whether romantic or descriptive, are fantacies of erratic imagination and unworthy of notice. The suppression or distortion of facts, is only to be corrected.

I am, with consideration, very truly,

Your friend and obedient servant,

(Signed) HENRY B. CARRINGTON, U.S.A. (Retired) Late Colonel Eighteenth U.S. Infy., Comdg. Rocky Mountain Dist., Dept. of the Platte.[95]

Had the Fetterman battle been won by any other fighting force than the Indians, the victory would have been followed up by an attack on the hated fort of Phil Kearney, which, with its depleted fighting force, might have been completely overcome, destroying that symbol of invasion, and wiping out all evidence of the white

[95] Brigadier General Henry B. Carrington, U.S.A., retired, a veteran of the Civil War, and one of the most experienced Indian fighters of the old days, died at his home in Hyde Park, Mass., October 26, 1912. General Carrington was born in Connecticut, March 24, 1824. He was appointed from Ohio colonel of the Eighteenth U. S. Infantry, May 14, 1861, and was made brigadier general of volunteers, November 29, 1862. He was unassigned as colonel March 15, 1869, and was retired December 15, 1870, for wounds in line of duty. He was complimented by the Secretary of War and by Generals Scott and Wool as Adjutant General of Ohio when the war began in 1861, for forwarding two regiments in sixty hours from the first call and organizing and placing in West Virginia nine regiments of the State Militia before the muster of three months U. S. Volunteers. At the conclusion of the Civil War, after a brilliant record, General Carrington was later ordered with his regiment to the plains, and commanded Fort Kearney, Nebraska, in December, 1865, and also the expedition of 1866 to open the wagon road to Powder River in the Indian country. He established the line during the harrassing warfare with the Sioux. He commanded Fort Phil Kearney and the "Rocky Mountain District," 1866; Fort McPherson, Nebraska, 1867, and Fort Sedgwick, Colorado Territory, 1868 and 1869. The General was subsequently professor of military science and tactics at Wabash College, Indiana. He was the author of numerous works, receiving literary honors at home and abroad. General Carrington was twice married and outlived both wives. He is survived by a son, James B. Carrington, of New York City, and two daughters, Mrs. Freeman (Henrietta Carrington) the wife of Dr. G. F. Freeman, a surgeon of the U. S. Navy, and Miss Jane Carrington, who resides in Hyde Park. – *Army and Navy Journal*, October, 1912.

man's possession of the Powder River country. The American Indian, with his semi-trained mind, did not possess the genius in military warfare of following up a victory after an advantage ground had been won – an art of war which seems to be the special property of the white man. For a successful skirmish, the red man was well trained in war tactics, such as for ambush or surprise, but he was wanting in strategy. In this particular our Indians followed out the methods of fighting as used in the art of war during the Middle Ages. It is to be remembered that the fighting Magyars (Turks) were lighthorse men, fighting with javelins and savage looking curved swords, but relying chiefly upon their skill with the bow and arrow. They also were noted for their ambushes and for their scouting and individual outpost guards. As with our Indians, these ancient warriors battled, not in a single advancing mass, but in small scattered bands, sweeping mounted along the enemies' front, then to the rear, punishing, as the opportunity might offer, with a rain of arrows. On a fair, open field, the Magyars, as our Indians, would not fight, nor were they ever at an advantage when dismounted. These conditions of warfare among the Indians at the time of the Fetterman battle, account for the fact that Red Cloud did not follow up his temporary and great victory. The taking of a fort by open battle, facing a trained and well armed enemy, made no appeal to the red man. This lack of the use of modern warfare, coupled with the unusual and unprecedented climatic conditions, seemed to present a sufficient explanation as to the reason why the hated forts on the Bozeman Trail were not destroyed, and the occupants massacred on the days immediately following the Fetterman disaster.

Of course after the Fetterman fight extreme precaution was observed, so that no person, or small party of soldiers, might be surprised outside of Fort Phil Kearney, for not an individual was permitted to go beyond the limits of the eight-foot stockade, except under the necessity of bringing in the wood for fuel. The Indians made no direct attack on Phil Kearney, though there were wild demonstrations easily to be seen from the fort, and piercing yells frequently to be heard. But above all this, there was a paramount reason for the lack of further depredation – Nature – with her extreme severity of weather – the storms, the deepening snow (now as high as the stockade) the cold, with the thermometer forty degrees below zero, and at times too low to be recorded, the mercury retiring into the bulb. Not only did this condition of weather continue through the month of January, in 1867, but spring was forgotten, and the snow, in its great depth, did not disappear until the coming of summer days. In fact, the snow was so deep on the level that the wood trains had to be discontinued. As a matter of fact, if the Indians had known the exact condition of affairs at Fort Phil Kearney during the day following the Fetterman fight, before reinforcements came from Fort Laramie, a dashing, united attack would have worked grave disaster, if not annihilation, to all concerned. In addition to all of this, the Indians thought the fort impregnable, as Colonel Carrington had always made a particular effort to impress the red men.

In the early months of the year 1867, there came from Fort Laramie constant demands, which were sent to the warring Indians, that they must surrender, but Red Cloud was emphatic in his refusal to give up the war only on condition of evacuation of the Powder

River country and the dismantling of the three detested forts on the Bozeman Trail. Red Cloud always brought the councils with the white men to a sudden termination with the haughty statement that "the white man could have peace as soon as he left the country, and not before."

Repeated overtures were made to this warring chief, setting forth the fact that the entire matter of the abandonment of the Sioux territory was under advisement by the Great White Chief; that it was possible to send more troops to guard and protect the forts; that more soldiers could be placed on the Bozeman Trail. All these arguments, it was so stated, should thoroughly demonstrate to Red Cloud that the white men wished peace. Skeptical of the motives of the officers, Red Cloud concluded that if the government really had a superior force with which to annihilate the red man, the Fetterman disaster would have been avenged long before the snow had melted from the prairies and the plains. No proof being offered that our government was able to place in the Powder River country a force sufficient to drive the red man back to the Yellowstone River, the chief spurned all ovations for peace, concentrating and bringing together all of the allied tribes south of the Yellowstone and north of the North Platte.

In July, 1867, the government authorized a commission, consisting of army officers and civilians, to meet the Indians, in order to negotiate for a permanent peace. No desired results followed; it only served to make Red Cloud steadily and stealthily add new warring chiefs to his forces. The sweeping victory of the Fetterman fight was the justification, if justification were needed, for Red Cloud's continued hostilities; the hope, ever present, that the forts, particularly Fort Phil Kearney, might be surprised, as were the troops at Lodge Trail Ridge. Gradually the hostile tribes were being centered, until, with the coming of the first days of August, 1867, there was witnessed two fights – one on August 1st, near Fort C. F. Smith, the "Hayfield fight," the other on August 2d, near Fort Phil Kearney, the "Wagon Box fight," while during these two days, frequent demonstrations were made near Fort Reno. Numerous Indians assembled in the surrounding country of Reno, though no depredations were committed, due more to the fact that no opportunity was given the red man to engage in warfare with the soldiers on duty outside of the fortification, as was the case at Fort C. F. Smith and Fort Phil Kearney.

Index